A Garland Series

The English Stage
Attack and Defense 1577 - 1730

A collection of 90 important works
reprinted in photo-facsimile in 50 volumes

edited by
Arthur Freeman
Boston University

The Anatomie of Abuses

by

Phillip Stubbes

with a preface
for the Garland Edition by

Arthur Freeman

Garland Publishing, Inc., New York & London

1973

Library of Congress Cataloging in Publication Data

Stubbes, Phillip.
   The anatomie of abuses.

   (The English stage: attack and defense 1577-1730)
   Reprint of the 1583 ed. printed at London, by R.
Jones.
   1. Theater--Moral and religious aspects.
2. Theater--England.   I. Title.   II. Series.
PN2047.S8 1973   792'.013   71-170409
ISBN 0-8240-0590-2

Printed in the United States of America

Preface

In terms of publication and response certainly the most popular of puritan "abuses" texts, Stubbes's Anatomie *was registered on 1 March 1583; an independent* Second Part *was issued later in the same year, but may well have been intended to capitalize upon the success of the earlier volume. While the anti-theatrical reflections which pepper Stubbes's catalog of vices in "Ailgna" (i.e., "Anglia") stimulated memorable retorts by John Lyly (*An Almond for a Parrot*) and Thomas Nashe (*Pierce Pennilesse *and* The Anatomie of Absurditie*), the author—who, incidentally, was* not *a clergyman—shows little enough practical experience of play-going. In one instance, at least, his dependence on prior testimony is rather amusing: Stubbes declares on L7, "that the arguments of tragedies, is anger, wrath, immunitie, crueltie, iniurie, incest, murther & such like: the Persons or Actors, are Goddes, Goddesses, Furies, Fyends, Hagges, Kings, Queenes, or Potentates. Of Commedies, the matter and ground is loue, bawdrie,*

5

cosenage, flattery, whordome, adulterie: the Persons or agents, whores, queanes, bawdes, scullions, Knaues, Curtezans, lecherous old men, amorous yong men, with such like of infinit varietie." Compare Stephen Gosson, Playes Confuted *(1582), C5^{r-v}:"The argument of Tragedies is wrath, crueltie, incest, iniurie, murther eyther violent by sworde, or voluntary by poyson. The persons, Gods, Goddesses, furies, fiendes, Kinges, Quenes, and mightie men. The ground worke of* Commedies, *is loue, cosenedge, flatterie, bawderie, slye conueighance of whordome. The persons, cookes, queanes, knaues, baudes, parasites, courtezannes, lecherouse olde men, amorous yong men. . . ."*

The Anatomie of Abuses *appears first with the date 1 May on the title page, containing a preface of some importance eliminated from later settings (STC 23376). A variant issue, dated 29 May (STC 23376.5) is known only in the Peterborough copy, now deposited at Cambridge. It was set anew without the conciliatory preface (excusing some plays, forms of amusement, dancing in private, and gentlemanly gaming from his general censure) with a title dated 16 August 1583 (STC 23397), and appears again, dated 12 October 1584, as "now*

6

PREFACE

*augmented the third time" (*STC *23377.5). A variant of the last version is dated 1585 (*STC *23378), and finally, with the preliminaries revised and "Ailgna" now called plainly "England,"* The Anatomie *resurfaces in 1595 (*STC *23379). Modern reprints begin with W. D. Turnbull's of 1836 (from* 1585*), and follow with J. P. Collier's of 1870 and F. J. Furnivall's (*New Shakspere Society, *1877-9). E. K. Chambers,* Elizabethan Stage, *IV, 221-5, took his text from Furnivall, with concomitant errors. Our reprint is prepared from Huntington 15594, Richard Farmer's copy of the first (1 May) edition, collating* $\P^8 A^2 B\text{-}P^8 Q^4 r^2$, *with Richard Jones's device on R2^V. STC 23376; Lowe-Arnott-Robinson 257 [not seen].*

January, 1973   A.F.

7

The Anatomie

of Abuses:

Contayning

A DISCOVERIE, OR BRIEFE
Summarie of such Notable Vices and Imperfections, as now raigne in many Christian Countreyes of the Worlde : but (es-
peciallie) in a verie famous ILANDE
called AILGNA : Together, with
most fearefull Examples of Gods Iudge-
mentes, executed vpon the wicked for the
same, aswell in AILGNA of late, as in
other places, elsewhere. *Anglia.*

Verie Godly, to be read of all true Chzistians,
euerie where : but most needefull, to
be regarded in ENGLANDE.

Made dialogue-wise, by Phillip Stubbes,

Seene and allowed, according to order.

MATH.3.ver.2. Repent, for the kingdome of God
is at hande.
LVC.13. ver.5. I say vnto you (saith Christ) except
you repent, you shall all perish .

¶ Printed at London , by Richard
Jones. 1. Iaij. 1583.

To the Right Hono-

rable, Phillip Earle of Arundell : Phillip
Stubbes wisheth helth of body & soule, fauour
of God, increase of Godly honour, reward of laudable vertue, and eternall felicitie, in the Heauens,
by IESVS Christ.

NOBILITAS Patriæ DECVS

HE Lord our God (right
honorable) hauing by the power of
his word, created Heauen and Earth,
with all thinges what soeuer, for the
comfort and vse of Man : the last of
all other (euen the sixt daye) made
Man after his owne similitude and
likenesse, that in him he might be glorified aboue all
other Creatures. And therfore, wheras in making of
other thinges, he vsed onely this Woord, FIANT, be they
made, or let them be made: when he came to make Man,
as it weare aduysing himselfe, and asking councell at his
wisdome, he said, FACIAMVS HOMINEM, let vs make Man,
that is a wôderful Creature: and therfore is called in greek
MICROCOSMOS, a litle world in himself. And truely he
is no lesse, whether we consider his spirituall soule, or his
humaine body.   For what Creature is theare vppon the
face of the Earth comparable to man, either in body or in
mind? what creature hath a soule immortall inherent in
his body, but onely Man? what Creature can forsee thinges

¶.2.

to come, remember things paft, or iudg of things prefent, but onely man? what Creature beareth the ymage of God about with him, but Man? what Creature is made fo erect to behould the Heauens, as man? What Creature may be likened to man, either in proportiō or body, or gifts of the foule? And (finally) what Creature hath the promife of the refurrectiō & glorificatiō of their bodies, & of eternall life but onely Man ? Than feeing the Lorde hath made man thus glorious, and preferred him in euery degree, before al other Creatures (the Angelicall Creatures fet a part) it is manifeft, he hath done it to fome end & purpofe, namely, that he might be glorified in him, and by him aboue all othe; his works, according to the meafure of his integritie excellency and perfection. And hereby we may learn that it is the will of G O D, that we bend all our force to the aduauncing of his glorious Name, the edification of his People, and the building vp of his Church, which he hath redemed with the bloud of his deare Sonne.

Which thing (mee think) is notably figured foorth vnto vs in the. 25. of E X O D V S wher the Lord commaunded Moyfes to build him a Tabernacle, or howfe of prayer, to this end aud purpofe (doubtles) that therin his lawe might be read, his Ceremonies practifed, Sacrifices, Victimates & Holocauftes offred, and his glorious Name called vppon and obeyed. To the erection wherof, euery one conferred fome what, fome brought gold, fome filuer, & fome braffe, lead & tinne, other brought filk, purple, fkarlet, and other ornaments, and the meaneft brought fome what, namely, fkins heare, fand, lyme, morter, wood, ftone, and fuch like. Euen fo (right honorable) would the Lord haue euery one to conferre fome what, euen fuch as he hath, to the building of his fpirituall howfe, the Church, purchafed with the bloud of Chrift. Wherfore feeing it is fo, that euery one is to further this fpirituall building to his poffible power, I haue rather chofen with the fimpleft, and meaneft fort to bring, though but heyre, fand, fkins, lyme, morter,

wood,

wood or ſtones, than altogether to contribute nothing.

Not doubting, but that the chief Maiſter and Builder of this howſe, Chriſt Ieſus, will not diſlike, but accept of my poore contribution, no leſſe than he did of the poore wydowes Mite, to whom was imputed that ſhe had caſt more, in Gazophilatium Templi, into the treaſury of the Temple, than all the reſt : for what ſhe wanted in effect, that ſhe ſupplyed in affect, And for that alſo the Lord our GOD committing his taléts to euery one, whether more or leſſe, not onely requireth of vs the ſame againe ſimply, but alſo, as a ſtraight computiſt, demaundeth intereſt and gaine of euery one of vs: & for that not only, he is a mur-therer & a Homicide before God, who ſlayeth or killeth, a man with materiall ſword. but he alſo, vho may preuent the ſame, and will not. And not onely, he is guiltie of haynous tranſgreſſion that committeth any euill really, but alſo he who conſenteth to it, as he doth, who holdeth his peace, or he who by any means might auoid it, and ei-ther for negligence wil not, or forʼfeare of the world dare not. Therfore, albe it, that I haue receiued, but one poore talét, or rather the ſhadow of one, yet leaſt I might be re-proued (with that vnprofitable Seruaunt) for hyding my ſmall talent in the Earth not profiting therwith at all, ei-ther my ſelf, or others, I haue aduétured the making of this litle treatiſe, intituled, (The Anatomy of Abuſes,) hoping that the ſame (by diuyne aſſiſtance) ſhall ſomewhat con-duce to the building of this ſpirituall howſe of the Lord.

And although I be one (moſt honorable Lord) that can do leaſt in this Godly courſe of life (palpable barbariſme forbidding mee ſo much as once to enter into Wyſdomes ſchool) yet for that ſomewil not, for feare of loſing world-ly promotion (though in the meane tyme they loſe the Kingdome of Heauen,) Other ſome dare not for diſplea-ſing the world: I ſay, for theſe, & ſemblable cauſes toge-ther, with the zeale and goodwill I beare vnto my Coun-trey, and feruent deſire of their conuerſion and amendement, I haue taken vpon me the contryuing of this book: Which G O D, graunt may be with like plauſible alacritie recciued, as with paines and good will , I haue publiſhed it, for the benefit of my Cuntrey, the pleaſure of the God-ly , and amendement of the wicked. And I doubt not, that as none, but the wicked, and peruerſe whoſe gawld backes are tutched, will repyne againſt mee , ſo the Godly and vertuous , will accept of this my labour, and trauailé herein , whoſe gentle ſauour and goodwill, ſhall coun-terpoyſe, (and farre ſurmount with mee) the maligne ſto-macks, and ſtearn countenances of the other. After that I had (right honorable) fully perfected this booke , I was minded, notwithſtanding, both in regard of the ſtraunge-nes of the matter it intreateth of, and alſo in reſpect of the rudeneſſe of my penne, to haue ſuppreſſed it for euer, for diuerſe and ſundrie cauſes , and neuer to haue offred it to the viewe of the world. But, notwithſtanding, being ouer-come by the importunat requeſt, and infagitable deſire of my freinds, I graúted to publiſh the ſame, as now you ſee, is extant.

But , when I had once graunted to imprinte the ſame, I was in greatter doubt than before , fearinge, to whome I might dedicate the ſame ſo rude and impoliſhed a worke. And withall I was not ignorant, how hard a thing it is in theſe daies to finde a Patrone of ſuch books as this, which ſheweth to euery one his ſin, and diſcouereth euery Mans wicked waies, which indeed, the vngodly cã not at any hãd abyde , but as ir were mad- iné diſgorging their ſtonacks (Cum in Authorë tum in codicem plenis buccis, & dentibus pluſquàm caninis rabidè feruntur :) they rage, they ſume and rayle both againſt the A v ʈʜoʀ and his booke. Thus (vacillante animo) my minde wandring too and fro, and reſting , as it weare in extaſie of deſpaire, at laſt I called to mind your honorable Lord-ſhip, whoſe praiſes haue pearced the Skyes, and whoſe lau-dable vertues are blowen; not ouer the realme of England
onely

Dedicatorie.

onely, but euen to the furtheſt coſts and parts of the world.

All whoſe vertues, and condigne prayſes, if I ſhould take vppon mee to recounte, I might as well number the ſtarres in the Sky, or graſſe of the Earth.

For, for Godly Wvſdome, and zeale to the truth, is not your good Lordſhip (without offence be it ſpoken') comparable with the beſt? For ſobrictie, affabilite, and gentle curteſie to euerie one, farre excelling many.

For your great denotion and compaſſion to the poore oppreſſed, in all places famous : For Godly fidelitie, to your Soueraigne, loue to the CVNTREY, and vertues in generall, euerie where moſt renowmed.

But leaſt I might obſcure, your Worthie commendations with my vnlearned penne, (lytle, or no thing at all emphaticall) I will rather ſurceaſe, than further to proceed, contenting my ſelfe rather to haue giuen a ſhadowe of them, than to haue ciphered them foorth, which indeed are both infinit, and inexplicable.

In conſideration (whereof) not withſtanding that my Booke be ſimpler, baſer, and meaner, than that it may (without bluſhing) preſent it ſelf to your good Lordſhip (being farre vnworthie of ſuch an honorable Perſonage) yet accordinge to your accuſtomed clemency I moſt humbly beſeache your good Lordſhip to receiue the ſame into your honors Patrociny and protection, accepting it as an infallible token of my faithfull heart, ſeruice, and good will towardes your honorable Lordſhip : For proofe whereof, would GOD it might once come to paſſe, that if not otherwyſe, yet with my humble ſeruice, I might ſhewe foorth the faithfull and euer willing heart I beare in breſt to your good Lordſhip, proteſting before Heauen and Earth, that though power want yet ſhall fidelitie, and faithfulnes faile neuer.

And becauſe, this my Booke is ſubiect (my verie good Lord (to as many reproches, tauntes and reprooofes, as euer was any litle book (for that few cã abyde to haue their ſins

¶·4·   de-

detected) therfore I haue had the greatter care to commit the fame to the guardance and defence of your honour, rather than to manie others, not onely for that (; O D hath made your honour a Lamp of light vnt) the world, of true nobilitie and of al integritie and perfection, but alfo hath made you his fubftitute, or vicegerent, to reforme vices, punifh abufes, and correcte finne.

And as in mercie he hath giuen you this power and autoritie, fo hath he giuen you a hungrie defire to accomplifh the fame according to his will: Which zeal in your facred breft, the L O R D increafe for euer.

And as your Lordfhip knoweth, reformation of maners and amendement of lyfe, was neuer more needfull, for, was pride (the chiefeft argument of this Booke) euer fo rype? Do not, both Men and Women (for the moft part) euery one in generall go attyred in filks, veluers, damafks, fatins, and what not? which are attvie onely for the nobilitie and gentrie, and not for the other at anie hand? Are not vnlawfull games, Playes and Enterluds, and the like euery where vfed? Is not whordome, couetoufnes, vfune & the like daylie practifed without all punifhment or lawe?

But hereof I fay no more, referring the confideration, both of thefe and the reft, to your Godly wyfdome. Befeafeaching your good Lordfhip, to perdon my prefumption in fpeaking thus much, for (Zelus domini huc adegit me:) the zeal of my God hath dryuen me heather.

Knowinge, that the L O R D hath ordeined you, to himfelfe a chofen veffell of honour, to purge his Church of thefe Abufes, and corruptions, which as in a table are depainted and fet foorth in this litle booke.

Thus I ceafe to moleft your facred eares any further with my rude fpeaches, moft hubly befeaching your good Lord fhip not onely to admit this my Book into your honours patronage and defence, but alfo to perfift the iuft Defender therof, againft the fwynifh crew of rayling Z o ɪ L v s and flowting M o м v s, with their complices, to whome

it

Dedicatorie.

it is eafier to depraue all things, than to amend any thing them felues. Which, if I fhall perceiue to be accepted of your honour, befides that I fhal not care for a thoufand others, difliking the fame, I fhall not only think my fel to haue receiued a fufficiēt guerdon for my paines, & fhilbe therby greatly incoraged (if G O D permit) hereafter to take in hand fome memorable thing to your immortall prayfe, honour and renowne, but alfo fhall daylie pray to
G O D , for your good Lordfhip long to continue,
to his good pleafure and your harts defire,
with increafe of Godly honour, reward of laudable vertue, and
eternall felicitie in the
H E A V E N s, by
Iefus Chrift.
(.·.)

Columna gloriæ virtus.

Your Honors to commaund,
PHILLIP Stubbes.

A PREFACE
TO THE READER.

Thought it conuenient (good Reader, who soeuer thou art, ẙ shalt read these my poore laboures)to admonish thée (least haply ẙ mightest take my woordes otherwise than I meant them) of this one thing: That wheras in the processe of this my booke, I haue intreated of certen exercyses, vsually practised amongest vs, as namely of Playes and Enterludes, of dauncing, gaming, and such other like : I would not haue thée so, to take mée, as though my speaches tended, to the ouerthrowe and vtter disliking of all kynd of exercyses in generall : that is nothing my simple meaning. But the particulare Abuses, which are crept into euery one of these seuerall exercyses, is the onely thing, which I think worthie of reprehension.

For,otherwise(all Abuses cut away)who séeth not, ẙ some kind of playes, tragedies and enterluds in their own nature, are not onely of great anciétie, but also very honest and very commen-
d..ble

dable exercyses, being vsed and practised in most
Christian common weales , as which containe
matter (such they may be) both of doctrine, erudition,good example and wholsome instruction?
And may be vsed in tyme and place conuenient,
as conducible to example of life and reformation
of maners. For such is our grosse & dull nature,
that what thing we see opposite before our eyes,
do pearce further,and printe deeper in our harts
and minds,than that thing, which is hard onely
with the eares , as Horace, the hethen Poet can
witnesse. Segnius irritant animum, dimissa per
aures, quàm quæ sunt hominum occulis obiecta.
So, that when honest & chast playes, tragedies,
& enterluds are vsed to these ends, for the Godly
recreatió of the mind,for the good example of life,
for the auoyding of that,which is euill,and learning of that which is good , thã are they very tollerable exercyses. But being vsed(as now commonly they be),to the prophanation of the Lord
his sabaoth, to the alluring and inuegling of the
People from the blessed word of God preached,
to Theaters and vnclean assemblies,to ydlenes,
vnthriftynes,whoredome,wantónes,drunkénes,
and what not? and which is more , when they
are vsed to this end,to maintaine a great sort of
ydle Persons, doing nothing , but playing and
loytring, hauing their lyuings of the sweat of
other Mens browes, much like vnto dronets deuouring ý swéet honie of ý poore labouring bees,

than

than are they exercyses (at no hand) sufferable.
1 But being vsed to the ends that I haue said,
they are not to be disliked of any sober, and wise
Christian.

And as concerning dauncing, I wold not haue
thee (good Reader) to think that I condemne the
exercyse it self altogether, for I know the wisest
Sages and the Godlyest Fathers and Patriar-
ches that euer liued, haue now and than vsed the
same, as Dauid, Salomon, and many others: but
my words doo touch & cöcerne the Abuses thereof onely. As being vsed vppon the Sabaoth
day, from morning vntill night, in publique assemblies and frequencies of People, Men & women together, with pyping, flating, dromming,
and such like inticements to wantonnesse & sin,
together with their leapinges, skippings, & other
vnchast gestures, not a few. Being vsed, or rather abused in this sort, I vtterly discommend it.

But vppon the otherside, being vsed in a mans
priuat-chamber, or howse for his Godly solace,
and recreation in the feare of GOD, or otherwise abroade with respect had to the time, place
and persons, it is in no respect to be disalowed.

And wheras I speake of gaming, my meaning
is not, that it is an exercise altogether vnlawful.
For, I know that one Christian may play with
another, at any kind of Godly, honest, ciuile game, or exercise, for the mutuall recreation one of
the other, so that they be not inflamed with co-
ney-

ueitousnes, o2 desire of vnlawfull gaine : fo2 the
comaundemēt saith, thou shalt not couet: wher-
fo2e,if any be voide of these affections,playing ra
ther fo2 his Godly recreation , than fo2 desire of
silthie lucre, he may vse the same in the feare of
God : yet so as the vse therof be not a let,o2 hin-
derance vnto him,to any other Godly exploit.

But, if a man make(as it weare)an occupation
of it , spenting both his tyme and goods therein,
frequenting , gaming howses, bowling allyes,
and such other places, fo2 grædinesse of lucre, to
him it is an exercise altogether discommendable
and vnlawfull.   Wherfo2e, as these be exercyses lawfull, to them that know how to vse them
in the feare of G D D,so are they p2actises at no
hand sufferable to them that abuse thē,as I haue
shewed. But take away the abuses, the thinges
in themselues are not euill,being vsed as instruments to Godlynes, not made as spurres vnto
vice. There is nothing so good,but it may be a-
bused,yet because of ȳ abuses, I am not so strict,
that I wold haue the things`, themselues remo-
ued, no mo2e than I wold meat and d2inke , be-
it is abused,vtterly to be taken away.

And wheras also I haue spoken of the excesse
in Apparell,and of the Abuse of the same,as wel
in men,as in womeu generally , I wold not be
so vnderstood, as though my speaches extēded, to
any,either noble,hono2able.o2 wo2shipful:fo2,I
am so farre from once thinking that any kind of
sump-

sumptuous,oʒ goʒgeous attire is not to be woʒn of any of them , as I suppose them rather Oʒnaments in them,than otherwise.

And that they both may,and foʒ some respects, ought to were such attire(their birthes callings, functions and estats requiring the same)foʒ causes in this my Booke laid downe , as maye appeare , and foʒ the distinction of them from the inferiour soʒte,it is pʒouable both by the Woʒd of G O D , Ancient Wʒiters , and common pʒactise of all ages , People and Nations , from the beginning of the Woʒld,to this day.

And therfoʒe, when I speake generally of the excesse of Apparell , my meaning is of the inferiour soʒte onely,who foʒ the most parte do farre surpasse,either noble, honoʒable, oʒ woʒshipfull, ruffling in Silks,Ueluets, Satens, Damasks, Taffeties, Gold , Siluer , and what not ? with their swoʒds,daggers , and rapiers guilte , and reguilte,burnished,and costly ingrauen,with all things els , that any noble , honoʒable , oʒ woʒshipfull Man doth, oʒ may weare , so as the one cannot easily be discerned from the other.

These be the Abuses , that I speake of , these be the euills,that I lament,and these be the persons that my woʒds do concerne , as the tenure of my Booke consideratly wayed , to any indifferent R E A D E R doth purpoʒt.

This much I thought good (Gentle Reader) to infoʒme thee of, foʒ thy better instruction , as

well

To the Reader.

well in thefe few points, as in all other the like, wherefoeuer they fhall chaunce to occurre in my Booke. Befeaching thée, to conftrue al things to the beft, to beare with the rudenes therof, and to giue the fame thy good-woord, and gentle acceptaunce. And thus in the LORD, I bid thée, farewell.

Thyne to vfe in the Lord,

PHILLIP Stubbes.

Phillippus Stubeus

CANDIDO LECTORI.

Offendit nimia te garrulitate libellus
    forte meus, Lector miror id ipfe nihil.
Obfitus eft etenim verború colluuione
plufquàm vandalica, rebus & infipidis.
Quare fi fapias operam ne perdito poft hac
    noftra legendo, legas vtiliora, vale.

¶ Idem in Zoilum.

ZOILE cum tanta rabie exardefcis in omnes,
    nõ aliter rabidus, quàm folet ipfe canis:
Dente Theonino rodens alios, calamoque,
    inceffens hos, qui nil nocuere tibi:
Viperęam in cunctos vibrans O Zoile linguam,
    linguam quã inficiunt toxica dira tuam:
Cum Debacchandi finis fit Zoile nullus,
    hora quieta tibi nullaque prætereat:
Cum tumeas veluti ventrofus ZOILE bufo,
    demiror medius quòd minus ipfe crepes.

¶ Aliud in eundem.

Dæmones ad tetrum defcendat Zoilus antrum,
    hunc lacerent furiæ, Cerborus ore voret.
Imprecor at mifero quid pænas, cui fatis intus?
    dæmona circumfert pectore namque fuo.

¶ Eiufdem aliud.

Si tibi prolixus nimium liber ifte videtur
    pauça legas, poterit fic liber effe breuis.

A

A.D. In cõmen-
dation of the Au-
thor and his Booke.

IF Mortall-man may challenge prayse,
    For any thing done in this lyfe :
Than may our Stubbes, at all assayes,
    Inioy the same withouten stryfe.
Not onely for his Godly zeale,
    And Christian life accordinglie :
But also for this booke in sale,
    Heare present, now before thine eye :
Herein the Abuses of these dayes,
    As in a glasse thou mayest behold :
Oh buy it than, hear what he sayes,
    And giue him thankes an hundred fold.

I. F. In Commen-

dation of the AVTHOR
and his Booke.

Shall men prophane, who toyes haue writ,
    And wanton pamphlets store,
Which onely tend to noorish vice,
    And wickednes the more,
Deserue their praise, and for the same,
    Accepted be of all,
And shall not this our AVTHOR than
    Receiue the Lawrell pall?
Who for goodwill in sacred brest
    He beares to natiue soyle,
Hath published this Godly Booke,
    With mickle paine and toyle.
Wherein, as in a Mirrour pure
    Thou mayest behold and see,
The vices of the World displayed
    Apparent to thy eye.
He flattereth none, as most men do,
    In Hope to game a price:
But shewes to all their wickednesse,
    And Gods diuyne Iustice.
A Godlyer booke was neuer made,
    Nor meeter for these dayes:
Oh read it than, thank GOD for it,
    Let T'H AVTOR haue his praise.

                       The

THE AVTHOR
AND HIS BOOKE.

Now hauing made thee, seelie booke,
and brought thee to this frame:
Full loth I am to publish thee,
lest thou impaire my name.

The Booke.

Why so? good Maister, what's the cause,
why you so loth should be,
To send mee forth into the World,
my fortune for to trye?

The Author.

This is the cause, for that I know,
the wicked thou wilt moue,
And eke because thy ignoraunce:
is such, as none can loue.

The Booke.

I doubt not, but all Godly Men,
will long and like mee well,
And for the other I care not,
in pride although they swell.

A. ij.   THE

The Author.

Thou art also no leſſe in thrall,
and ſubiect euery way :
To MOMVS and to ZOILVS crew,
who'le dayly at thœ bay.

The Booke.

Though MOMVS rage, and Zoilus carpe:
I feare them not at all,
The Lord my GOD in whom I truſt,
Shall ſone cauſe them to fall.

The Author.

Well, ſith thou wouldeſt ſo faine be gone,
I can thœ not withhold :
Adieu therfore, GOD be thy ſpeade,
And bleſſe thœ a hundred fold.

The Booke.

And you alſo good Maiſter mine,
GOD bleſſe you with his grace :
Preſerue you ſtill, and graunt to you
In Heauen a dwelling place.

Tl

The Anatomie of

the Abuses in AILGNA.

¶ The Interlocutors, or Speakers.

Spudeus.   Philoponus.

God geue you gœd moʒow, Maiſter Philoponus.

Philo. And you alſo, gœd Bʒother Spudeus.

Spud. I am glad to ſæ you in gœd health, foʒ it was bʒuted abʒoad euery where in our countrey (by reaſon of your diſcontinuance, I thinke) that you were dead, long agœ.

Flying fame oftentimes lyeth,

Philo. In dæde, I haue ſpent ſome tyme abʒoad, els where, then in my natiue countrey, (I muſt næds confeſſe) but, how falſe that Repoʒt is (by whom ſœuer it was firſt rumoʒed, oʒ how farre ſo euer it be diſperſed) your pʒeſent eyes can witneſſe.

B.i.   Spud:

Spud. I pray you, what course of lyfe, haue you lead in this your longe absence, sorth of your owne countrey?

The place wher the Author hath trauayled.

Philo. Truely (brother) I haue lead the life of a poore Trauayler, in a certaine famous Ilande, once named, Ainabla, after, Ainatirb: but nowe presently called Ailgna, wherein I haue liued these seuen winters, and more, trauailing from place to place, euen all the Land ouer indifferently.

Spud. That was to your no litle charges, I am sure?

Trauailing chargeable.

Philo. It was so: but what thā? I thank God I haue atchieued it, and by his dyuine assistāce prosperously accomplished it, his glorious name (worthie of all magnificence) bee eternally praysed therefore.

Spud. And to what ende, did you take in hand this great trauayle, if I may be so bould as to aske?

The causes that moued the author to take this trauaile in hand

Philo. Truely, to sée fashions, to acquainte my selfe with the natures, qualities, properties, and conditions of all men, to breake my selfe to the worlde, to learne nurture, good demeanour, & cyuill behauiour: to sée the goodly situation of Citties, Townes and Countryes, with their prospects, and commodities: and finally, to learne the state of all thinges in generall: all which I could neuer haue learned in one place. For who so sitteth at home, euer

com

commo2ante o2 abiding in one place, knoweth nothinge, in refpecte of him, that trauay-
leth ab2oade: and hee that knoweth nothing,
is lyke a b2ute Beafte, but hee that knoweth
all thinges (whiche thinge none doeth but
God alone) hee is a God amongeft men. And
feeing there is a perfectiō in knowledge, as in
euery thing els, euery man ought to defire
that perfection: fo2 in my iudgement, there is
as muche difference (almoft) betwixt a man
that hath trauayled much, and him that hath
dwelt euer in one place, (in refpect of knowledge, and fcience of things) as is betwen a
man lyuinge, & one dead in graue. And ther-
fo2e J haue had a great felicytie in trauay-
ling ab2oade.

The differēce
betwixt a mā
the hath tra-
uayled, and
a man that
hath not.

Spud. Seing that by diuyne p2ouidence, we
are heare met together, let vs (vntill we come
to y̆ end of our purpofed io2ney) vfe fome con-
ference of the ftate of the World now at this
daie, as well to recreate our minds, as to cut
of the tedyoufnes of oure io2neye.

Philo. J am very well contente fo to doe,
beinge not a litle glad of your good companie: Fo2, Comes facundus in via, pro ve-
hiculo eft. 1. A good Companion too trauayle withall, is in fteade of a Wagon,

The benefite
of a good
Companion
to trauayle
withall.

B ij   o2

or Chariot. For as the one doth ease the painfulnes of the way, so doth the other alleuiat ŷ yrksomnes of the iourney intended.

Spud. But, before I enter combat with you
A request to
auoid offēce. (because I am a countrey man, rude and vnlearned: & you, a Ciuilian, indued with great wisdome, knowledge and experience) I most humbly beseech you, that you wyl not be offended with me though I talke to you somwhat grossly, without eyther polished wordes, or syled speeches, which your wisdom doth require, and my insufficiencie and inabylitie is not of power to afforde.

Phil. Your speeches (I put you out of doubt) shal not be offensiue to mee, if they be not offensiue to God, first.

Spud. I pray you, what maner of Countrey is that Ailgna, where you say you haue trauailed so much?

Philo. A pleasant & famous Iland, immu-
Ailgna, a
goodly cūtry. red aboute with the Sea, as it were with a wall, wherein the aire is verie temperate, the ground fertile, and abounding with all things either necessary to man, or needefull for beast.

The people
of Ailgna. Spud. What kinde of people are they that inhabite there?

Philo. A strong kinde of people, audacious, bold, puissant, and heroycal, of great magnanimitie, valiauncie and prowes, of an incomparable feature, of an excellente complexion, and

in

in all humanitie, inferisur to none vnder the
Sunne.

Spud. This people, whome God hath thus
bleſſed, muſt nœdes bee a verie godly people,
eyther els they be mœre ingrate, to God the
authour of all grace, & of theſe their bleſſinges
eſpecially?

Philo. It grœueth me to remember their
liues, or to make mention of their wayes, for
notwithſtanding that the Lorde hath bleſſed
that Lande, with the knowledge of his truth
aboue all other Landes in the world, yet is
there not a people more abrupte, wicked, or
peruerſe, liuing vpon the face of the earth.

*The liues of
the people of
Ailgna.*

Spud. From whence ſpring all theſe euills
in man, for we ſœ euerie one is inclined to ſin
naturally, and there is no fleſhe which liueth,
and ſinneth not?

Philo. All wickednes, miſchiefe, and ſinne,
(doubte you not brother Spud.) ſpringeth of
our auncient ennemie the Deuill, the inuete-
rate corruption of our nature, and the inteſt-
ine malice of our owne hearts, as from the o-
riginals of all vncleannes, & impuritie whatſoeuer. But we are now newe creatures, and
adoptiue children, created in Chriſt Jeſus to
doe good woorkes, which God hath prepared
for vs to walke in. Wherefore wee ought to
haue no fellowſhip with the woorkes of dark-
neſſe, but to put on the armour of light Chriſt

*From whēce
all euilles
ſpring in mā.*

*We ought to
haue no dea-
ling with the
woorkes of the
fleſh,*

Jeſus, to walke in newneſſe of life and to worke our ſaluation in feare and trembling, as the Apoſtle ſaith, and our ſauiour Chriſt biddeth vs ſo work, as our workes may gloriſie our heauenlye Father. But (alas) the contrarie is moſt true, for there is no ſinne, that was euer broached in any age, which floriſheth not nowe.   And therfore the fearfull daie of the Lord cannot be farre of: at which day all the World ſhall ſtand in flaſhing fier, and than ſhall Chriſt our Sauiour come marching in ẏ clowdes of heauen, with his Taratantara ſounding in each mans eare:

The day of Dome not regarded.

ariſe you Dead, and come to iudgement, and than ſhall the Lord reward euery Man after his owne workes.   But how little this is eſteemed of, & how ſmally regarded, to conſider it greeueth me to the very harte, and there is almoſt no life in mee.

Spud. It is but a follie to greeue at them, who ſorowe not for them ſelues. Let them

Euery Man muſt anſwer for him ſelfe.

ſinck in their owne ſinne: lyue well your ſelfe & you ſhall not anſweare for them, nor they for you. Is it not written? vnuſquiſque portabit ſuũ onus. Euery one ſhall beare his own burden. Anima quæ peccauerit, ipſa morietur ẏ ſonle that ſinneth ſhall dy: wherfore ſurceaſe to ſorow or greeue any more for them: for they are ſuch, as the Lord hath caſt of into a reprobat ſenſe, & preiudicat opinion, & preordinat to de-

deſtruction, that his power, his glozie and iuſtice may appeare to all the Wozld.

Philo. Oh bzother, ther is no chziſtē mā, in whoſe hart ſhineth ſcintillula aliqua pietatis, any ſparke of God his grace, which will not grǣue to ſǣ his bzethzen & ſiſters in the Lozd, members of the ſame body, coheyzes of ỹ ſame kingdom, & purchaſed with one & the ſame ineſtimable pzice of Chziſt his bloud, to runne thus deſperatlie into the gulphe of deſtruction and laberinth of perdition. If the leaſt and meaneſt member of thy whole body, be hurt, wounded, cicatriced oz bzuſed, doth not the hart, and euerie member of thy body, fǣle the anguiſh and paine of the griǣued parte, ſeking & endeuouring them ſelues, euery one in his office & calling, to repaire the ſame, and neuer ſoying, vntill that be reſtozed again to his fozmer integritie & perfection? Which thinge in the balance of Chziſtian charity, conſideratly weighed, may mooue any good Man to mourn foz their defection, and to aſſay, by all poſſible means, to reduce them home again, that their ſoules maie be ſaued in the daye of the Lozd. And the Apoſtle commandeth vs, that we be (alter alterius emolumento) an ayde and helpe one to an other. And that we do good to all men, dum tempus habemus, whyleſt we haue tyme. To wǣpe with them that wǣpe, to mourne with them that mourne, and

The mutuall harmonie of one member with an other

B iiij   to

to be of like affection one towardes an other.
And common reason aduertiseth vs,that wee
are not borne for our selues onelie: for,Ortus
nostri partem patria,partem amici,partem pa
rentes vendicant. Our Countrey challengeth
a part of our byrth, our brethren and frendes

No mā born
for himselfe.

require an other parte,and our parentes(and
that optimo iure)doe vendicate a third parte.
Wherefore I will assay to doe them good(if I
can)in discouering their abuses,and laying o-
pen their inormities,that they seing the gree-
uousnes of their maladies, & daunger of theyr
diseases,may in time seeke to the true Phisiti-
on, & expert Chirurgion of their soules Christ
Iesus, of whome onelie commeth all health &
grace,and so eternally be saued.

　Spud. Seing that so many and so haynous
sinnes do raigne and rage in Ailgna, as your
wordes import, and which mooue you to such
intestine sorrowe,and griefe of minde,I pray
you describe vnto me more perticularly,some
of those Capitall crimes , and chiefe Abuses,
which are there frequented,and which dishonour the maiestie of God the most,as you suppose?

A parti-

A particuler descrip-
tion of PRIDE, the principall A-
buſe: and how manifold it is in AILGNA.

PHILOPONVS.

Ou do well to requeſt me to cipher foorth vnto you parte of thoſe great Abuſes (and Cardinall Uices) vſed in AILGNA, for no man in anie Catalogue, how prolixe ſoeuer, is able to comprehend the ſumme of all abuſes there in practiſe. And whereas you woulde haue mee to ſpeake of thoſe Capitall or chiefe Abuſes, which both are deadly in their owne nature, and which offende the maieſtie of God moſte. Mee thinke you ſhake hands with the ſworne enemies of God the Papiſtes, who ſay, there are two kindes of ſinne, the one beniall, the other lethall or deadly. But you muſt vnder-ſtand, that there is not the leaſt ſinne, that is committed eyther in thought, worde, or dæde, (yea, Væ vniuerſæ iuſtitiæ noſtræ, ſi remota miſericordia iudicetur. Wo be to all our righ-teouſnes, if mercie put away they ſhould bæ iudged:) but it is damnable, dempta miſeri-cordia Dei, if the mercie of God be not exten-ded. And againe, there is no ſinne ſo grænous, which the grace and mercy of God is not able

The number of Abuſes in-finite.

All ſinne in it owne na-ture is mor-tall.

B.v.   19

to counteruaile withal,& if it bee his pleasure to blot it out for euer. So y you see now, there is no sinn so veniall, but if the mercie of God, be not stretched out, it is damnable: nor yet anie sinne so mortall , which by the grace and mercie of God, may not bee done away. And therfore as we are not to presume of the one, so wee are not to despaire of the other. But to returne againe to y satisfying of your request.

The greatest abuse which offendeth god most,is pride. The greatest abuse, which both offendeth god mosse, & is there not a little aduaunced, is the execrable sinne of Pride', and excesse in apparell, which is there so ripe, as the filthie fruits thereof haue long since, presented themselues before the throne of the maiestie of God , calling and crying for vengeance day,and nighte incessantly.

Spud. Wherfore haue you inteded to speak of Pride the first of all,geuing vnto it the first place in your tractation? Because it is euill in it selfe, and the efficiente cause of euill,or for some other purpose?

Pride the beginning of all euill.

ECCLES. 10.

Philo. For no other cause , but for that I thinke it to bee,not onely euill and damnable in it owne nature, but also the verie efficient cause of all euills.And therfore the wise man was bolde', to call it Initium omnium malorum,the beginning and welspring of al euils. For as from the roote all natural thinges doe grow,& take their beginning:so from y cursed

roote

rœfe of pestiferous Pride do all other euilles
sproute, and thereof are ingencrate. Therfore
may Pride be called not improperly, Mater-
cula & origo omniu vitiorû, the mother and
nurse of al mischief : for what thyng so haynous, what cryme so flagitious, what deed so
perillous, what attemptso vèterous, what en-
terpriseso pernicious, or what thing so offésiue
to God or hurtful to mã, in all ŷ world, which
mã (of himselfe a very Sathanas) to maintain
his pride withall, wil not willingly atchieue?
hercof wee haue too muche experience euerye
day, more is the pittie.

Spud. How manyfold is this sin of Pryde,
whereby the glorie of God is defaced, and his
maiestie so grœuously offended?

Philo. Pride is tripartite, namely, ŷ pryde
of the hart, the pride of the mouth, & the pryde
of apparell, which (vnles J bee deceiued) offendeth God more then the other two. For as ŷ
pride of the heart & mouth is not opposite to ŷ
eye, nor bisible to the sight, and therefor intice
not others to banitie & sin (notwithstanding
they be grœuous sinnes in the sight of God) so
the pride of apparel, remaining in sight, as an
exemplarie of euill, induceth the whole man
to wickednes and sinne.

Spud. How is the pride of ŷ hart cõmitted?

Philo. Pride of the hart is perpetrate, whê
as a man lifting him selfe on highe, thinketh

of

of himselfe, aboue that which he is of himselfe:
dreamyng a perfection of himselfe, when he is
nothyng lesse: And in respect of himselfe, con-
tempneth, bilesieth and reproacheth all men,
thinking none comparable to him selfe, whose
righteousnes, notwithstanding, is lyke to the
polluted cloth of a menstruous woman :

What pride of the hart is. Therfore, the Pryde of the Heart, maye
bée saide, too bée a Rebellious elation, or
lyftyngz vppe of the mynde, agaynste the
Lawe of God, attrybutynge and ascry-
bynge that vnto himselfe, whiche is proper
to God onely. And although it bee the Lorde,
Qui operatur in nobis velle, & posse, who wor-
keth in vs both the wil and power to do good,
Ne gloriaretur omnis caro, leaste anie flesshe
should boste of his owne power and strength,
PHILAVTIA. yet Pride, with his Cosin germayn Philautia
which is Selfeloue, perswadeth him, ŷ he hath
néede of no mans helpe but his owne: that he
standeth by his own proper strength & power
and by no mans els, & that he is al in all, yea,
so perfect and good, as no more can be exacted
of hym.

Spud. How is Pride of wordes, or pride of
mouthe, committed?

How pride of wordes, or of the mouth is committed. Philo. Pride of the mouth, or of wordes, is,
when we boast, bragge or glorie, eyther of our
selues, our kinred, consanguynitie, byrth, parentage, and suche like: or when we extol our
selues

selues fo2 any bertue,sanctimonie of lyfe, sin-
certie of Godlynes, which eyther is in vs,o2
which we p2etend to be in vs. In this kinde
of P2ide(as in the other) almost euery one of-
fendeth:fo2 shal you not haue all(in a maner)
boast & vaunt themselues of their Auncetc2s,
and p2ogenito2s? saying, & crying with open
mouth: I am a Gentleman, I am wo2shipful,
I am Honourable , I am Noble , and I can
not tell what : my father was this,my father
was that: I am come of this house,and I am
come of that: Wheras,Dame Nature,b2yng-
eth vs all into the wo2lde,after one so2te,and
receiueth all againe , into the wombe of our
mother, I meane,the bowelles of the earth,al
in one and the same o2der and manner,with-
out any difference o2 diuersitie at all, wherof
mo2e hereafter shalbe spoken.

　Spud. How is P2ide of Apparell cõmitted?

　Philo. By wearyng of Apparell mo2e go2-
geous , sumptuous & p2ecious than our state,
callyng o2 condition of lyfe requireth , wherby, we are puffed vp into P2ide,and info2ced
to thinke of our selues, mo2e than we ought,
beyng but vile earth and miserable sinners.
And this sinne of Apparell (as I haue sayde
befo2e) hurteth mo2e then the other two: Fo2
the sinne of the heart , hurteth none, but the
Autho2,in whom it b2æeth,so long as it bursteth not fo2th into exteriour action:And the
　　　　　　　　　　　　　　　　P2ide

How pride of
apparel ¡is per
petrate & cõ-
mitted.

Pride of the mouth (whiche consisteth, as I haue sayd, in ostenting and bragging of some singular vertue, eyther in himselfe, or some other of his kinred, and which he arrogateth to himselfe (by Hereditarie possession, or lineall dissent) though it be meere vngodly in it own nature, yet it is not permanent, (for wordes fly into the aire, not leauing any print or character behinde them to offend the eyes.) But this sinne of excesse in Apparell, remayneth as an Example of euyll before our eyes, and as a prouocatiue to sinne, as Experience daylye sheweth.

Spud. Would you not haue men to obserue *A decorum to be obserued.* a decencie, a comlinesse & a decorum in their vsuall Attyre? Doeth not the worde of God commaund vs to do all things decenter, & secundum ordinem ciuilem: decently, and after a cyuile maner?

Philo. I would wish, that a decencie, a comly order, and as you say, a decorum were obserued, as well in Attyre, as in all things els: but, would God the contrarie were not true: For most of our nouell Inuentions and new fangled fashions, rather deforme vs then ad- *Our apparell rather defor- meth, than adorneth vs.* orne vs: disguise vs, then become vs: makyng vs rather, to resemble sauadge Beastes and stearne Monsters, then continent, sober and chaste Christians.

Spud. Hathe this contagious infection, of
Pride

Pride in Apparell, infected and poysoned any
other countrey, beside Ailgna, suppose you?

Philo. No doubt, but this poyson hath shed
forth his influence, and powred forth his stinking dregges ouer all the face of the earth, but
yet I am sure, there is not any people vnder
the Zodiacke of heauen, how clownish, rurall
or brutish soeuer, that is so poisoned with this
Arsnecke of Pride, or hath drunke so deepe of
the dregges of this Cup, as Ailgna hath, with
griefe of conscience I speake it, with sorow I
see it, and with teares I lament it.

Spud. But I haue heard them saye, that o-
ther Nations passe them, for exquisite brauery
in Apparell : as, the Italians, the Athenians,
the Spaniards, the Caldeans, Heluetians, Zuit-
zers, Venetians, Muscouians, and such lyke :
now, whither this be true or not, I greatly desire to knowe.

Philo. This is but a visour, or cloke, to hide
their Sodometrie withall: onelye spoken, not
proued: forged in the deceiptfull Mint of their
owne braynes : For (if credit may be giuen
to ancient writers,) the Egyptiãs are said, neuer to haue chãged their fashion, or altered the
forme of their first Attire, from the beginning
to this day: as Iacobus Stuperius, lib.de diuer
sis nostræ ætatis habitibus, Pag.16, affirmeth:
The Grecians, are saide, to vse but one kynde
of Apparell without any chaunge : that is to
wit:

No Cuntrey
so drunken
with pride as
Ailgna.

wit : a longe Gowne, reaching downe to the
grounde.

The Germaynes, are thought to be so pre-
cise in obseruing one vniforme fashion in Apparell, as they haue neuer recoded from their
first Origina: as the said Stuperius sayth, in
these wordes : Non enim mores leuiter mutare vetustos, Germanus vnqnam consueuit
incola : Which in Englysh Werse, is thus
muche in effect.

¶The Germayne people neuer vse,
     lightly to chop and chaunge
Their customes olde, or els Attyre,
     wherin abroade they range.

¶The Muscouians, Athenians, Italians,
Brasilians, Affricanes, Asianes, Cantabri-
ans, Hungarians, Ethiopians, or els, what
Nation soeuer, vnder the Sunne, are so farre
qehinde the people of Ailgna, in exquisitnesse
of Apparell, as in effect, they esteeme it litle or
nothyng at all, so it repell the colde, and rouer
their shame : yea, some of them are so smally
addicted therto, that settyng apart all honestie
and shame, they go cleane naked. Other some
meanly apparelled, some in Beasts skinnes,
some in haire, & what euer they can get: some
in one thing, some in another, nothing regarding cyther hosen, shoes, bands, ruffes, shirts,
or any thing els. And the ciuilest nations that
are, bee so farre estraunged from the pride of
                              Apparell

of apparell that they eſteme him as bꝛauelye attyred that is clothed in our carʒies, friʒes, ruggs, and other kinds of cloth, as we do him that is clad all ouer in ſilkes, veluets, ſatens, damaſks, grograins, taffeties, and ſuch like. So that herby you ſee, that they ſpeak vntruly that ſay, that other nations exceede them in bꝛauerie of apparell. Foꝛ it is manifeſt that all other Nations vnder the ſun how ſtrange, how new, how fine, oꝛ how comly ſoeuer they think their faſhiõs to be, when they be cõpared with the dyuerſe faſhions, & ſundꝛie foꝛmes of apparell in Ailgna, are moſt vnhandſame, bꝛutiſh and monſtrouſe. And herby it appeareth that no People in the Woꝛld is ſo curiouſe in new fangles, as they of Ailgna be. But graũte it were ſo, and admit that others excelled them, (which is falſe) ſhall we do euill, becauſe they do ſo? ſhall their wickedneſſe excuſe vs of ſinne, if we commit the like & woꝛſe? ſhall not the ſoule that ſinneth dye? Wherfoꝛe let vs not ſinne of pꝛeſumptiõ, with the multitude, becauſe they do ſo, leaſt we be plagued with them becauſe we doe the like. Moꝛeouer thoſe Cuntreyes are rich and welthie of them ſelues, abounding with all kinde of pꝛeciouſe oꝛnaments, and riche attyre, as ſilks, veluets, Satens, damaſks, ſarcenet, taffetie, chamlet, and ſuch like (foꝛ al theſe are made in thoſe foꝛaine cuntreyes) and therfoꝛe

Other countreyes not to be blamed though they, go in ſilks veluets, and why:

C　if

if they weare them, they are not muche to bee
blamed, as not hauing anie other kind of cloa
thing to couer themselues withall. So if wee
would contente our selues with such kinde of
attire, as our owne Countrey doeth minister
vnto vs, it were much tollerable. But wee
are so surpzised in Pzide, that if it come not
from beyond the seas, it is not wozth a straw.
And thus we impouerish our selues in buying
their trifling merchandizes, moze plesant thā
necessarie, and inrich them, who rather laugh
at vs in their slœues, than otherwise, to sœ our
gret follie in affcting of trifles, τ departing ω
gœd merchandizes foz it. And howe litle they
estœme of silkes, veluets, satens, damasks, and
such like, wee maye easely sœ, in that they sell
them to vs foz wolles, frizes, rugges, carzies,
and the lyke, whiche they coulde neuer doe, if
they estœmed of them as much as we doe. So
that you sœ they are forced of necessitye to
weare such riche attyze, wanting other things
(whereof we haue stoze) to inuest themselues
withall. But who sœth not (excepte wilfulhc
blynde) that no necessitie compelleth vs to
weare them hauing abundāce of other things
to attire our selues with, both hansomer, warmer, and as comlie as they in euerie respect?
But farre fetched, and deare boughte, is good
foz Ladyes they say.

Spud. Doe you thinke it not permitted to
any hauinge stoze of other necessary clothyng,

Other Coun-
tryes esteme
not so muche
of silkes, vel-
uets, as we do.

to weare, ſilks, veluets, taffeties, & other ſuche riche attyre, of what calling ſocuer they be of?

 Ph. I doubt not, but it is lawfull for ẙ po-teſtates, the nobilitie, the gentrie, yeomanrie, and for euerye priuate ſubiecte els to weare attyre euery one in his degræ, accordinge as his calling and condition of life requireth, yet a meane is to be kæpt, for, omne extremum vertitur in vitium, euery extreme, is turned into vice. The nobilitye (though they haue ſtore of other attyre) and the gentrie (no doubte) may vſe a rich, and preciouſe kẙnd of apparell (in the feare of God) to innoble, garniſhe & ſet forthe their byrthes, dignities, functions and callings, but for no other reſpecte, they may not in any maner of wyſe. The maieſtrats alſo, & Officers in the weale publique, by what tytle ſocuer they be called (accordinge to their abylities) may were (if the Prince, or Super-intendent do Godly commaund) coſtlie orna-ments and riche attyre, to dignifie their cal-lings, and to demonſtrat and ſhewe forth, the excelency, and worthines of their offices, and functions, therby to ſtrike a terroure & feare into the harts of the people, to offend againſt the maieſty of their callings : but yet would I wiſh, that what ſo is ſuperfluous or ouer-muche, either in the one, or in ẙ other, ſhold be diſtributed to the helpe of the pore members of Chriſt Ieſus, of whom an infẙnite number

C.ij.   hap-

Euery man may weare ap parell accor-ding to his callinge.

The nobility may weare gorgiouſe at-tyre, and why.

Maieſtrats may were ſumptuouſe attyre & why

daylie do perish , thozowe wante of necellarie
refectio , and due suﬆentation to their bodies.
And as foz the pziuat subiects,it is not at any
hand lawful that they ﬃould weare ﬁlks,vel-
uets, satens,damalks,gould, ﬁluer and what
they liﬆ(though they be neuer so able to main
tain it) except they being in some kinde of of-
ﬁce in the common wealth , do vse it foz the
dignifying and innobling of the same. But
now there is such a confuse mingle mangle of
apparell in Ailgna, and such pzepoﬆerous er-
cesse therof,as euery one is permitted to ﬂaunt
it out, in what apparell he luﬆ himselfe , oz
can get by anie kind of meanes. So that it is
verie hard to knowe , who is noble, who is
wozﬃipfull,who is a gentleman, who is not:
foz you ﬃall haue those , which are neither of
the noblilitie gentilitie.noz yeomáry, no, noz
yet anie Magiﬆrat oz Officer in the commen
welth,go daylie in ﬁlkes, veluets,satens,da-
malks,taffeties and such like , notwithﬆan-
ding that they be both base by byzthe, meane
by eﬆate,& seruple by calling.This is a great
confuﬁon & a general disozder,God be mercy-
full vnto vs.

Spud. If it be not lawfull foz euery one, to
weare, ﬁlks,veluets, satens, damalks, taffeties,gold, ﬁluer,pzeciouse ﬆones, & what not,
wherfoze did the Lozd make & ozdein them?

Philo. I denie not, but they may be wozne
of

Not lawfull
for priuate
subiectes to
weare sump-
teous attyre.

Hard to know
a Gentleman
from another
by apparell.

of them, who want other things to cloth them
withal, oz of ꝑ nobylity, gentilptie, oz magiſtra⸳
ry, foz the cauſes aboueſaid, but not of euery
pzoud ſtrnet indifferentlie, that haue ſtoze of
other attyze inough. And yet did not the Loźd
ozdeane theſe riche oznaments and gozgioule
beſtments to be wozne of all men, oz of anie,
ſo muche as to garniſh, bewtiſie, and ſet fozth,
the maieſty ⸲ glozie of this his earthly king⸳
dome: Foz, as cloth of gold, Araſe, tapeſtrie, ⸲
ſuch other riche oznaméts, pendices and han⸳
ginꬶs in a houſe of eſtate, ſerue not onely to
manuall bſes and ſcruyle occupatiös, but al⸳
ſo to decozate, to bewtiſie ⸲ become the houſe,
and to ſhewe the riche eſtate and glozie of the
owner: ſo theſe riche oznaments and ſump⸳
teouſe beſtments, of the earthly territozy of
this Wozld, do not onelie ſerue to be woźn of
them, to whome it doth appertaine (as befoze)
but alſo to ſhe n foźth, ꝑ powe⸳, welth, dignity
riches, and glozie of the Loźd, the Authoz of
all goodneſſe. And here in, the pzouidence
and mercy of God appeareth moſt plainclye,
foz wher there is ſtoze of other clothing there
hath be geuen, leſſe ſtoze of ſilks, beluets, ſa⸳
tens, damaſks, and ſuch like: and wher there
is plenty of them, there is no clothing els, al⸳
moſt, ⸲thus the Loźd did deale, foz that euery
cuntrey ought to contente themſelues, with
there owne kind of attyze: except neceſſytie
                              C iij   in⸳

foce the contrarie, fo2 than we are to v'e odr
libertie in the feare of God.

Spud. I pзaye you let mee intreate you, to
fhewe me wherefoze our apparell was giuen
vs, and by whome?

Philo. Your requeſte is both diffuſe and intricate, and moze than my weake and infirme
knowledge is able to compzehend: yet, leaſt I
might bee adiudged vnwilling to doe good, I
will aſſay to doe the beſt I can.

When the Lozd our God, a ſpiritual, intel-
lectible vnderſtanding ſubſtance, incompzehen-
ſible, immenſurable, e inacceſſible, had by his
wooзd, and heauenly wiſedome Chziſt Jeſus,
created and made ỹ woзld, e all things therin contayned, ỹ ſirſt day he created man, after
his own ſimilitude and likenes, in innocencie,
holines, rightcouſnes, e all kind of perfection,
he placed him in Paradiſe terreſtrial comaun-
ding him to tyl e manure ỹ ſame. Th̃ ỹ deuil,
an old maligner of mankind, who befoze was
an Angel in heauẽ, e thзough ſin of pзide in ar
rogating to himſelfe ỹ ſeate, e thзone of Gods
maieſty, caſt down into ỹ lake of hell, enuying
mans gloзious eſtate, which he than had loſt,
came vnto man in Paradiſe, e inticed him (oh
toзteouſe ſerpent) to eat of ỹ foзbidden fruite,
wherof the Loзde God had foзbidden him to
taſt, on pain of his life: notwithſtãding, Adam
condeſcending to his wife her perſwaſions, oз
rather

When, where,
and for what
cauſe our ap-
pirell was
gouen vs.

The fall of
man by the
malice of the
deuill.

father to the Serpent, hauing buzzed his ve-
nemous suggestions into their eares, tooke of
the apple, & did eat, contrary to ý expresse commandement of his God. This done their eyes
were opned, thei saw their nakednes, & were
not a litle ashamed (& yet before sin was committed, they being both naked, were not ashamed, but sin once committed, they became vncleane, filthie, lothsome, & deformed) & sewed
them garmēts of fig leaues together, to couer
their shame withall. Than the Lord pittying
their miserie, & loathing their deformity, gaue
thē pelts, & felles of beasts to make them garments withall, to the end that their shamefull
parts might lesse appeare: yet some are so bra-　_Impudent_
sen faced & so impudent, that to make ý deuill　_beasts._
& his members sport, will not sticke to make
open shew of those parts, which God cōmaun-
deth to be couered, nature willeth to be hid, &
honesty is ashamd once to behold or looke vpō.
Spud . I gather by your words three speciall
poynts. First, ý sin was the cause why our apparell was giuen vs. Secondly, ý God is the
author, & giuer therof. Thirdly, ý it was giuē
vs to couer our shame withall, & not to feed ý insatiable desires of mēs watō & luxurious eies.

Philo. Your collectiō is very true. Than see-
ing ý our apparel was giuē vs of god to couer　_Wherfor our_
our shame, to keep our bodies frō cold, & to be　_apparell was_
as prickes in our eies, to put vs in mind of our　_giuen vs._
　　　　　　C.iij.　　miseries, frailt-

frailties, imperfections and sin, of our backſliding from the cōmaundements of god and obedience of the higheſt, and to excite vs the rather to contrition, and compunction of the spirit, to bewayle our misery, & to craue mercy at ȳ mercifull hands of God, let vs be thākfull to God for them, be ſorie for our ſinnes, (which weare the cause therof) and vſe them to the glory of our God, & the benefyte of our bodies and ſoules, againſt the great day of the Lord appeare. But (alas) these good creatures, which the Lord our God, gaue vs for the respects before rehearsed, we haue so peruerſted; as now they ſerue in ſtead of the deuills nettes, to catche poore ſoules in: for euery one now adaies (almoſt) couet to deck and painte their liuing ſepulchres or erthly graues (their bodies I meane) with all kind of brauerie, what soeuer can be deuiſed, to delight ȳ eyes of the vnchaſt behoulders, wherby God is diſhonored, offence is encreaſed, and much ſinne daylie committed, as in further diſcourse ſhall plainly appeare.

Mens bodies lyuing sepulchres.

Spud. Did the Lord cloth our firſt parents in leather, as not hauing any thing more precious to attyre them withall, or for that, it might be a permanent rule, or patern vnto vs (his posterity) for euer, wherafter we are of force to make all our garments, so as it is not now lawfull to go in richer arraye, without offendinge his maiestie?

Philo. Although ẏ Lord did not cloth thē so
meanly, for that he had nothing els, more pre=
ciouse to attyre them withall (for Domini est
terra, & plenitudo eius, the earth is the Lords
and the fulnesse therof, saith the Lord by his
Psalmist: And by his Prophet. Gold is myne,
siluer is myne, and all the riches of the world
is my own) yet no doubt, but he would ẏ this
their meane & base attyre, should be as a rule,
or pedagogie vnto vs, to teach vs ẏ we ought
rather to walke meanelye, and simplye, than
gorgiously, or pompously: rather seruing pre=
sente necessitye, than regarding the wanton
appetits of our lasciuiouse mindes: Not with=
standinge I suppose not, that his heauenlye
maiestye would, that those garments of lether,
should stand as a rule or pattern of necessytie
vnto vs, wherafter we shold be boūd to shape
all our apparell for euer, or els greeuouslye to
offende: but yet by this, we may sée, his blessed
will is, that we should rather go an ace beneth
our degrée, than a iote aboue. And ẏ any sim=
ple couering pleaseth the Godly, so that it re=
pell the colde, and couer the shame, it is more
than manifest, as well by the legends both of
prophane Historyographers Cronologers, and
other writers, as also by the censures, exam=
ples and lyues of all Godly, since the begin=
ning of the world: And if the Lord would not,

C.b.   that

In our appa-
rell we ought
rather to ●-
by necessity,
than to feed
vanity.

Adã his mean kind of attire was a signe of mediocrity vnto vs in our apparell.

that the attyre of Adam, should haue beene a signe, or patterns of mediocritie vnto vs, he both in mercy would, & in his almighty power could haue inuested them in silks, veluets satens, grograins, gold, siluer, & what not. But the Lord our God foresawe, that if he had clothed man, in rich and gorgiouse attyre (suche is our proclyuitye to sinne) he wold haue bene proude therof as we sée it is come to passe at this day (God amend it) and therby purchase to himselfe, his body and soule, eternall damnation.

Spud. Than it seemeth a thinge materiall, and of great importãce, that we resemble our first Parẽts in austerity, and simplicity of apparell, so muche as maye be possible, doth it not?

No religion reposed in apparell.

Philo. I put no religion in goinge, or not goinge in the like simple attyre of our parẽts Adam, & Eua, (as our Papistes, Papists? no, Sorbonists, Sorbonists? no, Atheists, atheists? no, plaine Sathanists do, placing all thier religion in hethen garments, & Romish raggs) so that we obserue a meane and exceade not in pride. But notwithstanding, if we approched a litle nearer them, in Godly simplicitie and Christian sobrietie, both of apparell and maner of lyuinge, we should not onely please God a great deale the more, and enritche our Cuntrey, but also auoyd many scandals & offences,

ſetes, which grow daily by our exceſſiue ryot,
and ryotouſe exceſſe in apparell. For doth not
$\tilde{y}$ apparell ſtyrre vppe the heart to pride? doth
it not intice others to ſinne? and doth not ſin
purchaſe hell the guerdon of pride ?

The fruite of Pride.

Spud. But they ſay, they pleaſe God, rather
than offend him in wearing this gorgiouſe attyre, for therby the glory of his workmanſhip
in them doth more appeare. Beſides that, it
maketh a man to be accepted, and eſteemed of
in euery place: wheras otherwiſe, they ſhould
be nothing leſſe.

Philo. To think that the Lorde our God is
delighted in the ſplendente ſhewe of outward
apparell , or that it ſetteth forth $\tilde{y}$ glory of his
Creatures, and the maieſty of his kingdom I
ſuppoſe ther is no mã (at leaſt no perfect chriſtian man)ſo bewitched or aſſotted. For that
weare, as much, as to ſay, that ſtinking pride,
& filthie ſinne , tended to the glory of God, ſo
that the more we ſyn the more we increaſe
his prayſe and glory. But the Lord ours
God is ſo farre from dilighting in ſinne ,
that he adiudgeth them to eternall Death,
and damnation , that committe the ſame.
Than who is he that will take pleaſure in
vayne apparell, which if it be worne but
a whyle , will fall to ragges , and if it be
not worne , will ſoone rotte or els be eaten
with mothes. His wages are not ours
wayes

The Lord ac-cepteth no man after his apparell.

No attyre
can make the
creature of
God seeme
fayree.

Every one is
to contente
him selfe
with his crea-
tion and to
pnyse God
forit.

wayes, his iudgements, not our iudgements, as he sayth, by his Prophet: and wheras they holde, that Apparell setteth foorth the glory of his Maiestie in his creatures, makynge them to appeare fairer, than other wyse they would of themselues, it is blasphemously spoken, and muche derogateth, from ẏ excellency and glory of his name. For saith not God by his prophet Moyses, that after he had made all creatures, he beheld them all, & behould they weare (and especially mã, the excellentest of all other his creatures, whom he made after his own simi-litude & liknesse) exceedinge good? And were all creatures good & perfect, & only mã not perfect nor faire inough? If these their speeches were true (which in the fulnesse of their blasphemie they shame not to speake) thã might wee easily conuince the Lord of vntrue speaking, who in his sacred word, informeth vs, that mã is the perfectest Creature, & the fayrest of al others, ẏ euer he made (excepting the heuenly spirits, & Angelical creatures) after his own liknesse: as before. O mã who arte thou, that reasonest with thy Creator? Shall the clay say vnto the potter, why hast thou made me thus? Or can ẏ clay make himselfe better sauored than the potter, who gaue him his first stamp & propor-tion? Shall we think that stinking pride, can make the workmãshippe of the Lord to seeme fayrer? Than why did not the Lord cloth vs

so at

to as þ firſt ? oz at leaſt, why gaue he not com-
maundemēt in his will, & teſtament which he
ſealed with the pzice of the bleud of his ſonne
to cloth our ſelfes in riche & gozgiouſe apparel
to ſet ſozth his glozy þ moze? But away with
theſe dogs, & belliſh haggs, who retaine this
opiniō, that curſed pzide glozifieth God, & ſetteth ſozth oz bewtifieth his wozkmāſhippe in
his creatures. In vain is it, foz me to expoſtu-
lat with them, foz doubtles nō hould this, but
ſuch as be miſecreants (oz deuills incarnate)
& men caſt of into a repzobate ſence, whom I
beſeech the Lozd in the bowels of his mercy,
either ſpedely to cōuert that they periſh not,
oz els confounde, þ they hurle not, that peace
may be vppō Iſrael. Thus hauing ſufficiently (I truſt) refelled their falſe poſitiōs, I leaue
them to the Lozd, beſeechinge them (as they
tender their own ſaluation linguas cōpeſcere
digitis: to ſtoppe their ſacrilegiouſe mouthes
with ther fingers, & not to ſpit againſt heauen
oz kicke againſt the pzicke as they do, ani s
longer. Foz the Lozd our God is a cōſuming
fier, & vpon obſtinate ſinners ſhal raine down
fire & bzimſton, & conſume them in his wzath.
This is our poztion acquired by ſinne.

   Spud. But what ſay you to the other bzanch
of their concluſion, namely, that Apparell maketh them to be accepted, and well taken in
euery place ?

                              Philo.

The Lord our
God is a con-
ſuming fire,
to deſtroy all
impenitent
ſinners.

Philo. Amongeſt the wicked, and ignozant
Pezants, I muſt nedes confeſſe , they are the
moze eſtemed, in reſpect of their apparell, but
nothing at all the moze , but rather the leſſe,
amongeſt the godly wyſe. So farre of will all
wyſe men be, from accepting of any foz his gay
apparell onely, that (be he neuer ſo gallantly
painted, oz curiouſly plumed in the deceiptfull
fethers of pzide)they wil rather cótemne him
a great deale ÿ moze , taking him to be a mã,
puffed vp with pzide and vaine glozie, a thing
both odiouſe, & deteſtable to God & god men.
And ſeeing it cãnot ſtand with the rule of god
his iuſtice, to accept oz not to except any man
foz his apparell, oz any other externe ſhew of
deceiptfull vanytie, it is mãifeſt , that man
doinge the contrarie, is a Iudas to the truth, a
Traytoz to iuſtice, & an enemy to the Lozd :
Wherfoze farre be that from al god chziſtians
and if thoſe that go richely clothed ſhould be
eſtemed ÿ rather foz their rich apparel, than
a contrario muſt thoſe that go in meane , and
baſe attire, be the moze contemned, and reſpi-
ſed foz their pouertie. And then ſhould Chziſt
Jeſus our great Ambaſſadoz from the king of
heauen, & only Saulour, be comtemned:foz he
came in pooze, & mean array:but Chziſt Jeſus
is bleſſed in his pooze raggs, and all others are
cótemned in their rich & pzecious attyze. Vnder a ſimple rote, many tymes lyeth hid great
wiſdom & knowledg:& cótrarely vnder bzau

The wiſe
will not ac-
cept of any,
after apparell.

attyze somtime is couered great ydiotacy and
folly. Wherof euery daies successe offreth prose
sufficient, moze is the pytie.

Spud. Wherfoze would you haue men accepted, if not foz Apparell?

Philo. If any be so foolish to ymagin, that he
shalbe wozshipped, reuerenced oz accepted the
rather foz his apparell, he is not so wyse, as J
pzay God make me. Foz surely foz my part,
J will rather wozshippe ⁊ accept of a poze mā
(in his clowtes, ⁊ poze raggs) hauing ẏ gifts
and oznamēts of the mind, than J will do him
ẏ roisteth ⁊ flaunteth daylie ⁊ howzely, in his
silks, veluets, satens, damasks, gold oz siluer,
what soeuer, without ẏ induments of vertue,
wherto only al reuerence is due. And therfoze
as any mā is indued, oz not indued with vertue, ⁊ true godlynesse, so will J reuerence, oz
not reuerence, accept, oz not accept of him:
wherfoze if any gape after reuerēce, wozship,
oz acceptation, let them thirst after vertue, as
namely, wisdome, knowledge, discretion, mo-
destie, sobzietie, affability, gentlenesse, ⁊ suche
like, than can they be without reuerence, oz
acceptatiō no moze than ẏ sonne can be wout
light, the fire wout heat, oz the water wout
his naturall moysture.

Sp. Thā J gather you would haue mē accepted foz vertue ⁊ true Godlines, wold you not?

Ph. J would not only haue mē to be accepted ⁊ reuerenced foz their virtue (though the

Wisdom not
tyed to exte-
riour pompe
of apparell.

Reuerence
due to vertue
not to attyre.

Wherfore man is to be worshiped and had in reuerence.

chiefeſt reuerence is onely to be attributed to him, whoſe ſacred breſt, is fraught with ver tue, as it may well be called, the Promptuarie or Receptorie of true wiſdome and Godlines, but alſo (in parte) for their byrthes ſake, pa rentage and conſanguinitie, and not only that, but alſo, in reſpect of their callings, offices and functions, whether it be in the Temporal Ma giſtery a or Eccleſiaſtical presbitery (ſo lōg as they gouerne godly and well:) For, the A poſtle ſayth, that thoſe Elders which gouerne wel amongſt vs, are worthie of double honor: But yet, the mā whom God hath bleſſed with vertue and true godlynes, though he be ney ther of great byrth nor callynge, nor yet any Magiſtrate whatſouer, is worthie of more re uerence and eſtimation then any of the other, without the ornaments of ẏ minde & gifts of, vertue aboueſaid. For what preuayleth it to

Gentilitie without ver tue is no gē ulitie.

be borne of worſhipfull progenie, and to be deſtitute of all vertue, which deſerueth true worſhip? what is it els, then to carie a golden Sworde in a Leaden Scabbarde? Is it any thyng els, then a goldē Coffyn or painted Se pulchre, makyng a fayre ſhowe outwardly, but inwardly is full of all ſtinche, & lothſom nes? I remember once I red a certaine ſtorie of one, a Gentleman by byrth and parentage, who greatly reproched, and withall diſdayned an other, for that he was come to great autho
                                          ritie

rytie onely by vertue, being but a poze mans
rhild by byzthe : What? ſaith the Gentleman
by birth, arte thou ſo luſtie ? Thou arte but a
coblers ſonne, and wilt thou compare with
me, being a Gentleman by byzth, and calling?
To whome the other anſweared, thou arte no
Gentleman, foz thy gentilitie endeth in thee
and I am a Gentleman, in that my gentilitie
beginneth in me. Meaning (unleſt I be deceiued) that the wante of virtue in him, was the
decay of his gentility, and his vertue was the
beginning of true gentilitie in him ſelfe : foz
virtue therfoze, not foz apparell, is euerye one
to be accepted. Foz if we ſhould accept of men
after apparell onely reſpecting nothinge els,
thã ſhold it come to paſſe, that we might moze
eſteme of one, both meane by birth, baſe without virtue, ſeruyle by calling, & poze in eſtate,
moze than of ſome by birthe, noble, by virtue
honozable and by callinge laudable. And the
reaſon is becauſe euery one, tagge and ragge,
go bzauer, oz at leaſt as bzaue as thoſe that be
both noble, honozable and wozpſhipfull.

The exor-
dium of vir-
tue, is the ex-
ordium of
gentilitie, &
worſhip, and
want of the
one, is the de-
cay of the o-
ther.

Spud. But I haue hard ſay, there is moze
holyneſſe in ſome kynd of apparell, than in
otherſome, which makes them ſo much to af-
fecte varytie of faſhions, I thinke.

Philo. Indéd I ſuppoſe that the ſumme of
their religion, ooth conſiſte in apparell. And to
ſpeake my conſcience I thinke there is moze

No holynes
in apparell.

D   oz

oʒ as muche holynesse in the apparell, as in them, that is iust none at all. But admit that there be hoylnesse in apparell (as who is so infatuat to beleue it) than it followeth that the holynes pʒetended is not in them, & so be they plaine Hipocrits to make shew of that, which they haue not. And if ẙ holines by there attire pʒesaged be in them selues, thã is it not in the garments, & why do they than attribute that to the garments, whiche is neither adherente to the one noʒ yet inherent in the other? Oʒ if it wer so, why do they gloʒy of it to the woʒld, but I leaue them to their follie, hastinge to other matters moʒe pʒofitable to intreate of.

Spud. But I haue hard them reason thus. That which is good in it own nature, cannot

An argument
trimly con-
sryued. hurt: apparell is good, and the good Creature of God ; ergo no kynde of apparell can hurte.   And if there be anie abuse in it, the apparell knowethe it not.   Therfoʒe take awaye the abuse ; and let the apparell remaine still, foʒ so it maye (say they) without anie hurte at all.

Philo. These be well seasoned reasons, and substantiall asseuerations in dæd, but if they haue no better arguments to leane vnto, than these, their kingdome of Pʒide will shoʒtlie fall without all hope of recouerte againe.

The apparell in it owne nature is good and the good Creature of God (I will not de

ni

nie) and cannot hurte except it be thozowe
ouer owne wickednesse abuſed. And therfoze
wo be to them that make the good Creatures
of God inſtruments of dampnation to them
ſelues , by not vſing them, but abuſing them.
And yet not withſtanding, it maye be ſaid, to
hurte,oz not to hurte,as it is abuſed,oz not a-
buſed. And wheras they would haue the a-
buſe of apparell (if any be.) taken away,and
the apparell to remain ſtill, it is impoſſible to
ſupplant the one , without the extirpation of
the other alſo. Foz it is trulye ſaid, ſublata
cauſa,tollitur effectus: But not,ſubrepto effe-
ctu,tollitur cauſa. Take away the cauſe, and
the effecte falleth, but not contrarylye , take
away the effect , and the cauſe falleth. The
efficients cauſe of Pzide is gozgiouſe attire,
the effect is pzide it ſelfe ingenerate by attire:
But to begin to plucke awaie the effecte (to
wit pzide). and not to take awaye the cauſe
firſt (namelie ſumptuouſe attyze) is as if
a man intendinge to ſupplant a Træ by the
rootes , ſhould begin to pull the fruite, and
bzaunches onelye , oz to pull downe heauen, ſhould dig in the earthe, wozkinge altogether pzepoſterouſlie , and indyreclye.

And the reaſon is, theſe two collaterall
Cozins, apparell, and Pzide (the Mother
and Daughter of miſchiefe) are ſo combi-
nate together , and incozpozate the one in

Vnpoſſible
to take away
pride,except
ſumptuouſe
apparell be
take it away
alſo.

Apparell and
pride combi-
ned togethe-
as mother, &
daughter.

the other, as the one can hardlie be dyuorced from the other, without the distructiõ of them both. To the accomplishmente wherof God graunte that those holsome lawes, sanctions, and statuts, which by our most gracious and serene princesse (whome Iesus preserue for euer) and her noble, and renoumed Progenitors, haue beene promulgate, and enacted hertofore, may be put in execution. For in my opinion, it is as impossible for a man, to were pretiouse apparell, and gorgiouse attyre, and not to be proude therof (for if he be not proud therof, why doth he weare suche riche attire, wheras meaner is both better cheape, easier to be had, as warme to the bodie, and as decent, and comly to any chast christians eye?) as it is for a man to cary fire in his bosõe, and not to burne. Therfore would God euery mã might be compelled to weare apparell, according to his degrée, estat, and condition of life: which if it were brought to passe, I feare least some who ruffl now in silks, veluets, satts, damasks, golde siluer, and what not, shold be glad to weare frize cotes, & glad if they might get them.

Spud. What is your opiniõ? Did the people of the former world so much esteeme of apparell, as we doe at this present day, without respect had either to sex, kind, order, degrée estat, or callinge?

margin note: Unpossible not to be proud of rich attyre.

Philo.

Philo. No doubt but in all ages, they had
their imperfectiõs and faults, for Hominis eſt
errare, labi, & decipi, it is incident to man, to
erre, to fall, and to be deceiued. But notwith-
ſtandinge as the wicked haue alwayes affected not onelie pride in apparell, but alſo all
other bices whatſoeuer, ſo the chaſte Goodly,
and ſober Chriſtians, haue ener eſchewed this
exceſſe of apparell, hauing a ſpeciall regard to
weare ſuche attyre as might neyther offend
the maieſtie of God, prouoke them ſelues to
pride nor yet offend any of their Brethren in
any reſpecte. But (as I haue ſaid) not onely
the Goodlie haue deteſted and hated this baine
ſuperfluitye of apparell in all tymes ſince the
beginning of the World, but alſo the berie he-
panims, the heathen Philoſophers, who knew
not God (though otherwiſe, wyſe Sages, and
great Clarks) haue contemned it, as a peſtife-
rouſe euill: in ſo muche as they haue writ
(almoſt) whole volumes againſt the ſame, as
is to be ſcene in moſt of their Books yet extant.

Spud. Are you able to proue that?

Philo. That I am berie eaſilye, but of an
infinyte number, take a taſte of theſe few.
Democrates being demaunded, wherin the
bewtie, and comlie feature of man, or woman
conſiſted? aunſwered, in ſewnes of ſpeaches
well tempered together, in virtue, in integrity

D.iij.   of

The Godly
haue euer de-
teſted pride
of apparell.

The verie he-
then haue cõ-
temned ſump
tuouſe ap-
parell.

Teſtimonies
of hethen
people who
derided riche
attire.

of life,and suche like.   Sophocles seinge one
weare gorgeouse apparell , said to him, thou
foole,thy apparell is no ornamente to thee,but
a manifest shewe of thy follie.   Socrates being asked what was the greattest ornamente
in a woman ? answered, ẙ which most sheweth her chastitie , and good demeanoure of body,and mind & not sumptuouse attyre, which
rather sheweth her adulterate life. Aristotle
is so district in this point, that he would haue
men to vse meaner apparell , than are permitted them by the lawe : The Wife of Phi-

Virtue is the comlyest or-nament of all. lo the Philosopher , being vppon a tyme demaunded why she ware not gold , siluer, and
precïouse garments,said, she thought the vertues of her husbande sufficiente ornaments
for her.   Dionisius the king sente the richest
garments in all his wardrobes to the noble
Wome of the Lacedemonians, who returned
them from whence they came , sayinge,they
would be a greatter shame to them, than ho-
nore.   Kinge Pirrus sente riche attyre to
the Matrones of Rome , who abhorred them,
as menstruous clowtes.   The conceiued
opinion amongest the Grecians to this day is,
that it is neither gold , nor gorgiouse attyre
that adorneth either Man or Woman, but

Diogines his austerity. bertuous conditions,and such like. Diogines
so much contemned sumptuous attyre , that
he chose rather to dwell in wildernesse amongest

gest brute beasts, all his lyfe longe than in the pompouse courts of mightie kings one daye to be commorante.   For he thought if he had the ornaments of the minde, that he was than faire ynoughe, and fine inough also, not, needing any more.

A certen other Philosopher, addressed himselfe towards a kings courte in his Philosophers attyre, that is in meane, base and poore aray : But soe sone as the Officers espied him, they cried awaie with that rogue, what dothe he soe nie the kinges maiestyo courte.

The poore Philosopher seing it lighten so fast, retyred back, for feare of their thunder clappes, and repayringe home, appairelcd himselfe, in riche Attyre, and came againe marchinge towards the court, he was no sooner in sight, but euery one receiued him plausiblie, and with great submission, and reuerence.   When he came in presence of the kinge, and other mightie potentats, he kneled down, and ceased not to kisse his garmêts. The king and nobles marueylinge not a litle therat, asked him, wherfore he did so?

Who aunswered, O noble kinge, it is no marueyle, for that whiche my vertue and knowledge could not doe, my Apparell hath brought to passe.   For I comminge to thy gates in my PHILOSOPHERS

D.iij.   weede

The example of a Philosopher deriding the pompe of the World.

weede, was repelled, but hauing put vpon me
this riche attyre, I was brought to thy presence with as great veneration and worship
as could be. Wherby is to be séene in what
detestation he had the stinkinge Pride of apparell, takeing this occasion to giue the King
to vnderstand the inormious abuse thereof,
and so to remoue the same as a pestilent euill
out of his whole dominion & kingdome. I read
of a certen other Philosopher that came before a king, who at the same tyme, had inuited his nobles, to a feast or banquet, the Philosopher comming in, and seinge no place to
spit in (for euery place was hanged with cloth
of gold, cloth of siluer, tinsell, arrace, tapestrie,
and what not) came to the kinge and spat in
his face, saying, it is méet (o king) that I spit
in the fowlest place. This good Philosopher
(as we may gather) went about to withdraw
the king from taking pleasure or delight, in
the vaine glistering shewe, either of apparell
or any thing els, but rather to haue considera-
ration of his owne filthynes, miserie, & sinne,
not rysing vp into pride, and spitting against
heauen, as he did, by dilighting in prowde attyre and gorgeouse ornaments. Thus we sée
the verie painims, and heathen people, haue
from the beginning dispysed this excesse of apparell, both in them selues, and others, whose
examples héerin god graunt we may folowe.

Spud.

The exãple
of a Philoso-
pher who spat
in the kings
face.

Spud. But you are not able to proue that
any good Christians, euer set light by precious attire, but alwayes esteemed it as a speciall ornament to the whole man, As for these
Heathen they were fooles, neyther is it materiall, what they vsed, or vsed not?

Philo. I am able to prooue, that euen from
the beginning of the world, the chosen and pe-
culiar people of God, haue contemned proude
Apparel, as things (not onely) not necessarie,
but also as very euilles themselues, and haue   Probatio, that
gone both meanely and poorely in their vsuall   the former
attyre. What say you to our Grandfather A-   world hath
dam, and Eua our Mother? Were they not clo-   contemned
thed in peltes, and skins of beasts? Was not   pompouse
this a meane kinde of Apparell thinke you?   attyre.
Was it not vnsitting to see a woman inuested
all ouer in leather? But yet the Lord thought
it precious, and seemelie ynough for them.
What saye you to the noble Prophet of the
world Elias, did hee not walke in the solitude   Elias.
of this worlde in a simple playne mantell or
gowne, girded to him with a girdle of leather?
Elizeus the Prophet, did not he in a manner the   Elizeus.
verie same. And what say you to Samuell the   Samuell.
golden mouthed Prophet, notwithstanding y
hee was an Archprophet, and a chiefe seer of
that time, did hee not walke so meanely, as
Saul seking his fathers Asses, could not know
him from the reste, but asked him, where was

the ſeers houſe? This muſt needs argue that he went not richer then the common ſorte of people in his time.   The Childzen of Iſraell being the choſen people of God, did they not weare their Fathers attire fortie yeeres togither in the wildernes? was not Iohn the Baptiſt clothed with a garment of Camels heare? girded with a thong of the ſkin of the ſame in ſted of a girdle oz ſuccinctorie about his loines

The children of Iſraell.

Iohn Baptiſt.

Peter the deero Apoſtle of our Sauiour, was not diſtinct from the reſt of his Felowes, Apoſtles by any kinde of rich apparel, for then the maid would not haue ſaid I know thee by thy tung, but rather by thy apparel.

Peter.

The Apoſtle Paul wziting to the Hebrues ſaith, that the perſecuted Church, bothe in his time, and befoze his dayes were clothed ſome in Sheep ſkinnes, and ſome in Gote ſkinnes, ſome in Camels heare, ſome in this and ſome in that, and ſome in whatſoeuer they coulde get, for if it would hide their ſhameful parts, and kept them from the colde, they thought it ſufficient, they required no moze: but to ſpeak in one woze for all, did not our Sauiour Ieſus Chriſt weare the very ſame faſhion of apparell, that his Cuntrey-men vſed, that is a cote without a ſeame either knit oz weaued? which faſhions the Paleſtynians vſe there, yet to this day, without any alteration oz chauge as it is thought.   This his attyre, was not

The humility and pouertie of Chriſte vppon earth.

very

bery hanſome (one would think,) at the leaſt
it was not curious, oʒ new fangled, as ours
is, but as the Poet wel ſaid, initimur in ve-
titum ſeper cupimusq; negata, deſired things
foʒbid, and couet things are denied vs, lothing
the ſimplicitie of Chʒiſte, and abhoʒring the
chʒiſtian pouertie and godly mediocritie of
our Foʒefathers in apparel, are neuer content except wee haue ſundʒy ſutes of apparel,
one diuers from an other, ſo as our Pʒeſſes
crack withall, our Cofers bʒuſe, and our
backs ſweat with the cariage therof: we muſt
haue one ſute foʒ the foʒenwne, another foʒ ẏ
afternwne, one foʒ the day, another foʒ the
night, one foʒ the woʒkeday, another foʒ the
holicday, one foʒ ſommer, another foʒ winter,
one of the newe faſhion, an other of the olde,
one of this colour, another of that, one cutte,
an other whole, one laced, another without,
one of golde, and other of ſiluer, one of ſilkes
and veluets, and another of clothe, with moʒe
difference and varietie than I can expʒeſſe:
god be merciful vnto vs and haſten his king-
dōe that all imperfectious may be don away.

Superfluitie
of apparell
With dyuer-
ſitie of faſhi-
ons.

A peculiare Diſcrip-

tion of apparell in Ailgna by degrees

Y Ou haue boʒne me in hand of many and
grieuous abuſes reigning in Ailgna, but
now ſetting aparte theſe ambagies and
ſuperfluous

superfluous vagaries) I pray you describe vnto me moze particularly the sundzie abuses in
Apparell there vsed, running ouer by degrées
the whole state thereof, that I maye sée as it
were the perfect Anatomie of that Nation in
Apparell, whiche thinge I greatlye desire to
knowe.

Philo. Pour request sémeth both intricate,
and harde, considering there bee Tot tantæ
mæryadæs inuentionum, So manie, and so
fonde fashions, and inuentions of Apparell e-
uerie day. But yet, lest I might be iudged vnwilling to shewe you what pleasure I can, I
will assay (pro virili mea, omnibus neruulis
vndiqʒ extensis) with all the might and foʒce
I can, to satisfie pour desire. Wherefoʒe to begin first with their Hattes.

Sometimes they were them sharp on the
crowne, pearking vp like a sphere, oʒ shafte of
The diuersity a stéeple, standing a quarter of a yard aboue ẏ
of hattes in crowne of their heades, some moze, some lesse,
Ailgna. as please the phantasies of their mindes. O-
thersome be flat, and bzoad on the crowne, like
the battlements of a house. An other soʒt haue
round crownes, sometimes with one kinde of
bande, sometime with an other, nowe blacke,
now white, now russet, now red, now gréene,
now yellowe, now this, now that, neuer content with one colour, oʒ fashion two dayes to
an ende. And thus in vanitie they spende the

LOʒD

Lozde his treasure, consuming their golden
yeares, and siluer dayes, in wickednes & sin.
And as the fashions bee rare and straunge, so
are the thinges wherof their Hattes be made
diuerse also: foz some are of silke, some of veluet, some of taffetie, some of sarcenet, some of
wooll, & which is moze curious, some of a certaine kind of fine haire, far fetched, and deare
bought you maye bee sure. And so common a
thinge it is, that euerie Seruingman, Coun-
treyman, and other, euen all indifferently, do
weare of these hattes. Foz he is of no account
oz estimation amongst men, if hee haue not a
veluet, oz a taffatie Hatte, and that muste bee
pincked and cunningly carued of the beste fashion. And good pzofitable Hattes bee they, foz
the longer you weare them, the fewer holes
they haue. Besides this, of late there is a new
fashion of wearing their Hattes spzung vp a-
mongst the, which they father vpon ŷ French-
men, namely, to weare them without bandes,
but how vnseemelie (I will not say how Asse)
a fashion that is, let the wise iudge. Notwithstanding howe euer it bee, if it please them, it
shall not displease me. An other sozt (as phan-
tasticall as the rest) are content with no kind
of Hatt, without a great bunche of feathers of
diuerse and sundzie colours, peaking on toppe
of their heades, not vnlyke (I dare not say)
Cockscombes, but as sternes of pzide and en-

                        signs

The sundrie
things wher-
of hattes be
made.

Wering of
hattes with-
out bandes.

Wering of
Feathers in
hattes.

signes of vanitie, and these fluttering sayles and sethered flags of defiance to vertue (for so they are) are so aduaunced in Ailgna that euery Childe hath them in his hat or cap, many get good liuing by dying and selling of thē, and not a fewe proue them selues more then fooles in wearing of them.

Spud. These Fethers argue the lightnes of their fond imaginations, and plainly conuince them of instabilitie and folly, for sure I am, hansome they cannot be, therefore Badges of pride they must nods be, which I think none wil weare but such as be like them selues.

But to your intended discourse.

Philo. They haue great and monsterous ruffes, made either of Cambrick, holland, lawn or els of some other the finest cloth that can be got for money, whereof some be a quarter of a yard deep, yea some more, very few lesse.

So that they stand a full quarter of a yarde (and more) from their necks hanging ouer their shoulder poynts, insted of a baile. But if Aeolus with his blasts, or Neptune with his stormes, chaunce to hit vppon the craue bark of their brused ruffes, then they goe flip flap in the winde like rags flying abroad, and lye vpon their shoulders like the dishcloute of a slutte. But wot you what? the deuil, as in the fulnes of his malice, first inuented these

great

great ruffes, ſo hath hée now found out alſo
two great ſtayes to beare vp and maintaine
this his kingdome of great ruffes (for the deuil is king and prince ouer all the children of
pride) the one arch or piller wherby his kingdome of great ruffes is vnderpropped is a certaine kinde of liquide matter which they call
Starch, wherin the deuill hath willed them
to waſh and diue his ruffes wel, which when
they be dry wil then ſtand ſtiffe and inflexible
about their necks.

   The other piller is a certain deuice made of
wyers creſted for ÿ purpoſe, whipped ouer either with gold, thred, ſiluer or ſilk, & this hée
calleth a ſupportaſſe or vnderpropper. This
is to be ſupplyed round about their necks vnder the ruffe, vpon the out ſide of the band, to
beare vp the whole frame & body of the ruffe,
from falling and hanging down.

Spud. This is a deuice paſſing all the deuices that euer I ſawe or heard of. Then I perceiue the deuill not onely inuenteth miſcheif,
but alſo ordaineth inſtrumentall meanes to
continue the ſame.

   Theſe bands are ſo chargeable (as I ſuppoſe that but fewe haue of them, if they haue,
they are better monyed then I am?
Philo. So few haue them as almoſt none is
without them, for euery one how meane or
                     ſimple

Two arches
or pillers to
vnder proppe
the kingdom
of great ruffes
withall, vide-
licet ſupport-
taſſes, and
ſtarche.

ſimple ſoeuer they bee otherwiſe, will haue of
them three oꝛ foure apéece foꝛ fayling. And as

*Euery peſant
hath his ſta-
tely bands &
monſtrouſe
ruffes. how
coſtlie ſoeuer
they be.*

though Camericke, Holland, Lawne, and the
fineſt cloth that maye bee got anie where foꝛ
money, were not gꝺ inough, they haue them
wꝛought all ouer with ſilke wooꝛke, and peraduenture laced with golde, and ſiluer, oꝛ o-
ther coſtly lace of no ſmall pꝛice. And whether
they haue Argente to mayntaine this geare
withall oꝛ not, it foꝛceth not muche, foꝛ they
will haue it by one meane oꝛ other, oꝛ els they
will eyther ſell oꝛ moꝛgage their Landes, (as
they haue gꝺ ſtoꝛe) on Suters hill, & Stan-
gate hole, with loſſe of their lyues at Tiburne
in a rope.

Spud. The ſtate and condition of that Land
muſt néedes be miſerable, and in tyme growe
to greate ſcarcitie and dearth, where is ſuch
vayne Pꝛodigalitie, and exceſſe of all thynges
vſed.

Philo. Their Shirtes, which all in a manner doe weare (foꝛ if the Nobilitie oꝛ Gentrie
onely did weare them, it were ſomedeal moꝛe
tollerable) are eyther of Camericke, Holland,

*The ſhirts
vſed in Ailg-
na.*

Lawne, oꝛ els of the fineſt cloth that maye be
got. And of theſe kindes of Shirts euerie one
now doth weare alike: ſo as it may be thoght,
our Foꝛefathers, haue made their Bandes &
Ruffes (if they had any at all) of groſſer cloth,
and baſer ſtuffe, than the woꝛſt of our Shirtes
are

are made of now a dayes.   And theſe ſhurts
(ſomtimes it happeneth) are wrought through
out with nedle work of ſilke, and ſuche like,
and curiouſlie ſtitched with open ſeame, and
many other knackes beſydes, mo than I can
deſcribe.

Spud. Theſe be goodly ſhurts indeed, & ſuch
yet as will not chafe their tēder ſkinnes, no2
vlcerat their lyllie white bodyes, o2 if they do,
it wil not be much to their grœuances I dare
be bound. Is it anie maruell, ſi Criſtas eri-
gant & cornua attollant, if they ſtand vppon
their pantoffles, and hoyſe vp their ſayles on
highe, hauinge theſe dyamond ſhurts on their
delicate bodies: but how ſoeuer it is, I gather
by your wo2ds, that this muſt nœds be a nice,
and curious People, who are thus nuſſled vp
in ſuch daintie atty2e.

Philo. It is very true, fo2 this their curio-   Nicenes of
ſity, and nicenes in apparell (as it were) tran-   apparell ma-
ſnatureth them, makinge them weake, tender   keth the bo-
and infirme, not able to abide ſuch ſharp con-   dy tender.
flicts and bluſtering ſto2mes, as many other
people, both ab2oade farre from them, and in
their confines nie to them, do daylie ſuſtaine.
I haue hard my Father, with other wyſe Sages affirme, that in his tyme within the com-
paſſe of foure o2 fyue ſco2e yeres, when men
went clothed in black, o2 white frize coates, in
toſen of Huſwyues car2ie of the ſame colo2e,
                    E.   that

that the shæp boze them (the want of making
and wering of which clothe, together with the
excessiue wering of silks, veluets, satens, damasks, taffeties, and such like, hath and doth
make many a thousand in Ailgna, as poze
mendicãts to begge their bzead) wherof some
weare strait to the thigh, othersome litle bigger: and when they ware shurts of hempe, oz

Our prede- flax (but now these are to grosse, our tder sto-
cessours we - macks cannot easilye disgest such roughe and
ringe meaner crude meats) men weare stronger than we,
apparell were helthfuller, fayzer complectioned, longer ly-
stronge than uinge, and finallye, ten tymes harder than
we. we, and able to beare out any sozowe oz pay-
nes whatsoeuer. Foz be sure this pampering
of our bodies, makes them weker, tenderer,
and neshet, than otherwyse they would be if
they were vsed to hardnesse and moze subiect
to receiue anye kind of infection oz maladie.
And rather abbzeuiat oure dayes by manye
yeres than extenuate our liues one minut of
an houre.

Spud. I thinke no lesse : Foz how stronge
men were in tymes past, how lõg they lyued,
and how helthfull they weare, befoze suche
Nicenes, and vayne pamperinge curiositie
was inuented, we may reade, and many that
lyue at this daye, can testifie.   But now
thzough our fond toyes and nice inuentions,
we haue bzought our selues into suche pusil-
lant-

lanimitie, and effeminat condition, as we
may ſeeme rather nice dames, and yonge
gyrles, than puiſſante agents, or manlie men,
as our Forefathers haue bene.

Philo. Their dublettes are noe leſſe mon-
ſtrous than the reſte : For now the faſhion
is, to haue them hang downe to the middeſt of their theighes, or at leaſt to their pri-
uie members, beeing ſo harde-quilted, and
ſtuffed, bombaſted and ſewed, as they can
verie hardly eyther ſtoupe downe, or decline
them ſelues to the grounde, ſoe ſtyffe and
ſturdy they ſtand about them.

    Now what handſomnes can be in theſe
dubblettes whiche ſtand on their bellies, like
or muche bigger than a mans codpeece, (ſo
as their bellies are thicker than all their bodyes beſyde) let wyſe men iudge. For, for
my parte, handſomnes in them, I ſee none,
and muche leſſe profyte.

    And to be plaine, I neuer ſawe any weare
them : but I ſuppoſed him to be a man inclined to gourmandice, gluttonie and ſuche
like.

    For what may theſe great bellies ſignifie
els, than that either they are ſuche, or els are
affected that way. This is the trueſt ſigni-
fication, that I could euer preſage, or diuyne of them.   And this maye euerye one

The mon-
ſtrous dublet
in Ailgm.

Great bellied
dublets beto-
ken gourmi-
dice, gluttony
and ſuch like.

                        C. ij.   iudge

iudge of them that seeth them, for certaine I
am there was neuer any kinde of apparell e-
uer inuented, that could more disproportion
the body of man then these Dublets w great
bellies hāging down beneath their Pudenda,
(as I haue said) & stuffed with foure, fiue or sir
pound of Bombast at the least: I say nothing

Dublettes of dyuerse fashions. of what their Dublets be made, some of Saten, Taffatie, silk, Grogram, Chamlet, gold
siluer, & what not? slashed, iagged, cut, carued,
pincked and laced with all kinde of costly lace
of diuers and sundry colours, for if I shoulde
stand vpon these particularities, rather time
then matter would be wanting.

Spud. These be the strangest doublets that
euer I heard of, and the furdest from hansom-
nes in euery respect, vnlesse I be deceiued.

Philo. Then haue they Hosen, which as
Hosen of di- uerse & sun- dry fashions. they be of diuers fashions so are they of sundry names. Some be called french-hose, some
gally-hose and some Uenitians. The french-
hose are of two diuers makings, for the cōmon
french-hose (as they list to call them) contay-
neth length, breadth, and sidenes sufficient,
and is made very round. The other contay-
neth neither length, breadth nor sidenes, (beeing not past a quarter of a yarde side) wherof
some be paned, cut and drawne out with costly ornaments, with Canions annexed reaching down beneath their knees,

The

The Gally-hosen are made very large, and wide reaching downe to their knees onely, with three or foure guardes a peece laid down along either hose. And the Venetian-hosen, they reach beneath the knee to the gartering place of the Leg, where they are tyed finely with silk points, or some such like, and laied on also with rewes of lace, or gardes as the other before. And yet notwithstanding all this is not sufficient, except they be made of silk, velvet, saten, damask and other such precious things beside: yea euery one, Seruing man, and other inferiour to them in euery condition, wil not sticke to flaunte it out in these kinde of hosen, with all other their apparel sutable therunto.

The great excesse in hosen.

In times past, Kings (as olde Historiographers in their Bookes yet extant do recorde) would not disdaine to weare a paire of hosen of a Noble, tenne Shillinges, or a Marke price, with all the rest of their apparel after the same rate: but now it is a small matter to bestowe twentie nobles, ten pound, twentie pound, fortie pound, yea a hundred pound of one paire of Breeches. (God be mercifull vnto vs.)

Spud. This is a wonderful excesse as euer I hearde of, worthy with the Sworde of Iustice rather to be punished, then with paper and pen to be so gentle confuted.

C. 3.   Philo.

Philo. Then haue they nether-ſtocks to
The diuerſity
of neither-
ſtocks worne
in Ailgna.
theſe gay hoſen, not of cloth (though neuer ſo
fine) for that is thought to baſe, but of Iarnſey
worſted, ſilk, threed and ſuch like, or els at
the leaſt of the fineſt yarn y̆ can be, and ſo cu-
riouſlye knit with open ſeam down the leg,
with quirks and clocks about the ancles, and
ſometime (haply) interlaced with gold or ſiluer
threds, as is wunderful to behold. And to ſuch
inſolency & outrage it is now growen, that e-
uery one (almoſt) though otherwiſe verie por
hauing ſcarce fortie ſhillings of wages by the
yær wil be ſure to haue two or three paire of
theſe ſilk neither-ſtocks, or els of the fineſt
yarne that may be got, though y̆ price of them
be a Ryall or twentie ſhillinges, or more,
as commonly it is, for how can they be leſſe?
when as the very knitting of them is worth
a noble, or a royall, and ſome much more?

The time hath bæne, when one might haue
clothed all his body well, for leſſe then a pair
of theſe neither-ſtocks wil coſt.

Spud. I haue ſeldome hearde the like, I
The miſerie
of theſe daies
think verely that Sathan prince of darknes &
Father of pride, is let looſe in y̆ land, els it
could neuer ſo rage as it doth, for y̆ like pride
(I am fully perſwaded), is not uſed vnder the
ſonne, of any nation or people how barberous
ſo euer, wherfore wo be to this age and thriſe
accurſed be theſe dayes, which bring forth
ſuch

such sowꝛe frutes, & vnhappie are that people, whom Sathan hath so bewitched, & captiued in sin. The Lord holde his hād of mercy ouer vs.

Philo. To these their nether-stocks, they haue coꝛked shoes, pinsnets, and fine pantofles, which beare them vp a finger oꝛ two frō the ground, wherof some be of white leather, some of black, and some of red: some of black veluet, some of white, some of red, some of gréen, raced, carued, cut and stitched all ouer with silk and laid on with golde, siluer, and such like: yet notwithstanding, to what good vses serue these pantofles, except it be to wear in a pꝛiuate house, oꝛ in a mans Chamber, to kéepe him warme? (foꝛ this is the onely vse wherto they best serue in my iudgement) but to go abꝛoad in them as they are now vsed altogether, is rather a let oꝛ hinderāce to a man then otherwise, foꝛ shall he not be faine to knock, and spurn at euery stone, wall oꝛ poste to kéep them on his féet? wherfoꝛe to disclose euen the bowels of my iudgement vntoyou, I think they be rather woꝛne abꝛode foꝛ nicenes, thē either foꝛ any ease which they bꝛing, (foꝛ the contrary is moste true) oꝛ any handsones which is in them. Foꝛ how should they be easie, when as the héele hangeth an inch oꝛ two ouer the slipper on the ground? Insomuchjas I haue knowen diuers mens legs swel with the same.

And

Corked shoes
Pantoffles,
and pinsnets.

Pantoffles, &
slippers are a
let to those
that go abrod
in them.

Pantoffles
vneasie to
go in.

And handsome how should they be, when as
with their flipping & flapping vp and down in
ỹ dirte they exaggerate a mountain of mire &
gather a heape of clay & baggage together, lo-
ding the wearer with importable burthen?

Spud. Those kinde of pantoffles, can neither be so handsome, nor yet so warme as o-
ther vsuall commō shoes be, I think. Therfore the weringe of them abrode rather importeth a Nicenes (as you say) in them that
weare them, than bringeth any other commodytie els, vnlesse I be deceiued?

Philo. Their coates, and Ierkins, as they
be diuerse in colors, so be they diuerse in fashions: for some be made with colors, some
without, some close to the bodie, some loose, couering the whole body downe to the theighe,
like bagges, or sacks that weare drawen ouer
them, hidinge the dimensions, and proportiōs
of the body: some are buttened downe the
brest, some vnder the arme, & some downe the
back, some with flappes ouer the brest, some
without, some with great sleeues, some with
small, and some with non at all, some pleated and crested behind, & curiouslye gathered,
some notso, & how many dayes (I might say
houres or minuts of houres in the yeare,) so
many sortes of apparell some one man will
haue, and thinketh it good prouision in faire
weather, to lay vp against a storme. But if
they)

The varytie
of coates and
Ierkins.

they would conſider that their clothes (except
thoſe that they weare vppon their backs) be
non of theirs, but the poores, they would not
heap vp their preſſes, and wardrobes as they
do. Do they think that it is lawfull for them
to haue millions of ſundry ſortes of apparell
lying rotting by them, when as the poore mēbers of Ieſus Chriſte die at their dores for
wants of clothing? God commaundeth in his
law, that there be no miſerable poore man nor
begger amongeſt vs, but that euery one be
prouided for and maintained of that abundāce, which God hath bleſſed vs withal: But we
thinke it a great matter if we geue them an
old ragged coate, dublet, or a paire of hoſen, or
els a penny or two, wheras not withſtanding,
we flow in abundance of all things. Than we
thinke we are halfe way to heauen, and we
need to do no more. If we geue them a peace
of brown bread, a meſſe of porredge (nay the
ſtocks & priſon, with whippinge cheare now
and than is the beſt portion of almes which
many Gentlemen geue:) at our dores, it is
counted meritorious, and a worke of ſupere-
rogation when we fare full delicatelye oure
ſelues feeding on many a danity diſh. There
is a certen Citye in Ailgna called Munidnol,
where as the poore lye in ÿ ſtreats, vppon pal-
lets of ſtraw, and well if they haue that to, or
els in the mire and dirt, as commonlie it is

            C.b.   ſane

*The poore
ought to be
prouided for.*

*Our ſmal re-
gard to the
poore.*

*Cold charitie
to the poore.*

hauing neither house to put in their heads, couering to kéep them from the cold, nor yet to
hide their shame withall, penny to buy them
suftenance, nor any thing els, but are permitted to dye in the streats like dogges, or beasts
without anie mercie, or compassion shewed
to them at all.　　And if anye be sicke of the
plague (as they call it,) or any other disease,
their Maisters and Maistres are so impudent
(being, it should séeme at a league with Sathan, a couenante with Hell, and as it were
obliged them selues by obligation to the deuil
neuer to haue to do with¥ workes of mercy) as
straight way, thei throw them out of their dores. And so being caried forth either in carts,
or otherwyse, and thrown in the streats, there

**The Turkish
impietie of
some towards
the poore di-
seased.** they end their dayes most miserably. Truely
Brother if I had not séen it, I would scarsly
haue thought, that the like Turkish cruelty,
had bene vsed in all the World. But they say,
vnus testis occulatus plus valet, quàm mille
auriti: one eye witnesse, is better to be bely-
ued, than a thousand eare witnesses besydes.
But to leaue these excursions, and to returne
from whence I haue digressed, I think it the
best: For I am perswaded they will as much
respect my wordes (or amend their maners)
as the wicked World did at the preaching of
our Saniour Christe Iesus, that is, iust nothing at all.

　　　　　　　　　　　　　Spud.

Spud. Well then , ſeeing they are ſuche a ſtifneckned People, leaue them to the Lord, and proceed to your former tractation.

Philo. They haue clokes there alſo in nothing diſcrepante from the reſt, of dyuerſe and ſundry colors, white, red, tawnie, black, græene yellowe, ruſſet, purple, violet, and inſynite other colors: ſome of cloth, ſilk, veluet, taffetie, and ſuch like, wherof ſome be of the Spaniſh, French, & Dutch faſhion. Some ſhort, ſcarſely reachinge to the gyrdleſtead, or waſt, ſome to the knée , and otherſome traylinge vppon the ground (almoſt) liker gownes, than clokes. Theſe clokes muſt be garded, laced, & thorowly faced : and ſomtimes ſo lyned, as the inner ſide ſtädeth almoſt in as much as the outſide: ſome haue ſléeues, otherſome haue none, ſome haue hoodes to pull ouer the head , ſome haue none, ſome are hanged with points & taſſels of gold, ſiluer, or ſilk, ſome without al this. But how ſoeuer it be, the day hath bene, when one might haue bought him two clokes for leſſe, thä now he can haue one of theſe clokes made for , they haue ſuch ſtore of workmanſhip beſtowed vppon them.

The ſundry faſhions of cloks.

Spud. I am ſure they neuer learned this at the hands of our Proconſul and chief Prouoſt Chriſt Jeſus, nor of any other ẙ euer lyued godly in the Lord : but rather out of the deceiptfull forge of their own braines haue they drawen

The coũting houſe of all euill, is mans braine.

drawen this curſed Anatomy to their owne
deſtruction in the end, except the repente.

Philo. They haue alſo bootehoſe, which are
to be wondered at , for they be of the fyneſt
cloth, that may be got, yea fine inough to make any band, ruffe, or ſhurt needful to be worn:
yet this is bad inough to were next their gre-
ſie boots. And would God this weare all : but
(oh phy for ſhame) they muſt be wrought all
ouer, from the gartering place vpward , with
nedle worke, clogged with ſilk of all colors,
with birds, foules, beaſts, and antiques purtrayed all ouer in comlie ſorte. So that I haue knowen the very nedle work of ſome one
payre of theſe bootehoſe to ſtand, ſome in. iiij.
pound, vi. pound, and ſome in x. pound a peece.
Beſides this, they are made ſo wyde to draw
ouer all, and ſo longe, to reach vp to the waſte
that as litle or leſſe clothe would make one a
reaſonable large ſhurte. But tuſh, this is nothing in compariſon of the reſte.

Spud. I would thinke that bootehoſen of
groſſer lynnen, or els of wollen clothe , weare
both warmer to ride in , as coly as the other,
though not ſo fine , and a great deal more durable. And as for thoſe gengawes wherwith
you ſay they be bldunched and trimmed, they
ſerue to no end, but to feade ỹ wanton eyes of
gazing fools, & plainly argue ỹ vertigime, & in-
ſtability of their more than ſataſtical brains.
Philo

The vain ex-
ceſſe of bote
hoſen.

The varitie
of faſhions
conuince vs
of follie.

Phil. To theſe haue they their Rapiers, Swoords and Daggers gilt, twiſe oꝛ thꝛiſe o-uer the hilts, with ſcabeꝛds and ſheathes of Swords and daggers guile & damaſked. Veluet oꝛ the like, foꝛ leather, though it be moꝛe pꝛoffitable and as ſœmely, yet wil it not carie ſuch a poꝛte oꝛ countenance like the o-ther. And wil not theſe golden ſwoꝛds & dag-gers almoſte apale a man (though otherwiſe neuer ſo ſtout a Martialiſt)to haue any deling with them? foꝛ either to ẏ end they be woꝛne oꝛ els other ſwoꝛds, daggers and rapiers of bare yꝛon and ſtœle were as hanſom as they, & much moꝛe conducible to that end, whereto ſwoꝛds and rapiers ſhould ſerue, namely foꝛ a mans lawful and godly defence, againſt his aduerſarie in time of neceſſitie. But wher-foꝛe they be ſo clogged with gold and ſiluer I know not, noꝛ yet wherto this exceſſe ſerueth I ſee not, but certain I am, a great ſhewe of pꝛide it is, an infallible token of vain gloꝛie, and a grœuous offence to God, ſo pꝛodigallie, and licentiouſlie to lauiſh foꝛth his treaſure, foꝛ which we muſt reder accoūts at the day of Judgement, when it ſhall be ſaide to euerie one, Redde rationem Vilicationis tuæ. Come give accounts of thy Stewardſhip. Luce. 16.

A

A particulare Discri-

ption of the Abuses of Womens apparell in Ailgna.

Thus hauinge geuen thœ a superficiall
biewe, or small tast, (but not discouered
the hudreth part) of the guyses of Ailgna
in mésapparel, & of the abuses cōtained in the
same, now wil I with like celeritie of matter
impart vnto thœ, the guyse and seuerall Abuses of the apparell of wemen there vsed also :
Wherfore geue attentiue eare.

Sp. My eares be prest to heare, begin when
you wil, and truely herin you shal pleasur me
much, for I haue greatly desired to know thorowly the state of ý Lād, euen a crepundiis (as
they say (from my tender yeres, for the great
prayse I haue hard therof) Wherfore, I pray
you proceed to the same, & though I be vnable
tŏ any benefit to coūteruail your great pains,
yet ý Lord I doubt not, wil supplie my want.

Ph. The Lord our God is a mercifull God,
& a boūtiful Rewarder of euery one, that tru-
steth in him, but yet (such is ý magnificency &
liberalitie of that gētle sex) that I trust I shall
not be vnrewarded at their hands, if to be called a thousād knaues be a sufficiēt guerdō for
my pains. But though it wilbe a corrosiue tŏ
their hautie stomacks , & a nippitatū to their
tender brests to heare their dirtie dregs ript
vp and cast in their diamond faces, yet hope-
ing

The reward
of the femall
sex.

ing that they , ſæing the horrour of their impieties , and tragicall abuſes laide open to
the world, (for now they ſlæp in the graue of
obliuion) wil at the laſt like good Conuertes
and Penitentiaries of Chriſte Ieſus leaue of
their wickednes, call for mercie at the hands
of God, repent and amend. I will proceed to
my intended purpoſe.

The Women of Ailgna vſe to colour their
faces with certain oyles , liquors , vnguents
and waters made to that end , whereby they
think their beautie is greatly decored : but
who ſæthe not that their ſoules are thereby
deformed, and they brought dæper into the
diſpleaſure and indignation of the Almighty,
at whoſe voice the earth doth tremble and at
whoſe preſence the heauens ſhall liquifie,and
melt away . Do they think thus to adulterate the Lord his workmanſhip, and to be
without offence ? Do they not know that he
is Zelotipus a ielous God , and cannot abide
any alteration of his workes,otherwiſe then
he hath commaunded ?

Adulteration
of the Lord
his workma-
ſhip in his
Creatures.

If an Artificer , or Craftſman ſhoulde
make any thing belōging to his art or ſcience
& a cobler ſhould preſume to correct the ſame:
would not ȳ other think him ſelf abuſed , and
iudge him worthy of reprehenſion?
And thinkeſt thou (oh Woman) to eſcape the
Iudgement of God, who hath faſhioned thæ,

10

to his glo2y , when thy great and mo2e then
p2efumptuous audacicitie dareth to alter , ¢
chaunge his wo2kman$hip in thæ ?

Thinkeft thou that thou canft make thy
felf fairer then God who made vs all? Thefe
muft nædes be their inuentions , o2 els they
would neuer go about to coulour their faces ,
with fuch fibberfawces. And thefe bæing
their inuentions what can derogate mo2e frõ
the maieftie of God in his creation ? Fo2 in
this dwing they plainly conuince the Lo2d of
vntrueth in his wo2d who faith he made man
glo2ious, after his owne likenes, and the fay2-
reft of all other terreftiall Creatures. If he be
thus faire then what næd they to make them
fayrer ? Therfo2e this their colouring of their

They that
colour their
faces deny
the Lord of
glory to bee
true God and
fo no God at
all.

faces impo2teth , (as by p2obable coniecture
may be p2efuppofed) that they think them felues not faire enough, and then muft G Đ Đ
næds be vntrue in his wo2d.

And alfo they deny the Lo2d to be either
mercifull o2 almightie o2 bothe , and fo confe-
quently no God at all:fo2 if hæ could not haue
made them faire , |then is hæ not almightie ,
and if hæ could and would not, then is hæ not
a merciful God, and fo euery way they fall in
to the finck of offence , bæing afhamed of the
gwd creation of the Lo2d in them , but it is to
be feared leaft at the day of Iudgement , the
Lo2d wil be afhamed of them, ¢ in his w2ath
denounce

denounce this beaule and ineuitable ſentence
condemnatorie againſt them, Departe from
, mee you curſed into euerlaſting fire prepa-
, red for the deuil, and his Angels , I knowe
, you not: (I ſay) departe, for you were aſha-
, ined of mee, and of my creation in you .

Spud. Wherof do they make theſe waters,
and other vnctions wherwith they beſmeare
their faces, can you tel?

Philo. I am not ſo ſkilful in their matters
of pride, but I holde this for a Maxime, that
they are made of many mixtures, and ſundry
compounded ſimples, bothe farre fetched and
dér bought, cunningly couched together, and
tempered with many godly condiments and
holſome confections, I warrant you , els you
may be ſure they woulde not applye them to
their amorous faces, for feare of harming or
blemiſhing the ſame.

Philo. S. Ciprian amongſt all the reſt, ſaith,
a Woman thorow painting and dying of her
face , ſheweth her ſelf to be more then whoriſh. For (ſaith hée) ſhée hath corrupted and
defaced (like a filthie ſtrumpet or brothel) the
workmanſhip of GOD in her, what is this
els , but to turne trueth into falſhod , with
painting and ſibberſawces, wheras the Lord
ſaith , Thou canſt not make one haire white
, or black. In an other place hée ſaith, Qui ſe
, pinguunt in hoc ſeculo, aliter quam creauit

Inuectiues of
the Fathers
againſt payn-
ting and cou-
louring of
faces.

F.　　　Deus,

, Deus, metuant ne cum dies resurrectionis ve
, nerit, artifex creaturam suam, non recog-
, noscat. Those which paint or collour them
, selues in this world otherwise then G O D
, hath made them, let them feare least when
, the day of iudgement commeth, the Lorde
, wil not know them for his Creatures.

Againe, Feminæ crines suos inficiunt malo
, præsagio, capillos enim sibi flammeos aus-
, picari non metuunt. Whosoeuer doe color
; their faces or their haire with any vnnatu-
, rall collour, they begin to prognosticate of
, what colour they shalbe in hel.

S. Ambrose saith that from the coullouring
of faces spring the inticements to vices, and
that they which color their faces doo purchase
to them selues the blot and stain of chastitie.

For what a dotage is it (saith hœ) to chaunge
thy naturall face which God hath made thœ,
for a painted face, which thou hast made thy
selfe If thou beest faire, why paintest thou thy
selfe to seeme fairer? and if thou be not faire,
why doest thou hippocrittically desire to seeme
faire, and art nothing lesse? Can those things
which besides that they be filthie, doe cary the
brand of God his curse vpon their backs for
euer, make thœ to seeme fayrer? I could show
you the sharp Inuections, and grounded reasons of many inoe, as of Augstine, Hierome
Chrisostome, Gregorie, Caluin, Peter Mar-
tyr, Gualter, and of an infinite number moe:

No painting
can make a-
ny to seem
fairer but
fowler.

yea of all generally ſince the beginning of the
woꝛld, againſt this whoꝛiſh and bꝛothellous
painting and coulouring of faces, but to auoid
prolixitie, I will omit them, deferring them
to further opoꝛtunitie, foꝛ pauca ſapienti, To
a wiſeman few woꝛds are ſufficient.

Spud. It muſt nædes be graunted, that the
dying and coulouring of faces with artificiall colours, and vnnaturall Oyntments is
moſte offenſiue to God, and derogatoꝛie to
his Maieſtie: foꝛ do they think that the God
of all gloꝛie, and who only decketh and adoꝛneth the Sun, the Moon, the Starres and all
the hoaſt of heauen with vnſpeakable gloꝛie,
and incomparable beautie, cannot make the
beautiful and faire enough (if it pleaſe him)
without their ſibberſawces? And what are
they els then the Deuils inuentions to intangle pooꝛe ſoules in the nets of perdition?

Colouring of faces, the deuils net

Philo. Then followeth the trimming and
tricking of their heds, in laying out their hair
to the ſhewe, which of foꝛce muſt be curled,
friſled and criſped, laid out (a Woꝛld to ſæ) on
wꝛeathes & boꝛders from one eare to an other.
And leaſt it ſhould fall down it is vnder pꝛopped with foꝛks, wyers & I can not tel what, rather like grime ſterne monſters, then chaſte
chꝛiſtian matrones. Then on ye edges of their
bolſtred heir (foꝛ it ſtandeth creſted roūd about
their frontiers, & hanging ouertheir faces like

Trimming of their heds.

Simia erit ſimia etiam ſi aurea geſtet inſignia.

Laying out of their haire

F.v.   pꝛndices

pedices with glasse windowes an euery side)
there is layd great wreathes of gold, and siluer curiouslie wrought, & cunninglie applied
to the temples of their heads. And for feare
of lacking any thing to set forth their pride
withal, at their heyre thus wreathed and crested, are hanged, bugles (I dare not say, ba-
bles)ouches,rings,gold,siluer, glasses, & such
other gewgawes and trinckets besides.which
for that they be innumerable,and I vnsailfull
in wemens termes, I can not easily recount.
But God giue them grace, to giue ouer these
vanities,and studie to adorn their heads with
the incorruptible ornaments of vertue,& true
Godlynesse.

*Gold wrea-
thes circum-
gyring the
temples of
their heads.*

*Gewgawes
haged about
their Fron-
tiers.*

Spud. The Apostle Paul (as I remember)
commaundeth wemen to cherish their heyre,
saying,that it is an ornament to them,& therfor me think,this abuse of curling and laying
it out(if eyther were lawfull) is muche more
tollerable than dying their faces.

Philo. If curling,& laying out of their own
naturall heyre weare all (which is impious,
and at no hand lawfull,notwithstanding,for
it is the ensigne of Pride, and the stern of
wantonnes to all that behould it) it were the
lesse matter, but they are not simply contente
with their owne haire, but buy other heyre,
dying it of what color they list themselues: &
this they were in the same order as you haue
heard

*Curling and
crisping, and
laying out of
heyre.*

*Bought heyre
and colored,
vsed to be
worn.*

beard, as though it weare their owne natural heir: and vppon ý other ſide, if any haue heyre, which is not faire inough, than will they dye it into dyuerſe colors almoſt chaunginge the ſubſtance into accidentes, by their dyueliſh & more than thriſe curſed deuyſes. So, wheras their heire was geuen them, as a ſigne of ſubiection, and therfore they were commaunded to cheriſh the ſame, now haue they made (as it were) a Metamorphoſis of it, making it an ornament of Pride, and deſtruction to them ſelues for euer, except they repent.

Spud. This is a ſtyfnecked People, & a rebellious, I ſée well, that thus dareth in euerie reſpecte, to peruert the ſtraight wayes of the Lord, digginge vp to them ſelues ceſterns of iniquity, & pittes of aduerſity, which in th, end without the great mercy of God will be their vtter confuſion.

Philo. Than on toppes of theſe ſtately turrets (I meane their goodly heads, wherin is more vanitie, than true Phlloſophie now and than) ſtand their other capitall ornaments, as french hood, hat, cappe, kercher, and ſuche like, wherof ſome be of veluet, ſome of taffatie, ſome (but few) of woll, ſome of this faſhion, ſome of that, and ſome of this color, ſome of that, accordding to the variable fantaſtes of their ſerpétine minds. And to ſuch exceſſe is it growen, as euery artificers wyfe (almoſt) wil

F.iij.   not

Hattes of veluets, taffaty, worn in common.

not stick to goe in her hat of Veluet euerye day, euery marchants wyfe, and meane Gentlewomen, in her french-hood, and euerye poore Cottagers Daughter, in her taffatie hat, or els of woll at least, wel lined with silk, veluet, or taffatie. But how they come by this (so they haue it) they care not, who payeth for it they regard not, nor yet what hurt booth to them selues, and others it doth bring they feare not : But runne daylie a malo, ad

Trahit sua quenque voluptas.

pcius, as they say) from one mischiefe te an other, vntill they haue filled vp the mesure of their euill to their owne perdition at that day.

They haue also other ornaments befydes these to furnish foorth their ingenious heads, which they cal (as I remember) cawles, made

Cawles made Netwyle.

Netwyse, to th'ende, as I thinke that the clothe of gold, cloth of siluer, or els tinsell (for that is the worst) wherwith their heads are couered and attyred withall vnderneath their cawles maye appeare, and shewe it selfe in the brauest maner. So that a man that seeth them (there heads glister and shine in suche sorte) wold thinke them to haue golden heads.

Golden heads fraught with leaden wit.

Thus lauishe they foorth the goods of the Lorde, which are none of their owne (but lent them for a tyme) vppon Pride and naughtinesse, delighting (as it seemeth) in nothing so much

muche, as in the ſtincking puddle of vanitie
and ſinne, which will be their owne decay at
the laſt.   Another ſorte of diſſolute minions,
& wantō Sempronians (for I can term thē no
better) are ſo far bewitched, as they are not
aſhamed to make holes in their eares, wherat they hang rings, and other Iewels of gold
and precious ſtones.   But what this ſigni-
fieth in them, I will hould my peace, for
the thing it ſelfe ſpeaketh ſufficiently. There
is a certen kinde of People in the Orientall
parte of the World (as Writers affirme)
that are ſuche Philautoi louers of them ſelues and ſo prowde with all, that hauing plentie of precious Stones, and Margarits amongeſt them, they cut and launce their ſkinnes,
and fleſhe, ſetting therin thrſe precious Stones, to the end they maye glitter and ſhine to
the eye.

So, except theſe Women weare minded
to tread their pathes and folowe their dire-
full wayes in this curſed kind of vnhard of
Pride, I wonder what they meane.

But becauſe this is not ſo muche frequented, amongeſt Women as Men, I will ſay
noe more thereof, vntill further occaſion be
offred.

Spud. Except it weare a People wedded
to the deuills eldeſt Daughter Pride, for I
thinke, chaſtitie amongeſt them maye dwell
                     F.iij.   a vir-

Making of
holes in their
eares, to hang
rings and Ie-
wels by.

A people who
cut their ſkin
toſet precious
ſtones in
them ſelues.

a Uirgin fo2 any that wil marry her) and gi
uen ouer of God, J neuer heard the like.

J am perſwaded, neither the Libertines, the
Epicures no2 yet the vile Atheiſts euer excœ
ded this people in p2ide, no2 the wickednes
of them might euer counterpeaſe, with the
wickednes of theſe people. God be merciful
vnto them.

Philo. You heare not the tenth parte, fo2 no
pen is able ſo wel to diſcribe it, as the eye is
to diſcry it.   The Women there vſe great

Great ruffes
Neckerchers.
and partlets
vſed of Wo-
men.

ruffes, ꝯ neckerchers of holland, lawne, came-
rick, and ſuch cloth, as the greateſt th2ed ſhall
not be ſo bigge as the leaſt haire that is, then
leaſt they ſhould fall down, they are ſmeared
and ſtarched in the deuils liquo2e, J meane
Starch: after that d2yed with great diligence,
ſtreaked, patted and rubbed very nicely, and
ſo applyed to their godly necks, and withall,

Supportaſſes
he pillers of
2ride.

vnderp2opped with ſuppo2taſſes (as J tolde
you befo2e) the ſtatelie arches of p2ide:beyond
all this, they haue a further fetch nothing in
feriour to the reſt, as namely th2œ o2 foure
deg2œs of minor ruffes, placed gradatim,ſtep
by ſtep one beneath another, and all vnder ỹ

tinor ruffe.

Maiſter deuil ruffe, the ſky2ts then of theſe
great ruffes are long and ſide euery way ple-
ted and creſted ful curiouſly, God wot. Then
laſt of all, they are either clogged w̄ golde,ſil-
uer, o2 ſilk lace of ſtately p2ice, w2ought all

ouer

ouer with næble woozk, speckled and spark-
led hær & there with the sonne, the mœne, the
starres and many other antiquities straunge
to beholde. Some are wzought with open　*The great*
woozk dowpn to the midst of the ruffe and fur-　*curiosity of*
ther, some with purled lace so cloyd and other　*ruffs and neck-*
gewgawes so pestred, as the ruffe is the least　*erchers.*
parte of it self. Sometimes, they are pinned
vp to their eares, sometimes they are suffered to hang ouer their shoulders, like wind-
mil sayles fluttering in the winde, and thus
euery one pleaseth her self with her fœlish de-
nices, foz suus cuiusq; crepitus sibi bene olet,
as ý pzouerb saith: euery one thiketh his own
wayes best, though they leade to distruction
of body and soule, which I wish them to take
hœd of.

Spud. As in a Camelion are said to be all
coulours, saue white, so I think, in these peo
ple are all things els, saue Uertue and chzisti
an sobzietie. Proteus that Monster could ne-　*Proteus*
uer chaunge him self into so many fourmes &
shapes as these women do, belike they haue
made an obligation with hel and are at agrœ-
ment with the deuil, els they would neuer
outrage thus, without either feare of God oz
respect to their weak Bzetheren, whom hær-　*Women we-*
in they offend.　　　　　　　　　　　　　　　*ring dublets*

Philo The Women also there haue dublets　*and Ierkins.*
& Ierkins as men haue hær, buttoned vp the
　　　　　　　　　　　　　　　　　bzest

brest, and made with wings, welts and pinions on the shoulder points, as mans apparel is, for all the world, & though this be a kinde of attire appropriate onely to man, yet they blush not to wear it, and if they could as wel chaunge their sex, & put on the kinde of man, as they can weare apparel assigned onely to man, I think they would as verely become men indæd as now they degenerat from godly sober women, in wearing this wanton lewd kinde of attirs, proper onely to man.

A curse to them that weare cõtrary apparell to their sex.

It is written in the 22. of Deuteronomie, that what man so euer weareth womans apparel is accursed, and what woman weareth mans apparel is accursed also. Now, whether they be within the bands and lymits of that curse, let them sæ to it them selues. Our Apparell was giuen vs as a signe distinctiue to discern betwixt sex and sex, & therfore one to weare the Apparel of another sex, is to participate with the same, and to adulterate the veritie of his owne kinde.　　Wherefore these Women may not improperly be called Hermaphroditi, that is, Monsters of bothe kindes, half women, half men.

Hermaphro-diti.

Spud. I neuer read nor heard of any people except drunke with Cyrces cups, or poysoned with the exorcisms of Medea that famous and renoumed Sorcerelle, that euer woulde weare suche kinde of attire as is not onely stinking

ſtinking before the face of God, offenſiue to
mã, but alſo painteth out to the whole world,
the venereous inclination of their corrupt con
uerſation.

Philo. There Gownes be no leſſe famous
alſo, for ſome are of ſilk, ſome of veluet, ſome
of grograin, ſome of taffetie, ſome of ſcarlet,
and ſome of fine cloth, of ten, twentie or fortie ſhillings a yard. But if the whole gowne
be not ſilke or veluet, then the ſame ſhall be
layed with lace, two or three fingers broade,
all ouer the gownc or els the moſte parte.

Or if not ſo, (as lace is not fine enough
ſometimes) then it muſt be garded with great
gardes of veluet, foure or ſix fingers broad at
the leaſt, and edged with coſtly lace, and as
theſe gownes be of diuers and ſundrie colors
ſo are they of diuers faſhions changing with
the Moon, for ſõe be of the new faſhion, ſome
of the olde, ſome of this faſhion, and ſome of
that, ſome with ſleeues hanging down to their
ſkirts trayling on the ground, and caſt ouer
their ſhoulders, like Cow-tayles.

Some haue ſleues much ſhorter, cut vp the
arme and pointed with ſilk-ribons very gallantly, tyed with true-loues knottes, (for ſo
they call them.)

Some haue Capes reaching downe to the
middeſt of their backs, faced with Veluet
or els with ſome fine wrought ſilk Taffatie,

The diuerſity
of Gownes.

Simiæ in pur
puris.

Coſtly
gownes.

Diuers faſhi-
ons of
Gounes.

ai

at the leaſt, and fringed about very brauely: & (to ſhut vp all in a word) ſome are pleated, & rvueled down the back woderfully, with more knacks, than I can declare. Than haue they

Peticots.

Petticots of the beſt cloth that can be bought and of the faireſt dye that can be made. And ſometimes they are not of cloth neither, for that is thought to baſe, but of ſcarlet, grograin taffatie, ſilk, and ſuche like, fringed about the ſkirts with ſilk fringe, of chaungable coloure. But which is more vayn, of whatſoeuer their petticots be, yet muſt they haue kyrtles (for

Kyrtles.

ſo they call them) eyther of ſilk, veluet, grograin, taffatie, ſaten, or ſcarlet, bordered with gards, lace, fringe, and I cannot tell what beſydes. So that when they haue all theſe goodly robes vppon them, women ſéme to be the ſmalleſt part of themſelues, not naturall wo-

Women the least part of themſelues.†

men, but artificiall Women, not Women of fleſh, & blod, but rather puppits, or mawmets of rags & clowtes compact together. So farre hath this cancker of pride eaten into the body of the common welth, that euery pore Yeomã his Daughter, euery Huſband mã his daugh-ter, & euery Cottager his Daughter will not

Poore Mens Daughters excelſ.

ſpare to flaunt it out, in ſuche gownes, petti-cots, & kirtles, as theſe. And not withſtanding that their Parents owe a braſe of hundred pounds more than they are worth, yet will they haue it quo iure quaué iniuria, eyther

by

by hooke, oꝛ crooke, by right oꝛ wꝛong as they
ſay, wherby it commeth to paſſe, that one can
ſcarſly know, who is a noble woman, who is
an honoꝛable, oꝛ woꝛſhipſull Woman, from
them of the meaner ſoꝛte.

Spud. Their parents & Freinds are muche
to be blamed, foꝛ ſuffering them to go in ſuchs
wanton attyꝛe. They ſhould not allowe them
ſuch large pittāce, noꝛ ſuffer them to meaſure
their apparell, after their own licentious yar-
des of ſelfe will, and wicked deſires.

Parents to blame.

Philo. Than ſhall they be ſure, neuer to haue good day with them. Foꝛ they are ſo impudent, that all be it, their pooꝛe Parents haue
but one cow, hoꝛſe, oꝛ ſheep, they wil neuer let
them reſt, til they be ſould, to maintain them
in their bꝛaueries, paſt all tongue can tell.
And to ſay the truth, ſome Parents (woꝛthie
to be inaugured with the lawrell Crowne of
triple follie) are ſo buxome to their ſhameleſſe
deſires, and ſo eroꝛable to their pꝛoſtitute re-
queſts, ẙ they graūt to their too too nice daughters moꝛe than they can deſire themſelues, taking a ſingular felicity & ſurmoūting pleaſure
in ſing them to go plumed and decked in the
Feathers of deceiptfull vanity.

The impu-decy of proud harlots.

Our remiſſe leuitie of Pa-rents to their Children.

Sp. This ouer great lenitie, & remiſſe libertie in the educatiō of youthe, in reſpect of the
euent, and ſucceſſe in the end, maye rather be
counted an extrem cruelty, than a Fatherly
pitis

pitie of them towards their children : For
what maketh them so soone whores, strumpets, and bawdes, as that cockering of them
doth ?

what maketh whores, and strumpets.

What maketh them apt & prone to all kind
of naughtynesse, but this? Nothing in the
World soe muche.   For giue a wild horse
the libertie of the head neuer so litle, and he
will runne headlonge to thyne and his owne
destruction also.

So long as a sprigge twist or braunche, is
yong, it is flexible and bowable to any thing
a man can desire, but if we tarie till it be a
great trææ, it is inflexible and vnbowable:
If war be taken whyleft it is hote, anye
character maye be easilye imprinted, but ta-
rying till it be hard, it receiueth no printe at
all.

So, correct Children in their tender yeres,
and you may bow them to what good lore you
will your selfe, but tarie till they be old,
than is it to late, as experience teacheth
daylie.

Netherstocks of gernsey or silk.

Corked shoes pinsnets, pa-toffles,& such like sor wo.

Philo. Their netherstockes in like maner
are either of silke gearnsey, worsted, crewell,
or at least of as fyne yarn, thread, or cloth as
is possible to be had cunningly knit, and curiously indented, in euery point, wherto they
haue korked shoes, pinsnets, pantoffles, and
slip-

flippers: some of black veluet, some of white, some of gréene, and some of yellowe : some of spanish leather, and some of English lether, stitched with silk and imbrodered with Gold, and siluer all ouer the sowe, with other gew-gawes innumerable : All which if I should endeuoure my selfe to exprectse, I might with more facilitye number the sands of the Sea, the Starres in the Skye, or the grasse vp-pon the Earth so infinit, and innumerable be their abuses .

The innu-merable fa-shions of wo-mens attire.

For weare I neuer soe experte an Arith-metrician, or Mathematician, I weare neuer capable of the halfe of them, the deuill bro-cheth soe many new fashions euery day.

Wherfore to their Author I leaue them, not omittinge to tell you by the way (as an interim) of a certen kynde of sweete Pride vsed amongest the Gentlemen and Gentle-women in Ailgna.

Pride stin-king before the face of God.

Spud. I haue learned but of the Booke of God, that all Pride is stincking before the face of GOD, wherfore I greatlye desyre to knowe what abortyue Miscreant this is, for it is some portenteous mishapen monster, I am perswaded.

The hauing of ciuet, muske

Philo. Is not this a certen sweete Pri-de, to haue cyuet, muske, sweete powders,
                              fragrant

and other perfumes a sweet kind of Pride.

fragrant Pomanders, odorous perfumes & such like, wherof the smel may be felt and perceiued not only all ouer the house or place where they be present, but also a stones cast of, almost, yea the bed wherin they haue layed their delicate bodies, the places where they haue sate, the clothes and thinges which they haue touched shall smell a weeke, a moneth, and more after they be gon. But the Prophet Esai. Cap. 3· Esaias telleth them, instead of their Pomaunders, musks ciuets, balmes, sweet odours and perfumes, they shall haue stench and horrour in the nethermost hel. Let them take heed to it and amend their wicked liues.

And in the Sommer-time whilst floures be graene and fragrant, yee shall not haue any Nosegayes, & posies of flow ers, worn and caried abrod. Gentlewoman almost, no nor yet any droye or pussle in the Cuntrey, but they will carye in their hands, nosegayes and posies of floures to smell at, and which is more, two or three Nosegayes sticked in their brests before, for Beware the Spanish pip. what cause I cannot tel, except it be to allure their Paramours to catch at them, wherby I doubt not but they get many a slabbering kisse, and paradeuenture more fraendship be· sides, they know best, what I mean.

Spud. You wil be thought very straght la ced to speak against these thinges, for I haue heard it said, that these sweet smels are bothe corroborratiue to the sences and comfortatiue

110

to the spirits , and which dw biuiffe and recre
ate aswel the body as the minde.

Philo. They are so far from comforting the
braines, or lightning the spirits of men, that
as myftes and exhalations which euaporate
from these earthly bodyes, and are drawen
vp by the attractiue power of the Sun, Mon,
and starres dw rather obnubilate and darken
the beames of the Sun, not suffering his ra=
diatiõs to disparcle abrode. So these(in a ma=
ner) palpable odors, sumes, vapours, smells
of these musks,cyuets, pomanders,perfumes
balmes & suche like ascending to the braine,do
rather denigrate, darken and obscure ȳ spirit
and sences,then either lighten them , or com
fort them any manner of way . But howsoe=
uer it falleth out,sure I am,they are ensignes
of pride , allurements to sinne and prouocati=
ons to vice.   After all this, when they haue
attired thē selues in the midst of their pride,
it is a world to consider their coynesse in gestu=
res, their minsednes in words and speaches,
their gingerlynes in trippinge on toes like
yong goats , their demure nicitie and babish=
nes and withall their hawtie stomackes and
more than Cyclopicall countenãces: their fin=
gers are decked with gold,siluer,and precious
stones , their wristes with bracelets , and
armlets of gold, and other preciouse Iewels,
their hands are couered with their sweet wa=

Q.   shed

These curious smelles obnubilat the spirits & darken the sences.

Sweet smells of musks cy= uet,and such like, do anoy the spirits.

The vain ge= stures & coy= nes of women in the mid= dest of their pecok fethers. Fingers clog= ged with rings. Womens trinckets. Sweeted gloues.

shed gloues imbrodered with gold, siluer, and what not, & to such abhominatió is it grown, as they must haue their loking glasses caryed with thê whersoeuer they go: And good reason, for els how cold they see the deuil in them? for no doubt, they are the deuils spectacles to allure vs to pride, & cõsequently to distructió for euer: and aboue al things they must haue their silk scarffes cast about their faces & fluttering in the winde with great tassels at euery end, either of gold, siluer or silk. But J know wher for, they wil say they weare these scarfes, namely, to kéep them from Sun-burning. But J wold aske these Nice lings one question, wher in if they cã resolue mé, thê J willsay as they say, ý scarffes are necessary, and not flags of pride. Can that thing which is moste glorious & fair of it self, make any thing soule or ilsauored? the sun is a most glorious & fair creature, & therfor cánot make thê fowler, then they are of their own nature. Frõ whence then is it, ý the Sun burneth them & altereth their orient colour into woorser hue? The cause therof proceedeth from their own genuine corruptió and natural imperfectió, for no more is their fowlenes to be ascribed to the stelliferous beames of ý glittering sun, then ý stench of a dead carcasse, may be said to come of ý Sun, & not rather of it own corruptió, & filthines. They bustle theselues in preseruing the beautie of their bodyes, which lasteth but for a time, & in time

is cauſe of his own corruptiō, & which in effect
is nothing els then putrifactiō it ſelf, & a dung-
hil couered with white & red, but for y beautie
of y ſoule they care nothing at all. When they
vſe to ride abrod they haue inuiſories or viſors
made of veluet, wherwith they couer all their
faces, hauing holes made in thē againſt their
eyes, whercout they look. So that if a man
that knew not their guiſe before, ſhould chaunce to meet one of them he would think he
met a monſter or a deuil, for face he can ſee
none, but two brode holes againſt her eyes,
with glaſſes in them. Thus they prophane y
name of God & liue in al kinde of voluptuouſ-
nes, & pleaſure wurſſe thē euer did the hethen.

Viſors, or ſu-
uiſories of
veluet, to ride
abrode in.

Sues voluta-
bris verſan-
tur.

Sp. What think you, are not the inuētors, &
firſt finders out of theſe new toyes & dyueliſh
deuices in great daunger, and partakers with
them of the euill committed.

Philo. It cannot be, but the Inuentors of
theſe new toyes, are in great daunger before
God, as they who ſhall render accoūts to god
not only for the inuentiō of them, but alſo for
the euil cōmitted by them. For whoſoeuer, is
author of any euil muſt needs anſwer for the
euil. And ſurely y authors of theſe newfāgles,
are not vnworthy to be canonized ſaints whē
the yeere of Iubilie cōmeth (I meane ſaints of
ſathan) for there is no deed ſo flagicious, no fact
ſo dangerous, nor any thing ſo hainous, which
with alacritie is not plauſibly cōmitted for the

The firſt fin-
ders, and in-
uentors of
new faſhions,
are culpable
of all the euil
that cōmeth
by them.

maintenance of these Diuelish toyes and deuices : And albeit that the Persons themselues who offend this way shal dye in their sinnes , their owne bloud being powred vppon
their owne heads , yet the Authors of these
new toyes, wherthorow they offended,shalbe
giltie of their deathes and surely answear for
their destruction in the day of the LORD.

Spud. But say they, if I make them not, an
other wil, & it is as good for me to make them,
as an other, & it is my lyuing, wherfore I am
discharged of blame , if I make them (being
comaunded)with sweat of my face, and with
trauaile and paine to get my lyuing?

A vaine ex-
cuse.

Philo. We are commaunded indeed to get
our lyuing with the sweate of our face , but
how ? Not in doing those things , which are
euill of themselues,and also drawe and intice
others to euill,but in things lawful and good,
& which induce to goodnesse. And to say,others
will make them if I do not,no more excuseth
them of offence, thā for a Murtherer or Thief
to say,if I had not robbed , or killed this man
another wold , dischargeth him from the pe-
naltie of the iudiciall lawe to be inflicted a-
gainst him. Is it lawfull for vs to do euill,
because others do it ? Or doth the wickednes
of an other, delyuer me from blame,if I commit the same offence:no,nothing lesse. Wherfore,let Taylers and Artificers beware , how
they

We are bound
to get our ly-
uing in well
doing, not in
euill doing.

A caueat to
Artificers that
inuent new
fashions.

they eyther inuente oz make these new deuy-
res and Dyuelish fashions euery day : And
being requested to make them, if they perceiue them tende to vice, and allure to sinne, let
them refuse them in the name of God , moze
tendering the saluation of many, than the pziuat commodytie of themselues alone : which
thing, if euery one wold do , he should delyuer
his own soule, & suppozt an infinit number fro
falling into the gulphe of sinne, and so in shozt
tyme these new toyes , fond deuyces and chil-
dish babelries, (new fashions I should say,)
wold sone vanish away, and come to naught,
which God graunt may once be sæne.

Spud. Did the women of the fozmer wozld
attire themselues in suche sozte , as these women do ?

Philo. The Women of the fozmer age you
may be sure neuer appareled themselues like
one of these: But least you should thinke, that
$ Godly onelie lyued thus austerly , you shal
heare how litle the very hethé and barbarian
Women haue, and do at this pzesent estæmé
of apparell , as Stuperius witnesseth, whose
wozds are these speking of the Egiptian women : Vestimenta sciunt nec noua pristinis
mutare, verum semper his in cultibus gaudent
perpetuo tempore congredi, qualcunqae gen-
tes hunc per orbem visitent. Which may be
thus turned into English verse.

                      G.iij.   The

The Egiptian Matrones neuer vse
Their fashion of attyre to change,
But euer keep one forme to chuse
Although they visite Nations strange.

AND as all Writers do affirme, all the
Women there, indifferetly go with their
haire hanging downe, with a broade hat
vppon their heads, and other attyre as playne
as the rest, so farre are these People from
Pride, and hunting after strange fashions as
our Women do.

The Women of Affrica are witnessed
by the same Stuperius, and others, to be so
farre from affecting strange fashions, or curiosity in aparel, that they cloth themselues in
a manner al ouer, ferinis pellibus, with beasts
skinnes, furres, and such like.   And this they
think so riche attire, as they vse it altogether,
when they celebrat their festiual solene dates,
or when they go abrode to be seene.

The Brasilian Women esteeme so litle of
apparell also as they rather chose to go naked
(their secret partes onely being couered) then
they wold be thought to be proud, or desirous
of such vanities.

The Cantabrian Women likewyse with
many others do the same. In High Germany
the Women vse in effect one kind of apparel,
or habite, without any differece at all, nothing
like other Natios delighting in new fangles:

yes

yea the wiues there, are ſo far from pꝛide, that
they will not diſdaine to carie all their houſe-
hould ſtuffe and other trincliets about with
them vppõ their backs in tyme of extremitie.
Theſe Mayds & Virgins go very plain, with
kerchers only on their heads, their haire hanging down behinde, in token of Virginitie.

Thus you ſæ, euery Natiõ, how barbarous
ſoeuer, are much inferiour to ẙ people of Ailgna in pꝛide & exceſſe of apparell: and yet theſe
exainples I alledge not to th'end I wold with
all others to vſe ẙ ſame, oꝛ ẙ very like brutiſh
kind of auſter habite, but to ſhew how farre
they be from Pꝛide, & how much the other be
wedded to ẙ ſame. And as foꝛ the vertuous &
godly chꝛiſtian women from the beginning of
the woꝛld, they haue ſo litle cared foꝛ the vain
gloꝛy of apparell, & ſo litle (oꝛ rather nothing
at al) were they a quainted therwith, as they
hunted foꝛ nothing els ſo much as foꝛ the oꝛnaments of the mind, as wiſdom, continency,
chaſtitie, & true godlyneſſe, thinking the ſame
bewtie ſufficient. They coũted it great ſhame
to cloth their bodies with ſumpteous apparel,
& their minds to be naked, & voide of true vertue. So, if theſe womẽ wold ſæk after ẙ bewtie of ẙ mind, they wold not affect apparell ſo
much, foꝛ if they be faire iꞑ body alredy, than
nǣd they not goꝛgeous apparel to make them
fairer: & if they be defoꝛme in body, it is not ẙ

apparell, that

that can make them fairer. And either their
bewtie consisteth in them, or in their apparel:
If in them, than not in the Apparell, & so it is
meere foolery to were them. And if in apparel,
than not in them, and so cannot the garments
make them fayre, whome God, & nature hath
made otherwise: wherfor, look in what shape,
forme, or condition euerye one is created by
God, let him content himselfe with the same,
without any alteratiō or chaunge, with praise to his Creator.

Spud. They hold (notwithstanding) that it
is the pride of the heart, which God so muche
hateth, and detesteth.

Pride of the
heart.

Philo. It is verye true that G O D puni-
sheth the pride of the heart with eternal damnation (if they repent not,) for he will be serued, and obyed either with the whole man, or
els with none. Than if he punish the pride of
the heart with euerlasting damnatiō, he must
needs (in iustice) punish the pride of Apparell
with the like, being both ioyned in one predi-
camet of sinne, and the pride of apparell much
more hurting before the world, thā the other.

Pride of ap-
parel equiua-
lēt with Pride
of the heart.

Also, it is manifest, that the pride of apparel, riseth first from the corruptiō of the heart,
as the effects from the cause, the fruits from
the roote of the tree: than is the pride of y heart,
which, notwithstanding, it hurteth not outwardly, but is secret betwixt God, and himselfe

selfe, be damnable in it owne nature before
God, than must it néeds be, that the Pride of
apparell, (which sheweth it selfe to the world,
both offensiue to G O D, and hurtfull to mã,
and which also is the fruite of the pride of the
heart, and throweth almost as many as behold it, at least, as many as followes it, into the
déep dungion of hell) is much more pernicious
and damnable than the other.

Spud. Hath the Lord plagued this sinne of
pride, with any notable torture or punishmēt,
euer from the beginning of the World vnto
this day, or hath he omitted the reuenge therof as a thing of small force, or importance?

Philo. Most fearfull plagues, and dreadfull
iudgements of G O D haue in all ages béene
powred vppon them that offended herein, as
all Histories both holy, and prophane do beare
record. For proofe wherof, I will geue you a
taste but of a few, wherby may appeare how
wonderfully the Lord in all ages, tymes, kin-
réds & peoples hath punished those that thô-
row pride (like wicked recusants, and back-
slyders from God) haue rebelled against his
maiestie. The deuill, who before was an An-
gell in Heaué, arrogating to himselfe the im-
periall throane of the maiesty of God, was cast
downe into the déepth of Hell burning with
fire and sulphur for euer.

Adam, desiring to be a God (for the serpent
G.b.   tould

Examples of
God his pu-
nishmēts ex-
ecuted vppon
them that of-
fended in
Pride, in all
ages.

tould him he should be as God, knowing both
good & euill) was for the sin of Pride throwne
downe to the bottome of Hell, & not onely he,
but all his posteritie to the end of the World.
The hoast of Core, Dathan, and Abiram for
their exceding pride, in stirring vp mutenie,
rebelling against their lawfull Magistrats
were swallowed vp quick into hell, the earth
opening her mouth, & deuouring them, with
all their complices whatsoeuer. The People
of Babylon intēding to builde a tower, whose
top should tutche the Skye, thinking that if
God should drown ý world againe with water, they would be sure inough on the toppe of
their high turrets, yea they intending to sit
with God himselfe (if need weare) weare all
confounded, and a diuerse language put into
euery mans mouth, that none knew what an
other spake. And thus were they forced to leaue there building, and dispersed themselues a-
broad vppō the face of the earth, wherof sprāg
the first piuersitie of languages in the world.
Wherfore when we heare any language spoken we know not, it may be a memorandum

A memoran-
dum.

to vs to put vs in minde of our Pride, which
was the cause therof.

Goliah, the great Gyant, the huge Cyclops,
and sworne enemy to the Children of Israell,
for his pride against the Lord, was slaine by
Dauid, the faitfull Seruaunt of the Lord.

An-

Antiochus intending to ouerthrowe, and sacke Ierusalem, to spoile the Sanctuarie and Temple of the Lord, and to kill the people of God, was for his pride ouerturned in his charet ryding thetherward, his belly brust and all thy wormes crawled out, moste lothsomly, and in fine, beganne so to stinke and swell, as neither his Seruants nor he himselfe cold abide his owne sauoure, and thus ended his lyfe in great miserie, and wretchednesse.

Nabuchodonosor, was for his pride cast out of his kingdom and forced to eat grasse with wild beasts in the wildernesse.

King Saule, for his pride and disobedience, was deposed of his principallitie and kingly regimente, and in the end slewe him self on mounte Gelboe most desperately.

Sodoma and Gomorr:, were both destroyed with fire & brimstone frô heauen for their sin of pride, & contempt of the Lord. All the world in the daies of Noah was drowned with vniuersall deluge for pride & contumacy of heart.

King Hezekiahs for his pride in shewing to the Ambassadors of the king of Babylon, all his treasure (for he sent Messengers vnto him wt giftes & lettres congratulatorie, for ye recouerie of his helth) lost al his iewels, treasures & riches, wt his owne sonnes also, being transported captiues into Babilon: K. Dauid, for his pride in numbring ye people contrary the wil of god
was

Antiochr

Nabuchodo-
noser.....
Daniel.

K.

1 Reg. Cap. 10

was greuouslie puniſhed , and thꝛeeſcoꝛe and
ten thouſand of his People ſlaine with a grꝫe-
nous peſtilence foꝛ the ſame.

1.Samuel.1. c.
24.Verſ.15.

King Pharao foꝛ his pꝛide againſt the Loꝛd,
(foꝛ he thought him ſelfe a G O D vppon the
Earth, and therfoꝛe aſked he Moyſes in deriſi-
on, who is the Loꝛd) was dꝛowned in the
read Sea with all his hoaſt. The pꝛoude Pha-
riſey iuſtifying himſelfe, foꝛ his pꝛide was re-
pꝛoued of the Loꝛd, and reiected.

The proude
Pharisey.

King Herode foꝛ attiring himſelfe in ſumpteous aray, ꝗ not aſcribing gloꝛy to the Loꝛd,
was ſtrucken dead, by an Angel, and woꝛmes
conſumed his fleſh immediatly. Al theſe, with
infinit millions moe in al ages, haue periſhed
thoꝛow pꝛide, and therfoꝛe let not this people
think that they ſhall eſcape vnpuniſhed , who
dꝛinke vp pꝛide as it weare ſweet wyne, fade
vppon it, as vppon delicious meats, and wallowe in it, as a filthie ſwyne doth in the dirtie
myꝛe: will the Loꝛd puniſh his peculiare people, and elect veſſels, and let them go free ?
Wherefoꝛe I wold wyſhe them to be warned,
foꝛ it is a terrible thing to fall into ẏ hands of
G O D, who is a conſuming fire, ꝗ a fearfull
God. His bowe is bente, his arrowes of iudgements are dꝛawen to the head, his fire is
kyndled, his wꝛath is gone out, ꝗ ready to be
powꝛed vppon the contemners of his lawes.
Tempt not the Loꝛd any longer, pꝛouoke not

K. Herode.

God his Pla-
gues are pre-
pared, if we
repent not.

his

his wrath, exaſperate not his iudgements to∘
wards thee: for as mercy proceedeth frō him,
ſo doth iuſtice alſo: And be ſure of it, he payeth
home at the laſt. For as in mercie he ſuffreth
no good deed to be vnrewarded, ſo in his iuſt
iudgmente there is no wickednes, which he
leaueth vnpuniſhed. And yet notwithſtāding
their wickedneſſe and pride is ſuch, as ſtinc∘
keth before the face of God, and maketh the
Enemies to blaſpheme and ſpeake euill of the
wayes of the Lord: For ſay they, the men
of Ailgna are wicked, & licentious in all their
wayes, which eaſily appeareth by their appa∘
rell, & new fangled faſhions euery day inuen∘
ted. The beaſtly Epicures, the Drunkards,
& ſwilbowles vppon their ale benches, when
their heads are intoxicat with new wine, wil
not ſtick to belch forth, and ſay, that the inha∘
bitantes of Ailgna go brauelye in Apparell,
chaunging faſhions euerie daye, for no cauſe
ſo much as to delight the eyes of their harlots
withall, and to inamoure the mindes of their
fleſhly paramours.   Thus be this People a
laughing ſtock to all the world for their pride,
a ſlaunder to the word of God & to their pro∘
feſſion, ſcandalles to their brethren, a diſhonor
and reproch to the Lord, and very caterpillers
to themſelues. in waſting and cōſuming their
goods and treaſures vppon vanyties & trifles.
Spud. Seeing that by diuyne aſſiſtance, you
                                                                    haue

Our new fan∘
gles and toies,
are occaſions,
why all na∘
tions mocke,
and flouté vs.

Our ſlyuing a
ſlaunder to
the truth.

haue now finished your tractation of the Apparell of Ailgna, shew me (I pray you) what other abuses be there vsed, for I am perswaded, that pride the Mother of all sinne, is not without her Daughters of sinne semblable to her selfe?

The horryble vice

of Whordome in Ailgna.
Philo.

THE horryble vice of Whordome also is ther to to much frequented, to p great dishonor of God, the prouoking of his iudgements against them, the staine and blemish of their profession, the euill example of all the world, and finally to their owne damnation for euer, except they repente.

Spud. I haue heard them reason, that mutuall coition betwixt man and woman, is not so offensiue before God. For do not all Creatures (say they) as wel reptilia terræ, as volatilia Cœli, the creping things vpon the earth, as the flying Creatures in the aire, and all other Creatures in generall both small & great ingender together? hath not nature and kynd ordained them to? & geuen them mēbers incident to that vse? doth not p Lord (say they) (as it were to a stimule, or prick by his mandat, saing crescite & multiplicamini, & replete terrā, increase, multiplie, & fill the earth,) thrust p vp

Whordome in Ailgna too too rife.

Vain and vngodly reasons pretending that whordome is no sinne.

vp to the ſame? Otherwyſe the Woꝛld wold
become barren, and ſoone fall to decay: wherfoꝛe they conclude, that whoꝛdome is a badge **Oh wicked**
of loue, a cognizāce of amitie, a tutch of luſtie **Lybertynes.**
youth, a frendlie daliance, a redintegration of
loue, and an enſigne of vertue, rather meritorious than dānable: theſe with the like be ẏ ex-
ceptiōs which J haue hard them many times
to obiect, in defence of their carnal pollutions.

Philo. Curſed be thoſe mouths, that thus
blaſpheme the mightie God of Iſraell, and his
ſacred woꝛd, making the ſame clokes, to couer
their ſinne withall, woꝛſe are they than Ly-
bertines who thinke all things lawfull, oꝛ A-
theiſtes, who denie there is any God. The deuills themſelues neuer ſinned ſo hoꝛribly, noꝛ
erred ſo groſſely, as theſe, (not Chꝛiſtians, but
dogges) do, that make whoꝛdom a vertue, and
meritoꝛious:. but becauſe you ſhal ſee their de-
ceptiōs diſplayed ⁊ their dānable abuſes, moꝛe
plainly diſcouered, J will reduce you to ẏ firſt
inſtitutiō of this Godly oꝛdenāce of matrimo-
ny. The Loꝛd our God hauing created all **The firſt in-**
things in Heauen, earth, oꝛ Hell whatſoeuer, **ſtitution of**
created of euery ſex, two, male ⁊ female of both **matrimonie.**
kindes, and laſt of al other creatures, he made
man after his own likeneſſe, ⁊ ſimilitude, ge- **Gen.2 Mat.19**
uing him a womā, made of a ribbe of his own **Marc. Luc.16.**
body, to be his companion, ⁊ comfoꝛter, ⁊ linc- **1.Cor. 6.**
king them together in the honoꝛable ſtate of **Ephe. 5.**
vedse

venerable wedlocke, he bleſſed them both, ſaying, creſcite, multiplicamini, & replete terrã,
Increaſe, multiplie, & repleniſh ẏ earth: wherby it is moze than apparent, that the Lozde,
whoſe name is Iehouah, the mightie GOD
of Iſraell, is the Authoz of Godly matrimony,

*Mariage in
ſtituded for 4
cauſes.*

inſtituting it in the tyme of mans inconcency
in Paradice, and that as mee ſeemeth foz foure
cauſes. Firſt, foz the auoydauce of whozdom:

1

Secondly, foz the mutuall comfozte, & conſolatiõ, that the one might haue of the other in all
aduerſities & calamities whatſoeuer: Third

2

3

ly, foz the pzocreation, and Godly pzopagation

*All mutuall
copulation,
except mariage, is vnlawfull. 4*

of Childzen in the feare of the Lozd, that both
the wozld might be increaſed therby, and the
Lozd alſo in them glozified. And fourthlie, to
be a figure oz type of our ſpirituall wedlocke
betwixt Chziſt and his church both militant,
and triumphante. This congreſſion, and mutuall copulation of thoſe that be thus ioyned
together in the Godlye ſtate of bleſſed matrimony, is pure virginitie, and allowable befoze
God and man, as an action wherto the Lozde
hath pzomiſed his bleſſing thozow his mercy,
not by our merite, ex opere operato, as ſome
ſhame not to ſay. All other goinges together
and coitions are damnable, peſtiferous, and
execrable. So, now you ſee, that wheras the
Lozd ſaith, increaſe, multiplie, & fill the earth,
he alludeth to thoſe that are cheyned together

in

in the Godly state of matrimonie and wed-
lock, and not otherwyse : For to those that
go together after any other sorte, he hath de-
nounced his curse and wrath for euermore,
as his alsauing word beareth record.   And
wheras they say that all creatures vppon the
Earth do ingender together, I graunte it is
true. But how? in suo genere, in their owne
kinde. There is no creature creeping, on the
earth, or flying in the aire, how irrationable
soeuer that doth degenerate as man doth, but
keepeth the same state and order wherein
they were made at the first, and so if man did,
he should not commit abhominable whordom
and filthie sinne as hee doth. It is said of those
that write de natura animalium, that (almost)
all vnreasonable beasts and flying fowles after they haue once linked and vnited them selues togither to any one of the same kinde, and
after they haue once espoused them selues the
one to the other, wil neuer after ioyne them
selues w any other, til the one be dissolued fro
the other by death. And thus they keepe the
knot of matrimonie inuiolable to the end. And
if any one chaunce to reuolte and go togither
with any other during p life of his first mate,
al the rest of the same kind, assemble togither,
as it were in a councel or parliament, and either kil or greuously punish the adulterer or
adulteresse whether euer it be, which lawe I

Now all cre-
atures do goe
togither in
their kindes.

The fidelitie
of vnreasona
ble creatures
in mariage
one towards
an other.

would God were amongst Christians establi
shed . By all which it may appeer how horri
ble a sinne whoredome is in nature , that the
very vnreasonable creatures dw abhorre it.
The Heathen people who know not God , so
much lothe this stinking sinne of whordome,
that some burne them quick, some hang them
vn gibbets, some cut off their heds, some their
armes , legs and hands ,. some put out their
eyes, some burne them in the face , some cut
of their noses, some one parte of their bodye ,
some anether, and some with one kind of tor
ture, and so te with another: but none leaueth
them vnpunished: so that we are set to schole
to learn our first rudiments (like yung Noui
ces or Children scarce crept out of the shel,)
how to punish whoredome , euen by the vnrea
sonable creatures and by the heathen people
who are ignorant of the deuine goodnes.

> *How much the Heathen haue deteste d whordome.*

> *Sundery pu-nishments of whordome a-mongst the Heathen.*

God be merciful vnto vs.

Spud. I pray you rehearse some places out
of the word of God , wherin this cursed vice
of whordome is forbidden , for my better instruction.

> *Testimonies out of the woord of god wherin whor-dome is for-bid,*

Philo. Our Sauiour Christe in the eight of
Iohn speaking to the woman, whom the ma-
licious Iewes had apprehended in adulterie ;
bad her go her way and sin no more. If it had
not been a moste grœuous sin , he would neuer haue bid her to sin therin no more.

In

In the fift of Mathew he ſaith, who ſo luſteth after a woman in his hart, hath committed the fact alredy, and therfore is guiltie of death for the ſame. To the Phariſes, aſking him whether a man might not put away his wife for any occaſion? Chriſte anſwered, for no cauſe, ſaue for whoredome onely, inferring that whoredome is ſo hainous a ſinne, as for the perpetration therof it ſhalbe lawful for a man to ſequeſter him ſelf from his owne wife and the wife from her owne huſband. The Apoſtle Paul ſayth, know you not that your bodyes are the members of Chriſte, ſhall I then take the members of Chriſte (ſaith he) and make them the members of an whore? God forbid, knowe ye not that he who coupleth him ſelf with a harlot is become one body of her? flee fornication (ſaith he) therfore, for euery ſinne that a man committeth is without the body, but who committeth fornication ſinneth againſt his owne body. And in an other place, knowe you not, that your Bodyes are the temples of the holy ghoſt, which dwelleth within you? And who ſo deſtroyeth the Temple of God, him ſhall God deſtroy. In an other place, he ſaith: be not receiued, for neither Whoremonger, Adulterer, Fornicator, inceſtuous perſon nor ſuch like ſhall euer enter into the kingdome of heauen. Againe, Coniugium honorabile eſt inter omnes.

Mat. 5.

Mat. 19.
Mar. 10.
Luc. 16.

1. Cor. 6.

Mariage

Mariage is honorable amongst all men, and the bed vndefiled, but whoremongers and adulterers God shall iudge. In the Reuelation of Saint Iohn it is said, that they who were not defiled with women, doo waite vpon the Lamb, whethersoeuer he goeth. The Apostle Paul willeth vs to be so far from fornication, that it be not once named amongst vs, as becommeth Saints, with infinit such places, which for breefnes I omit, referring you in the olde Testament to these and such like places, namely, the 20. of Exodus. 20. of Leuiticus. Deutronomie 22. Deutro. 27. 2. Reg. 11. Leuit. 18. Exodus, 22. Num 5. Eccle. 9. Pro. 23. Pro. 7. verse. 24.

Spud. As you haue now proued by inuincible testimonies of holy Scripture, that whoredome is forbidden by the Lord: so I pray you shew mee the greuousnes thereof by some seuere & rare examples of Gods iust iudgement executed vppon the same from the beginning.

Genesis 7. 8.

Philo. The whole world was destroyed w water, not any liuing thing left vpon the erth, (saue in ye Ark of Noath) for the sin of whoredō incest & brothelry vsed in those daies. Sodoma and Gomorra two famous Cities were consumed with fire and brimstone from heauen for the like sin of whoredom adulterie and fornication. The citie of ye Sichemits, man, woman and childe weare put to the edge of the sworde;

Punishments of whordom in all Ages.

Genesis. 19.

Genesis 24.

sword, for the rauishing of Dina the daughter of Iacob. The Lord also tolde Abimelech,
that if he did not let go vntouched Sara, Abraham his wife, bothe he and all his housholde
should dye the death, notwithstanding he did
it ignorauntly. The very same hapned to I-
saac also. Iudas vnderstanding that his daughter in law was impregnate and great with
childe, and not knowing by whom, comman-
ded that she should be burned without any further delay. Was not Absalon, king Dauid
his sonne plagued all his life for going into
his Fathers Concubines? And did not Achi-
tophel who gaue councel so to do hang himself? Was not Ruben the first borne sonne of
Iacob, accursed for going vp to his Fathers
bed, and lost he not his birth-right, his dignitie and primacie ouer his Bretheren for the
same? Were there not aboue threescore and
fiue thousand men slain for the adulterie don
with one Leuits wife? Was not king Dauid
punished all ydaies of his life for his adultery
don with Bersabe, Vrias his wife? Was not
his sone Amon, for lying with Thamar, slain?
Was not Salomon being peruerted with hethen women cast out of the fauour of GOD,
notwithstanding, being otherwise, the wisest
Prince in all the world? Did not Achab at
the perswations of Iesabel, his cursed wife, falling to Idolatrie and worshiping of Idolles

P. 3.   and

Genesis. 20.

Ge.   26.

Ga: 18.

1. Reg. 16

Ge.   29.

Iudi. 20.

2. Reg. 13,
12,

1. Reg. 11

and deuils, suffer moste cruel punishment in this life all his dayes, besides what he suffereth now God onely knoweth. Were not the Israelite, and Madianitish woman both slain by that woorthy man Phinees, who ran them both thorow the priuy members with his Iauelin or sword? Was not Sampson brought to a miserable end, his eyes being bothe put out, and he made to be a laughing stock to all men, thorow his too much fauouring of wantō women? Was not King Pharao wunderfully plagued for but intending euil in his hart towards Sara Abraham his wife? Did not the Lord slay (with a moste græuous mortalitie) foure & twentie thousand of ỹ Israelites in one day, for whoredome and adulterie with the women of the Moabites and Madianits?

By these and such like fearful Examples of the iustice of God powred vpon these whoremongers & adultrers, we may learn to know the græuousnes of the same, and the punishment due to all whoremongers and fornicatours either in this life, or in the World to come, or els in both: for if the Lord deferre the punishment of whoredome in this life, hæ reserueth it for the world to come, suffering the wicked to wallow in their sinne, and to fil vp the measure of iniquitie, that their damnation may be iust. And if the Lord list not sin vnpunished, no, not in his most dær Saints, what

Numer. 25.

Iud: 16.

Gene: 12.

what he wil do in them who dayly crucifie him a new, let the world iudge?

Spud. Now am I fully perswaded by your inuincible reasons, that there is no sin greater before the face of God, then whordome, wherfore, God graūt that all his may auoid it.

Philo. You haue said true, for there is no sinne (almost) comparable vnto it, for besides that, it bringeth euerlasting damnation to all that liue therin to the end, without repentāce, it also bringeth these inconueniences, with many mo, vidilicet, it dimmeth the sight, it impairsth the hearing, it infirmeth ÿ sinewes, it weakneth the ioynts, it exhausteth the marow, consumeth the moisture and supplemēt of the body, it riueleth the face, appalleth the coūtenance, it dulleth ÿ spirits, it hurteth the memorie, it weakneth ÿ whole body, it bringeth it into a consūption, it bringeth vlcerations, scab, scurf, blain, botch, pocks & biles, it maketh hoare haires, & bald pates: it induceth olde age, & in fine, bringeth death before nature vrge it, malady enforce it, or age require it.

What euil whordome bringeth to mans body in this life.

Sp. Seing ÿ whordome bringeth such soure sauce with it, namely, death euerlasting after this life, and so many discomodities besides in this life, I wonder that men dare cōmit the same so securely as they do now a dayes?

Philo.   It is so little feared in Ailgna, that vntill euery one hath two or three Bastardes a péece, they estéeme him no man,

(for that, they call a mans deede) insomuch as euery scuruie boy of twelue, sirtéen or twenty yéeres of age wil make no conscience of it , to haue two or thrée , peraduenture half a dosen seuerall women with childe at once , and this exploite béeing don , he showes them a faire pair of héeles, and away goeth he, Euro voloci-uskas quick as a Bée (as they say) into some strange place where he is not knowen where, how he liueth , let the wise iudge , for coelum non animum mutant qui trans mare currunt , though they chaunge their place of abode , yet their naughtie dispositions they retaine stil.

The small care to auoid whordome in Ailgna.

Then hauing estraunged them selues thus for a small space, they returne againe , not to their pristine cursed life I dare say , but vnto their cuntrey, and then no man may say, black is their eye, but all is wel, & they as good chri-stians as those that suffer them vnpunished .

Whormon-gers Runagates.

Spud. The state and condition of that Cuntrey is most miserable if it be true you report, it weare much better that euerye one had his lawful wife, and euery woman her lawfull husband, as the Apostle commaundeth , then thus to be drowned in the filthie sin of whor-dome.

Mariage, an antidotarie a gainst Whor-dome.

Philo. That is the only salue and soueraine remedy, which the lord ordained against whor-dome, that those who haue not the gift of con-tinencie might mary, and so kéep their vessels
                                                        vndefiled

vndefiled to the Lord. But notwithſtāding, in
Ailgna there is ouer great libertye permitted
therin: for litle infants, in ſwadling clowts,
are often maried by their ambicious Parents
and frends, when they know neither good nor
euill, and this is the origene of much wickedneſſe, & directlie againſt the word of God, and
examples of the primitiue age.   And beſydes
this, you ſhall haue euery ſawcy boy, of x.xiij.
xvi. or xx. yeres of age, to catch vp a woman &
marie her, without any feare of God at all, or
reſpect had, either to her religion, wiſdom, integritie of lyfe, or any other vertue, or which
is more, without any reſpecte how they maye
lyue together with ſufficient maintenance for
their callings and eſtat. No no, it maketh no
matter for theſe things, ſo he haue his pretie
puſſie to huggle withall, it forceth not, for that
is the only thing he deſireth. Than build they
vp a cotage, though but of elder poals, in euery
lane end, almoſt, wher they lyue as beggers al
their life. This filleth the land with ſuch ſtore
of poore people, that in ſhort tyme (except ſome
caution be prouided to preuent the ſame) it is
like to growe to great pouertie and ſcarſnes,
which G O D forbid.

Sp. I cānot ſée how this geare ſhold be holpē?

Ph. What if a reſtraint were made, y̆ none
(except vppon ſpeciall and vrgente cauſes)
ſhould marie before they come to xx. or xxiiij.
                                                           yeres,

**Maring of
infants in
ſwadling
cloths.**

**Euery Boy
ſnatcheth vp
a Woman to
wyfe..**

**A reſtraint of
mariage.**

yæres, o2 at ẜ leaſt, befo2e they be .riij. o2 rbiiȝ yæres old , would not this make fewer beggers, than now there are ?

Sp. But if this were eſtabliſhed, thã ſhould we haue moe Baſtards, and of the two, I had rather we had many legittimats, than many illegittimates.

How whordome may be suppreſſed.

Philo. The occaſion of begetting of manye Baſtards were ſoone cut of, if the puniſhment which either God his lawe doth allowe, o2 els which good pollicy doth conſtitute, were aggrauated, and erecuted vppon the Offenders.

The puniſhment for whordome ouer remiſſe.

Fo2 the puniſhment appointed fo2 who2dom now is ſo light, that they eſtæme not of it, thei feare it not, they make but a ieſt of it.   Fo2 what great thing is it, to go ij. o2 th2æ dayes in a white ſhæte befo2e the congregation, and that ſomtymes not paſt an how2e o2 two in a day, hauing their vſnall garmẽts vnderneth, as commonly they haue ?   This impunitie (iu reſpecte of condigne puniſhement , which that vice requireth) doth rather animate and imbolden them to the acte, than feare them from it.   In ſo much, as I haue heard ſome miſcreants impudently ſay , that he is but a beaſt, that fo2 ſuch white lyuered puniſhment would abſtaine from ſuche gallant paſtyme: but certen it is, that they who thinke it ſuche ſwæt meate here , ſhall find the ſawce ſow2e

and

and ſtiptick enough in Hell.

Spud. What punishment would you haue
inflicted vppon ſuch as commit this horrible
kinde of ſinne?

Philo. I would wiſh that the Man or
Woman who are certenlye knowen without all ſcruple or doubte, to haue committed
the horryble fact of whordome, adulterie,
inceſt, or fornication, eyther ſhould drinke a
full draught of Moyſes cuppe, that is, taſt
of preſent death, or els, if it be thought too ſe-
uere (for in euill, men will be more mercifull, than the Author of mercie him ſelfe,
but in goodneſſe, fare well mercy,) than
wold G O D they might be cauterized, and
ſeared with a hote yron on the cheeke, fore-
head, or ſome other parte of their bodye that
might be ſeene, to the end the honeſt and chaſt
Chriſtians might be diſcerned from the a-
dulterous Children of Sathan : But (alas)
this vice (with the reſt) wanteth ſuch due
puniſhement, as G O D his Word doth
commaunde to be executed thervppon.

The Magiſtrates wincke at it, or els as
looking thorow their fingers, they ſee it,
and will not ſee it.

And therfore, the Lorde is forced too take
the ſword into his owne hands, and to exe-
cute puniſhment him ſelfe, becauſe the Magiſtrates will not.

What kind
of puniſhmēt
whordome
ought to
haue.

Fe2

Fo2 better p2œf wherof marke this ſtrange ⁊
fearful iudgment of god ſhewed vpon two adulterous perſons there, euen ẏ laſt day in effect,
ẏ remēb2āce wherof is yet grǣn in their heds.

There was a man whoſe name was W.
Ratſurb, being certenly knowen to be a noto-
rious vſerer (and yet p2etending alway a ſingular ʒeale to religion, ſo that he wold ſeldom
tymes go without a byble about him, but ſœ
the iudgements of God vpon them that will
take his wo2d in their mouthes, and yet lyue
cleane contrarie, making the wo2d of God a
cloke to couer their ſinne and naughtyneſſe
withall) who vppon occaſion of buſines viſi-
ting Lewedirb a place appointed fo2 the co2-
rectiō of ſuch that be wicked lyuers, ſaw there
a famous whoze, but a very p2oper Woman,
whō (as is ſaid) he knew not, but whether he
did, o2 not, certē it is, that he p2ocured her de-
lyuery from thence, bayled her, ⁊ hauing put
away his owne wife befo2e, kept her in his
chamber, vſing her at his pleaſure. Whyleſt
theſe two mēbers of ẏ deuil were playing the
vile Sodomits together in his chamber, ⁊ hauing a litle pan of coles befo2e them wherin
was a very litle fire, it pleaſed G D D euen
in his w2ath, to ſtrike theſe two perſons dead
in a moment. The Woman falling ouer the
pan of coles, was burned that all her bowels
guſhed out, the man was founde lying by, his
                                                    cloths

cloths in some partes being scorched and bur=
ned, & some partes of his body also. But which
is most wonderfull, his arme was burned to
the very bonne, his shirte sleeue, and dublet, not
once perished, nor tutched with the fire. Wher
by may be thought & not without great proba=
bilitie of truth, that it was euē the fire of God
his wrath from Heauen, and not any natural
fire from the earth. And in this wonderfull, &
fearsull maner weare these cupple founde:
which God graunt may be a documēt to all y
heare or read the same, to aboyde the like of=
fence, and to all Magistrates, an Example to
see the same punished with more seueritie, to
the glorie of God, and their owne discharge.

But so farre are some, from suffering con=
digne punishment for this horrible sinne, that
they get good maintenance with practising the
same. For shall you not haue some, yea many
thousands, that liue vppō nothing els, and yet
go clothed Gentlewomenlike, both in their
silks and otherwyse, with their fingers clog=
ged with rings, their wrists with braccelets, &
Jewels, and their purses full of gold and sil=
uer? And here of they make no conscience, so
their Husbands know it not. Or if they do,
some are such peasants, and such maycocks,
that either they will not, or (which is truer)
they dare not reproue them for it. But & if the
Husband once reproue them for their misde=
meanour,

meanwur, than they conspire his death, by some
meane or other.   And all this commeth to
passe, because the punishment therof is no ex-
tremer, as it ought to be. And some both Gentlemen and others (wherof some I know)
are so nusled herein, that hauing put away
their owne wyues, do kepe whores openly,
without any great punishment for it, and hauing bene conuented before the magistery,
and there bene deposed vppon a booke to put
away their whores, haue put them forth
at one doore, and taken them in at the other.

And thus they dally in their othes with the
Lord, and stoppe the course of the lawe, with
rubrum argentum, wherof they haue store to
bestowe vppō such wickednesse, but haue not
a mite to giue towards any good purpose.

Wherfore, in the name of GOD, let all
men that haue put away their honest wyues
be forced to take them again, and abandon all
whores, or els to taste of the law. And let all
whores be cut of with the sword of right iudgement. For, as long as this immunitie and
impunitie is permitted amongest vs, let vs
neuer lowke to please GOD, but rather prouoke his heuie iudgements against vs. And
the reason is ; for that there is no sinne in all
the World, but these whores, and whores
maisters will willingly attempt, and atchei-
ue; for the inioying of their whoredome :

                                              And

And Hell, deſtruction, and death euerlaſting is the guerdon therof, and yet men cannot be aware of it. The Lord remooue it from all his Children, and preſent them blameles before his tribunall ſeate, without ſpotte, or wrincle at that great day of the Lord.

Spud. What niemorable thing els haue you ſeen there frequented: For ſeing you haue begun, in parte, I pray you deſcribe the wholer.

Gluttonie and

drunkenneſſe in Ailg.
Philo.

I Haue ſéene that which gréeueth mée to report. The People there are marueilouſly giuen to daintie fare, gluttonye, bellichéer, many alſo to drunkenneſſe, & gourmandice.

Daintie fare, gluttony and gourmandice vſed in Ailg.

Sp. That is a manifeſt argumét of good hoſpitality, which both is comended in y word of God, & which, I know you wil not reprehéde.

Ph. Godly hoſpitalitie is a thing in no wiſe worthy of reprehenſió, but rather of great comendatió, for many haue receiued Angels into their houſes, at vnawaris, by vſing y ſame, as Abraham, Lot, Tobias, & many others. Yet if hoſpitality flow ouer into ſuperfluitie & riotous exceſſe, it is not tolerable: for now adaies if y table be not couered frō the one end to y other as thick as one diſh can ſtãd by another,

Godly hoſpitalitie to be commended.

with

Varietie of dishes, and meats, with their curious sawces.

with delicat meats of sundry sorts, one cleane different from an other, and to euery dish a seuerall sawce appropriat to his kinde, it is thought there vnworthye ẏ name of a dinner. Yea so many dishes shal you haue pesseruing the table at once, as the insaciablest Helluo, the deuouringest glutton, or the greediest cormorant that is, can scarse eat of euery one a litle. And these many shall you haue at the

Excesse of meats.

first course, as many at the second, and peraduenture, moe at the third, besydes other sweet contyphricks, and delicat confections, of spiceries, and I cannot tell what. And to these dainties, all kind of wynes are not wanting, you may be sure.   Oh what nisitie is this? what vanitie, excesse, ryot, and superfluitie is heare? Oh farewell former world? For I

The austerity and Godly simplicity of the former World in meats, and drinkes.

haue heard my Father say, ẏ in his dayes, one dish, or two of god wholsome meate was thought sufficient, for a man of great worship to dyne withall, and if they had three or four kinds, it was reputed a sumptuous feast. A god pece of beef was thought thã, god meat, and able for the best, but now, it is thought to grosse: for their tender stomacks are not able to digest such crude and harsh meats: For if

Nice, tender stomacks.

they shold (their stomacks being so quease as they be, and not able to concoct it) they should but euacuat the same againe, as other filthie excrements, their bodies receiuing no norishment

ment therby, or els they ſhould lye ſtincking
in their ſtomacks, as dirte in a filthie ſinck or
pryuie.　If this be ſo, I marueile how oure
fore-Fathers lyued, who eat litle els, but cold
meats, groſſe and hard of diſgeſture? Yea, the
moſt of them fead vppon graine, corne, roots,
pulſe, herbes, wads, and ſuch other baggage,
and yet liued longer then wée, helthfuller then
we, were of better complection then we, and
much ſtronger then we in euerie reſpect: wherfore I cannot perſwade my ſelf otherwiſe,
but that our nicenes and curiouſnes in dyet,
hath altered our nature, diſtempered our bodies, and made vs more ſubiect to millions of
diſcraſies and diſeaſes, then euer weare our
Forefathers ſubiect vnto, and conſequently
of ſhorter life then they.

The ſaraginie or rough fare of our Fore-fathers.

Our nice fare hath altered our bodies and chaunged our nature.

　Spud. They wil aſke you again, wherfore
god made ſuch varietie of meats, but to be eaten of men, what anſwere giue you to that?

　Philo. The Lord our God ordained indéede,
the vſe of meat and drinks for man to ſuſtain
the fraile, caduke and brittle eſtate of his mor-
tall body withall for a time. But he gaue it
him not to delight and wallow therin continu-
ally, for as the olde Adage ſaith, Non viuen-
dum vt edamus, ſed edendum vt viuamus.
Wée muſt not liue to eat, but wée muſt eat ſo
liue, wée muſt not ſwill and ſingurgitate our
ſtomacks ſo ful, as no more can be crammed

Medietie to be obſerued in meat.

I.　　　in

in. The Lord willed that they should be ordinarie meanes to preserue the state of our bodyes a time whilste we liue, and soiourne in this vaste wildernes of the worlde, but not that they should be instruments of destruction to vs bothe of body and soule. And truely they

When meats
and drinks
are Instruments of destruction vnto vs.

Ge. 34.

are no lesse, when they are take inmoderatly without the feare of God. And doth not the simpletion and satietie of meates and drinks prouolke lust, as, Hiero saith, Venter Mero estuans, spumat in libidinem, the belly enflamed with wine, bursteth forth into lust. Doth not lust bring forth sinne, and sin bring forth death? The Children of Israel, giuing themselues to delicat fare & gluttony, fel to Idolatrie, sacrilegd & apostasie, worshipping stocks stones and deuils in-sted of the liuing God. The sonnes of Heli the Priest, giuing themselues to dainite fare & belly-chœre, fell into such lust as the Lord slew them all, & their father also, for that he chastisd them not for the same. The Children of blessed Iob in midst of all their banquetings & ryot, were slain by the Lord, the whole house falling vpon them, and destroying them most pitifully. Balshasar, king of the Chaldeans, in midst of all his god thœr, saw a hand, writing vpon the wall these words, mene techel upharsin, signifying y his kingdoe should be taken from him, and so it was, and he slain the same night by the

1. Reg. 2.

Daniel. 5.
Verse. 5.

hand

hand of ꝩ lozd. The rich glutton in the Goſ-
pel, foz his riotous feaſtings ꝑ pzopoſterous li
uing was cōdemned to ꝩ fire of hel. Our Fa-   Luc. 16.
ther Adam with all his of-ſpzing (to the end
of ꝩ wozld) was cōdemned to hel-fire, foz taking one apple to ſatiſfie his glotonus deſire
withall. Gluttony was one of the chicfeſt ca-   Mat. 4
nons , wherwith the deuil aſſailed Chziſte ,
thinking therby to batter his kingdome ꝑ to
win the fæld foz euer , yet not withſtanding,
ꝩ græuouſnes hærof, the ſame is thought to be
a coutenāce, ꝑ a great credit to a mā in Ailg.
But true hoſpitality conſiſteth not in many
diſhes noz in ſundzy ſozts of meats (the ſubſtance wherof is chaunged almoſte into acci-
dents thozow their curious cœkries, ꝑ which
dœ help to rot ꝩ bodies ꝑ ſhozten their daies,   Wherin hoſ-
but rather in giuing liberally to the poz, and   pitalitie con-
indigent members of Jeſus Chziſte , helping   ſiſteth.
them to meat, dzink, lodging, clothing ꝑ ſuch
other neceſſaries wherof they ſtand in næd.
But ſuch is their hoſpitality ꝩ the poz haue ꝩ
leaſt part of it: you ſhal haue 20.40.6c,yea,a   The ſmall
C. li. ſpent in ſome one houſe in bāqueting ꝑ   leef of the
feſting, yet ꝩ poz ſhall haue litle oz nothing,if   poore.
they haue any thing, it is but ꝩ refuge meat,
ſcraps ꝑ patrings, ſuch as a dog wculd ſcarſe
eat cōtimes, ꝑ wel if they can get ꝩ tœ: inſted
wherof, not a few haue whipping thærto ſed
thē withall, it is coūted but a ſuial matter foz

a man that can scarslie dispend fortie pound
by the yeer, to bestow against one time, ten or
twentie pound therof in spices. And truely so
long & so grieuously hath this excesse of gluttonie and daintie fare surffeted in Ailgna,
as I feare mee, it will spue out many of his
Maisters out of dores before it be long. But
as some be ouer largeous, so other some are

Locking vp
of Gates whē
meat is stir-
ring.

spare enough, for when any meat is stirring
then lock they vp their gates, that no man
may come in. An-other sorte haue so many
houses, that they visit them once in vij. yeer,
many Chimnies, but little smoke, faire houses, but small hospitalitie. And to be plaine,
there are three cankers which in processe of
time wil eat vp the whole common Welth,

Three deuou
ring Cankers

if speedy reformatiō be not had, namely, daintie Fare, gorgious Buildings, and sumptuous Apparel, which three Abuses, especially,
yet not without their cosin germanes do flo-
rish there. God remooue them thence for his
Christes sake.

Spud. I had thought that dainty fare & good
cheer had both noorished y body perfectly, and
also prolōged life, & dooth it not so think you?

Who more
subiect to in-
firmities then
they that fare
best?

    Philo. Experience, as my former intimati-
ons you may gather, teacheth cleane contrary:
for who is sicklier thē they, that fare deliciou-
sly euery day? who is corrupter? who beleeth
more? who looketh wurse? who is weaker,
                                                              and

and fæbler then they? who hath moze filthie
colour, flegme and putrifaction(repleat with
groſſe humozs) then they? and to be bzéef,
who dyeth ſoner then they? Do wæ not ſée
the poz man that eatcth bzown bzead, wherof ſome is made of Rye, barlie, peaſon, beans
oates and ſuch other groſſe grains) ẓ dzink-
eth ſmall dzink, yea ſometimes water, fædeth
vpon milk, butter and cheeſe, (J ſay) do wæ
not ſée ſuch a one, helthfuller, ſtronger and
longer liuing then the other, that fare dain-
tily euery day? And how ſhould it be otherwiſe? foz wil not the eating of diuers and ſun
dzy kindes of meats of diuers operations and
qualities (at cne meale) engender diſtempe-
rance in the body? And the body diſtempered,
wil it not fall into ſundzy deſeaſes? one meat
is of hard diſgeſture, another of light, ẓ whilſt
the meate of hard diſgeſture is in concoctiug
the other meat of light diſgeſture dœth putri-
fie and ſtink, ẓ this is the very mother of all
diſeaſes: one is of this qualitie, another of ẏ,
one of this operatiõ, another of that, one kind
of meat is gœd foz this thing, another is naught foz that. Then how can all theſe contra-
rieties ẓ diſcripancies agræ togither in one
body at one ẓ the ſame time? wil not one cen
trary impugne his contrary? one enemy reſiſt
an other? Then what wiſeman is he that wil
reeeiue allthese enemies into the caſtle of t is

eating of di-
uers meats
at one time
hurtful.

J. 3.   body

The spedy
ecay of those
hat geue thē
elues to
aintie fare.

body at one time ? Doo we not se by experiēcs
that they ꝥ giue thēselues to dainty fare, and
sweet meats, are neuer in helth?dooth not their
sight war dim, their eares hard of hering, their
teeth rot & fall out?dooth not their breth stink ,
their stomack belch foorth filthy humoꝛs, and
the ir memoꝛy decay? do not their spirits and
sences becōe heuie & dul by reason of exhalati
ons & impure vapoꝛs which rise vp in their
gingered bꝛests & spiced stomacks: & sumyng
vp to ꝥ hed, they moꝛtifie ꝥ vitall spirits & in
tellectiue powers? dooth not ꝥ whole body be
come pursie & coꝛpulent, yea somtimes decre
pit therwith & ful of all filthy coꝛruptiō. The
Lord keep his chosen from the tastingtherof.
Sp. You spake of dꝛūkēnes, what say you of ꝥ
Phi. I say, ꝥ it is a hoꝛrible vice & too too much
vsed in Ail. Euery cūtrey, citie, towne , vil
lage oꝛ other, hath abundāce of alehouses, ta
uerns & Innes, which are so fraughted with
mault-woꝛmes night & day, that you would
wunder to se them. You shal haue them there
sitting at ꝥ wine, and good ale all the day long,
yea all the night too, peraduenture a whole

The beastly
vice of drunk
nnes requen-
ced in Ailg

weēk togither , so long as any money is left,
swilling, gulling & carowsing from one to an
other, til neuer a one can speak a redy woꝛd.
Then when loo the spirit of the buttery they
are thus possesse'd , a woꝛld it is to consider
their gestures & demenoꝛs, how they shut and
stāmer, stagger & rele too & fro, like madmen,

ſome bomiting ſpewing ⁊ diſgorging their fil
thie ſtomacks, other ſome (Honor ſit auribus)
piſſing vnder the bord as they ſit, ⁊ which is
moſt horrible, ſome fall to ſwering, curſing ⁊
ſtaning, interlacing their ſpœches wᵗ curious
tearms of blaſphemie to ẙ great diſhonour of
God and offence of the godly eares preſent.
Sp. But they wil ſay ẙ god ordained wines ⁊
ſtrong drinks to chœr ẙ hart, ⁊ to ſuſtain the
body therfore it is lawful to vſe thẽ to ẙ end.
Phi. Meats (moderatly taken) corroborate ẙ
body, refreſh ẙ arteries, ⁊ reuiue the ſpirits,
making them apter euery niember to do his
office as god hath appointed: but being immo
deratly takẽ (as cõmonly they be) they are in-
ſtrumẽts of damnatiõ to ẙ abuſers of ẙ ſame,
⁊ noriſh not ẙ body but corrupt it rather, ⁊ ca
ſeth it into a world of deſeaſes : And a man
once drunk with wine or ſtrong drink, rather reſembleth a brute beaſte, then a chriſtian man: for, do not his eies begin to ſtare ⁊ to
be red, fiery ⁊ blered, blubbering forth ſeas of
teares? doth he not frothe ⁊ ſome at the mouth
like a bore? doth not his tung faulter ⁊ ſtãmer
in his mouth? doth not his hed ſœme as heule
as a millſtone, he not being able to bear it vp?
Are not his wits ⁊ ſpirits as it were drowned? Is not his vnderſtanding altogher de-
cayed? do not his hands ⁊ all his body quiuer
⁊ ſhake as it were with a quotidiã feuer? Beſides theſe, it caſtth him into a dropſie or plu-

The ſpirite
of the butte
ry, is drunk-
nes, and ex-
ceſſe.

The lothſo-
me qualities
of thoſe that
be drunke.

The transfi-
guration of
thoſe that b
drunke,

reſſe nothing ſo ſoon, it infæbleth the ſinewes,
it weakneth ẙ natural ſtrength, it coꝛrupteth

*The diſcom-
modities of
drunkennes.*

the blœd, it diſſolueth ẙ whole man atẙ legth,
and finally maketh him foꝛgetful of him ſelf
altogither, ſo that what he dœth being dꝛunk
he remembꝛeth not being ſober. The Dꝛun-
kard in his dꝛunkennes killeth his frænd, re
uileth his louer, diſcloſeth ſecrets and regar-
deth no man: he either expclleth all feare of
god out of his minde, all lœue of his frænds &
kinſſolkes, all remembꝛance of honeſtie, ciui-
litie & humanitie: ſo that I will not feare to
call dꝛunkerds beaſts, and no men, and much

*Drunkerds
wurſſe then
Beaſts.*

wurſſe then beaſts, foꝛ beaſts neuer excæd in
ſuch kind of exceſſe, oꝛ ſuperfluitie, but alway
modum adhibent appetitum, they meaſure
their appetites by the rule of neceſſitie, which
would God wee would doo.

Spud. Sæing it is ſo great an offence befoꝛe
God, I pꝛay you ſhow me ſome teſtimonies
of the holy Scripture againſt it, foꝛ whatſoeuer is euil, ẙ woꝛd of God I doubt not repꝛo-
ueth the ſame.

Philo. It ſæmeth you haue not read ẙ holy
ſcripture very much, foꝛ if you had, you ſhould
haue found it not only ſpoke againſt, but alſo
thꝛowẽ down euen to hel, foꝛ pꝛof whereof of
infinit places, I wil recite a few. The Pꝛo-
phet Eſaias thundereth out againſt it, ſaying,

Eſaie. f.

ve qui conſurgitis mane ad ebrietatẽ ſectandã
Wo

Wo be to them that ryſe earlie to follow
drunkenneſſe, wallowing therein, from morning to night , vntill they be ſet on fire with
wyne & ſtrong drinke. Therfore gapeth hell, &
openeth her mouth wyde, that the glory, multitude, and welth of them that delight therin,
may go downe into it, ſaith the Prophet.

The Prophet Hoſeas ſaith, fornicatio, vinũ,
& muſtum auferunt animum. Whordome,
wyne & ſtrong drinke infatuat ẙ heart of mã.

The Prophet Ioel, biddeth all Drunkards
awake, ſaying, wæpe and howle you winebib-
bers , for the wickedneſſe of deſtruction that
ſhall fall vppon you.

The Prophet Habacuck , ſoundeth a moſt
dreadfull alarme, not only to all Drunkards,
but alſo to all that make them drunken ſaying : wo be to him that geueth his Neighbour
drinke , till he be drunke, that thou mayſt ſæ
his priuities.   Salomon ſaith, wyne maketh
a Man to be ſcornfull, and ſtrong drinke maketh a Man vnquiet , who ſo taketh pleaſure
in it, ſhall not be wiſe. In an other place, kæp
not companie with wynebibbers, and riotous
Perſons, for ſuch as be Drunkards ſhal come
to beggerie. In the xxiij. of his Prouerbes he
ſaith. To whome is woo ? To whome is ſorow ? to whome is ſtrife ? to whome is mur-
muring? to whome are woũds without cauſe?
and to whome are red eyes ? Euen to thẽ that
                    I. b.   taris

Teſtimonies
againſt drun-
kenneſſe, out
of the word
of God.

Hoſeas. c. 4.

Ioel. 1.

Habacuck. 2.

Prouerb. 20.

Prouerb. 23.

tarie longe at the wyne, to them that go, and
seek mixt wyne. And againe : Looke not thou
vppon the wyne when it is red, and when it
sheweth his colour in the cup oz goeth downe
pleasantlie, foz in the end, it will bite like a
serpent, and hurt like a Cockatrise, oz Basili-

Prouerb. 31. cock, which stay oz kill men with the poison of
their sighte. Again, it is not foz kings to dzin-
ke wyne, noz foz Pzinces to dzinke strong

Luc. 21. dzinke. Our Sauiour Chzist in the gospell of
of S. Luke biddeth vs take heed that we be not
ouercome with surffeting and dzunknes and
cares of this lyfe, least the day of the Lozde
come vppon vs vnawares.

Ephe.5.   Paule to the Ephesians biddeth beware that
we be not dzuk with wine, wherin is excesse,
but to be filled with ÿ spirit. The same apostle
in an other place, saith, ÿ neither whozemöger
adulterer, Dzunkard, glutton, ryotous person,
noz such like, shal euer enter into ÿ kingdome
of Heauen. By these few places out of many,
you may see the inozmitie of this vice, which
is so much euery where frequented.

     Spud. Let me intreate you to shew me some
examples withall, wherby I may see, what
euill it hath done in all ages?

Gene.19.   Philo. Dzunknes caused Lot to commit
most shamefull incest with his owne two
Daughters, who got them both with Child,
be

be not perceiuing it, neither when they lay downe, nor when they roſe vp.   See how drunkenneſſe aſſotteth a man, depriuing him of all ſence, reaſon and vnderſtanding.

Drunkenneſſe cauſed Noah to lye with his prtuities bare in his Tabernacle, in ſuche beaſtlie ſorte, as his wicked Sonne Cham teſted and ſcoffed at the ſame.

Thorow drunkenneſſe, Holophernes, that great and inuincible Monarche of the Aſſyrians, was ouercome by a Woman, hauing his head cut from his ſhoulders with a fauchone. Thorow drunkenneſſe, King Herode was brought to ſuche ydiocie, and ſooliſhe dotage, that he cauſed the head of good Ihon Baptiſt, to be cut of, to ſatiſfie the requeſt of a dauncing ſtrumpet.   That riche Epulo of whom Luke maketh mention, was for his drunkenneſſe, and ryotous exceſſe condemned to the fire of Hel for euer, with many moe examples, which for ſhortnes I omit. Now ſeeing than that drunkenneſſe is both offenſiue to G D D, and bringeth ſuch euil's in this lyfe preſent, let vs in the name of G D D auoyde it, as a moſt wicked thing, and prenicious euill.   For euery Drunkard is ſo farre eſtranged from himſelfe, that as one in an extaſie of mind, or rather in a playne Phrenſie, he maye not be ſaid to be, ſui animi compos, or a man of ſounde wit, but rather a

very

very Bedlem, or muche worse, no Christian,
but an Antichristian, no member of Christ Iesus, but an impe of Satha, and a lymme of the
Deuill.　　Wherfore, in the name of God, let
vs auoyd al excesse, imbrace temperancie, and
sobrietie, & receiue so much meats and drinks
as may satisfie nature, not the insaciat appetits of our fleshly desires. Knowing thatexcept
the Lord blesse our meats and drinks within
our bodyes, and giue them power & strength
Whir if God to nourish and fœde the same, and our bodyes
blesse not our their naturall powers, euery member to do his
meats. office, and dutie, our meates shall lye in our
stomacks stincking, smelling, and rotting like
filthie carion in a lothsom sinck. So farre of
ought we to be from abusing the good creaturs
of God, by ryot, drunknesse, or excesse, that we
ought neuer to take morsell of bread, nor sope
of drinke, without humble thankes to ŷ Lord
for the same. For we neuer read, that our Sauiour Christ euer eat, or dranke, but he gaue
Geuing of thankes (or as we call it, said grace) both be-
thanks befor fore the receipt therof, and after. This nœded
meat, & after. be not to haue done in respect of himselfe, but
for our erudition & learning, accordding to this
saying, omnis Christi actio, nostra est instructio. Euery action of our Sauiour Christe is
our example and instructio, to follow as nœre
as we are able. And thus much of drukenesse,
which god graut may euery wher be auoided.
Spud,

Spud. Shew mœ I pray you ẙ ſtate of that
Cuntrey a litle further: is it a welthie Countrey with in it ſelfe, or otherwyſe poore and
bare?

Philo. It is a moſt famous Yland, a fertile
Cuntrey, & abounding with all maner of ſtore
both of riches, treaſure, & all things els whatſoeuer, but as it is a welthie and riche Countrey, ſo are the inhabitaunts from the higheſt,
to the loweſt, from the prieſt, to the populare
ſorte, euen all in generall, wonderfully inclyned to couetouſnes, and ambitiõ, which thing,
whileſt they follow, they cã neuer be ſatiſfied:
for, creſcit amor nummi, quantũ ipſa pecunia
creſcit. The loue of mony, doth by ſo much the
more increaſe, by how much more ẙ monie it
ſelfe doth increaſe: and ẙ nature of a couetous
man is ſuch, that tam deeſt quod habet, quam
quod non habet: as well that thing which he
hath, as ẙ which he hath not, is wanting vnto
him. A couetouſe man may wel be compared
to Hell, which euer gapeth and yawneth for
more, and is neuer content with inough. For
right as Hell euer hunteth after more, ſo a couetous mã drowned in the quagmire, or plaſh
of auarice and ambition, hauing his ſummam
voluptatem repoſed in momentaine riches, is
neuer content with inough, but ſtill thirſteth
for more; much like to a mã ſicke of the ague,
who the more he drinketh, the more he thyr-
ſteth,

Ailgna a fa-
mous Yland.

The nature
of a couetous
man.

The inſacia-
ble deſire of
a couetouſe
man.

keth: the moze he thursteth, the moze he drink
keth: the moze he drinketh, ỹ moze his diseas
increaseth: Wherfoze I hould it true, which is
wzit, bursa auari os est diaboli, the powch of
The purse of a riche Man. rich couetous Man, is the mouth of the deuill,
which euer is open to receiue, but alway shut
to giue.

Spud. But they will easily wipe away this
blot, namely in saying, are we not bound to pzo
uyde foz our selues, our wynes, our childzen
samelie? Doth not the Apostle hold him foz an
infidell and a deneger of the faith, who pzouy
deth not foz his Wyfe and Family? Is it not
good to lay vp somthing against a stozmie day?
wherfoze, they wil rather deeme thế selues good
husbands, than couetous oz ambitious persons.

How farre euery Man is bound to prouyde for his Familie. Philo. Euery Christen Mã is bound in cõ
science befoze God, to pzouide foz their hous
hould Family, but yet so as his immoderat
care surpasse not the bands, noz yet transcend
the limits of true Godlynes. His chiefest trust
care is to rest onely in the Lozd, who giueth
liberally to euery one ỹ asketh of him in veri
ty truth, repzocheth no mã, withall he is
to vse such ozdinarie meanes, as God hath ap
pointed, to ỹ perfozmaunce of ỹ same. But so
Immoderate care for riches reproued. farre frõ couetousnes frõ immoderate care
wold ỹ Lozd haue vs, ỹ we ought not this day
to care foz to mozow, foz (saith he) sufficient to
ỹ day, is the trauail of the same. After all these
things

ʒings(with a diſtruſtfull, ⁊ inoʒdinat care)do
ʒe heathen ſæk, who know not God, ſaith our
ſauiour chʒiſt, but be you not like to thē. And
ꝛet I ſay, as we are not to diſtruſt the pʒoui-
ence of God, oʒ deſpaire foʒ any thing, ſo are
de not to pʒeſume, noʒ yet to tempt the Loʒd
ur God, but to vſe ſuch ſecundary and inſtru-
nental meanes, as he hath commaunded and
ppointed to y end ⁊ purpoſe, to get our owne
ꝛuing ⁊ maintenance withall. But this peo-
ole leauing theſe Godly meanes, do all runne
ꝛeadlōg to couetouſnes ⁊ ambition, attēpting
ill waies, ⁊ aſſaying al meanes poſſible to ex-
aggerat ⁊ heap vp riches, y thick clay of damnatiō to thēſelues foʒ euer. So (likwiſe) Lād-

Land-Lordes racke their tenantes.

loʒds make marchandiſe of their poʒe tenāts,
racking their rents, raiſing their fines ⁊ inco-
mes, ⁊ ſetting thē ſo ſtraitely vppō y tēter ho-
kes, as no man cā lyue on them. Beſides y, as
though this pillage ⁊ pollage, were not rapa-
cious enough, they take in, and incloſe com-

Incloſing of commons from the Poore.

mons, moʒes, heaths, and other common pa-
ſtures, wher out the poʒe commonaltie were
wont to haue all their foʒage and fæding foʒ
their cattell, ⁊ (which is moʒe) coʒne foʒ them
ſelues to lyue vppon: all which are now in
moſt places taken from them, by theſe gree-
dye Puttockes, to the great impoueriſhing
and vtter beggering of whole townes and
pariſhes, whoſe tragicall cries and inceſſant
                              clamoʒs

clamo₂s haue long since, pearced the Skyes,
and presented them selues befo₂e the Maiestie
of God, saying: how long Lo₂d, how long wilt
thou deferre, to reuenge this villanie of thy
po₂e Saincts, and vnwo₂thie members vppon the earth? Take hæd therfo₂e you riche
men, that poll and pill the po₂e, fo₂ the bloud
of as manye as miscarie any maner of way,
tho₂ow your iniurious exactions, sinister op-
p₂essions, and indirect dealings shall be powred vppon your heads at the great daye of the
Lo₂d, Cursed is he (saith our Sauiour Christ)
that offendeth one of these litle ones, it were
better that a millstone were hãged about his
neck, ⁊ he cast into ẙ middest of the sea. Christ
so entierely loueth his po₂e members vppon
earth, that he imputeth the contumely which
is done to anie one of them, to be done to himselfe, and will reuenge it, as done to himselfe:
wherfo₂, G D D giue them grace to lay open
their inclosures againe, to let fall their rents,
fines, incomnes and other impositions, wherby G D D is offended, their po₂e B₂eth₂en
beggered, ⁊ I feare me, ẙ whole realme will
be b₂ought to vtter ruine ⁊ decay, if this mischiefe be not met withall, and incoûtred with
verie sho₂tlie. Fo₂ these inclosures be the causes, why rich men, eat vp po₂e men, as beasts
dô eat grasse.   These I say are the Caterpillers, and deuouring locustes that massacre the
po₂e

Iniurie to
Christ his
members, is
iniury to
Christ.

Inclosures.

poꝛe, & eat vp ẙ whole realme to ẙ deſtruction
of the ſame: The Lord remooue them.

Vpon the other ſide, the Lawyers they goe
ruſling in their ſilks, beluets and chaines of
Gold, they build goꝛgeous howſes, ſumptu-
ous edeſices, and ſtately turrets: they kæp a
poꝛt like mightie potētates, they haue bands,
and retinewes of men attendant vppon them
daylie, they purchaſe caſtels & towers, Lands
and Loꝛdſhips, and what not? And all vppon
the polling and pilling of the poꝛe commons.

They haue ſo good conſciences, that all iſ
ſiſh, that comes to the net, thei refuſe nothing
that is offred, and what they do foꝛ it in pꝛe-
ferring their Poꝛe clients cauſe, the Loꝛde
knoweth, and one day they ſhall ſinde it: If
you haue argent, oꝛ rather rubrum vnguen-
tum, I dare not ſay Gold, but red oyntment,
to greaſe them in the ſiſt withall, than your
ſute ſhall want no furtherance, but if this be
wanting, thā farewel clyent, he may go ſhoe
the gooſe foꝛ any good ſucceſſe he is lilie to
haue of his matter: without this, ſheriffes &
Officers wil returne wꝛits with a tarde ve-
nit, oꝛ with a non eſt inuentus, ſmally to the
poꝛe mãs pꝛoſit. So long as any of this oint-
mēt is dꝛopping, they wil beare him in hand,
his matter is good and iuſt, & all to kæp him
in vꝛe, till all be gon, and than will they tell
him his matter is naught: and if one aſke thē

Lawyers ru-
ſling io poore
Mens riches.

Oyntment to
greeſe lawiers
in the ſiſt
withall.

                    R.   why

The pretēsed excule of Lawers, when their cliants haue loost their plees.

why they could not their cliéts so in ẙ beginning:they will anſwere, J knew not ſo much ąt the firſt, ẙ fault is in himſelfe,he could me ẙ beſt, but not the woꝛſt:he ſhewed mée not this euidence ꝛ that euidence, this preſident, and ẙ preſidēt,turning al the fault vpō ẙ ſuggeſter whereas ẙ whole fault inꝺeeꝺ is in himſelfe, ąs his own conſcience rꝺ beare him witneſſe:

The slaightie practises of lawers.

Jn preſence of their clients, they will be ſo earneſt one with another, as one (that knew ñot their ſlaightes, wold thinke they would go together by the eares) this is to ꝺꝛaw on their cliéts withal(but immediatly after theïr clients being gōn, they laugh in their ſléeues, to ſée how pꝛetily they fetch in ſuch ſömmes of money,and ẙ vnder the pꝛetence of equitie, any Juſtice.But though thei cā foꝛ a time(preſtigiatorum inſtar)like cūning ꝺeceiuers,caſt ą miſt befoꝛe ẙ blinb woꝛlꝺ, yet the Loꝛꝺ who ſeeth (ſuboꝛned by none) ẙ ſecrets of all harts ſhall make them manifeſt to al the woꝛlꝺ,and reward them accoꝛding to their doings. The

The fraudulent dealing of marchant Men. Artificers.

marchāt mē by their marting, chaffering and changing,by their counterfait balances ꝛ vntrue waights, and by their ſurpꝛiſing of their wares,heap vp infinit treaſures. The Artificer ꝛ Occupyers,euen all in generall,will not ſell their wares foꝛ no reaſonable pꝛice, but will ſweare ꝛ teare pittifully, ẙ ſuch a thing coſt thē ſo much,ꝛ ſuch a thing ſo much, when

es

as they swear as false, as the lyuing Lord is true: But one day let them be sure ý the Lord (who saith, thou shalt not sweare at all, nor deceiue thy Brother in bargaining) will reuenge this villanie done to his Maiestie.

Into such a ruinous estat hath couetousnes now brought that Land, that in plentie of all things, there is great scarsitie and dearth of all thinges.   So, that, that which might haue bæn bought heretofor within this twentie, or fourtie Yéers, for twentie shillings, is now worth twentie nobles, or rr. pound. That which thā was worth twentie pound, is now worth a C. pound, and more :   Wherby the rich Men haue so balaunced their chests with Gold and siluer, as they cracke againe. And, to such excesse is this couetousnes growne, as euery one ý hath money will not stick to take his neighbors house, ouer his head, long before his yéers be expired : Wherthorow many á poore man, with his wyfe, childre, & whole fa= melie, are forced to begge their bread all their dayes after. Another sorte who flow in welth, if a poore mā haue eyther house or Land, they will neuer rest vntill they haue purchased it, giuing him not the thirde parte, of that it is worth.   Besides all this, so desperately gi= uen are many, that for the acquiring of siluer and Gold, they will not sticke to imbrew their hands, and both their armes in ý blood of their

Great dearth in plenty of all things.

Taking of howses ouer mens heads.

The desperat desire of Men to get money

owne Parents and friends most vnnatu-
rally.　Other some will not make any conscience, to sweare and forsweare themselues
for euer, to lye, dissemble and deceiue the dæ-
rest frends they haue in the world. Therfore
the heathen Poët Virgill said very well: O
sacra auri fames, quid non, mortalia pectora
cógis: Oh cursed desire of gold, what mischief
is it, but thou forcest Man to attempt it, for
ỹ loue of thæ? This immoderat thirst of Gold

Many brou-
ght to rufull
end thorow
meanes of
Gold and
siluer.

& monie, bringeth an infinit nüber to shame-
ful end: some, as homicides, for murthering &
killing: some as latrones, for robbing & stea-
ling: some for one thing, some for another: So
that surely I think, maior est numerus Ho-
sthnium, quos dira auaritiæ pestis absorpsit,
& quàm quos gladius vel ensis perforauit: the
number of those whom the pestilence of auarice hath swallowed vp, is greatter, than the
nüber of those whom the sword hath destroid:
the Lord asswage the heat hereof with ỹ oyle
of his grace, if it be his good pleasure and wil.

Spud. If I might be so bold, I wold request
you to shew me out of the word of god, where
this so detestable a vice is reproued ≠

Math. 6.
Testimonies
out of the
word of God
against coue-
tousnes.

Philo. Our Sauiour Christ Iesus, the Arch-
doctor of all truth in his Euangely, the sirt of
Mathew, saith: Be not carefull for to morow
day, for the morow shall care for it selfe.

Againe, be not carsull for Apparell, what
you

you shall put on, no2 fo2 meat what you shall
eat, but sœke you the Kingdome of Heauen, &
the righteousnes therof, and all these things
shal be giuen vnto you. He charged his Disciples to be so farre from couetousnes, as not to
cary two coates with them in their io2neys,
no2 yet any money in their purses. He toulo
his Disciples another time, strruing which of
them should be y greattest, that he who wold
be the greattest, must condescend to be seruãt
of all.　When the people wolo haue aduãsced
him to haue bœne King, he refused it, and hid
him self: He telleth vs, we cannot serue two
Maisters, God & Mammon : he biddeth vs not
to set our minds vppõ couetousnes, inferring
that wher our riches be, there will our harts
be also. He saith, it is harder fo2 a rich Man
(that is, fo2 a Man, whose trust is in riches) to
enter into the Kingdome of God, than fo2 a
Camell to go tho2ow the eye of a nœdle. The
Apostle biddeth vs if we haue meat & d2inke
and clothing, to be content, fo2 they that will
be rich (saith he) fall into diuerse temptations
and snares of the Deuill, which d2owne Men
in perditiõ. Dauid saith, Man disquieteth him
selfe in vaine, heaping vp riches, & cannot tell
who shall possesse them: Salom. cõpareth a couetous man, to him y murthereth & sheadeth
innocent bloud. Againe, Hell and destruction
are neuer ful, so the eyes of Men can neuer be

Luc. 6.
Math. x.]

1. Timo. vi.

Psalm. 39.

Prouerb.

Proue. xxvii.

B. iij.　Sa-

satiffied. The Apostle S. Paule, saith, neither Whoremongers, Adulterers, nor couetous persons, nor Extortioners shal euer enter into the Kingdom of Heauen. And saith further, ÿ the loue of monie is ÿ rot of al euil. Christ, biddeth vs be liberal, & lend to them that haue need, not loking for any restitutiõ again, & neuer to turn our face away frõ any pore mã, & thã ÿ face of the Lord shall not be turned away frõ vs. By these few places it is manifest how farre frõ al couetousnes ÿ lord wold haue al cristiãs to be.

Mat. 5.
Luc. 6.

Spud. Be their any examples in scriptures to shew forth the punishmentes of the same, inflicted vpon the Offenders therin?

Philo. The Scripture is full of such fearful examples, of the iust iudgements of God powred vpon thẽ that haue offended herein. Wherof I will recite three or four, for the satiffying of your Godly mind. Adam, was cast out of Paradice for coueting that fruit, which was inhibited him to eat. Giese, the Seruant of Elizeus ÿ Prophet, was smitten with an incurable leprosie, for ÿ he to satiffie his couetous desire, exacted gold, siluer, & riche garments of Naamã ÿ K. of Siria his seruant. Balaam was reproued of his asse, for his couetousnes in going to curse ÿ Children of Israel; at the request of K. Balac, who promised him aboundance of gold & siluer so to do. Achab ÿ K. for couetousnes to haue pore Naboth his vintard slew him and

The punishmen of couetousnes shewed by examples.

4. Reg. 5.

Num. 22.

and dyed after himſelfe, with all his progeny,
a ſhameful death. The Sōnes of Samuel were
for their inſaciable couetouſnes, deteined frō Sa. viii.
euer inioying their Fathers kingdome. Iudas
for couetouſnes of mony ſould the Sauiour of
the world, and betrayed him to the Iewes, but
afterward dyed a miſerable death, his bellye
burſting & his bowels guſhing out. Ananias &
Saphira his wiſe, for couetouſnes, in cōcealing Act. v.
part of ý price of ther lāds frō ý apoſtles, were
both ſlain, & dièd a fearful death. Achā was ſtoned to death by ý lord his cōmandemēt for his
couetouſnes in ſtealing gold, ſiluer, & Iewels,
at the ſacking of Iericho, & al his goods were
burned preſently. Thus you ſee how for couetouſnes of mony, in all ages, Men haue made
ſhipwrack of their conſciences, and in the end
by the iuſt iudgemēt of God haue dyed fearful
deaths whoſe iudgments I leaue to the Lord.

Spud. Sxring that couetouſnes, is ſo wicked
a ſin, & ſo offenſiue both to God & Man, & pernicious to the ſoule, I maruaile what moueth
Men to followe the ſame, as they do?

Ph. Two things moue mē to affect mony ſo What make.
ſo much as they do: ý one, for feare leaſt they men to affc̄-
ſhold fal into pouertie & beggery(oh ridiculous money.
inſidelitie) ý other, to be aduanced, & promoted
to high dignities & honors vpō earth. And thei
ſee, ý world is ſuch, ý he who hath moni enough
ſhalbe rabbied & maiſtered at euery word, and

         R. iij.   withal ſaluted with the

the vaine title of woꝛſhipfull, and right woꝛſhipfull, though notwithſtanding he be a dung-
ghill Gentleman, oꝛ a Gentleman of the firſt
head, as they vſe to terme them. And to ſuch

Euery Begger almoſt is called Maiſter at euery word.

outrage is it growne that now adayes euery
Butcher, Shoemaker, Tailer, Cobler, Huſ-
band-man, and other, yea euery Tinker, ped-
ler and ſwinherd, euery Artificer and other,
gregarii ordinis, of the vileſt ſoꝛte of Men that
be, muſt be called by ẏ vain name of Maiſters
at euery woꝛd. But it is certen, that no wyſe
Man, will intitle them, with any of theſe names, woꝛſhipfull and maiſter (foꝛ they are names and titles of dignitie, pꝛoper to ẏ Godly
wyſe, foꝛ ſome ſpeciall vertue inherent, either
els in reſpect of their birth, oꝛ calling one vnto thē,) but ſuch Ticiuillers, flattering Paraſits, and gloſing Gnatoes, as flatter them, ex-
pecting ſome pleaſure oꝛ benefit at their hāds,
which thing if they were not blowen vp with
the bellowes of pꝛide, and puffed vp with the
wind of vaingloꝛi they might eaſily perceiue.

Refuſing of vaine Titles.

Foꝛ certen it is, they do but mocke and flatter
them with theſe titles, knowing that they de-
ſerue nothing leſſe. Wherfoꝛe, like good Recu-
ſants of that thing which is euill, they ſhould
refuſe thoſe vaingloꝛious Names, remem-
bꝛing the woꝛds of our ſauiour Chꝛiſt, ſaying:
be not called Maiſter, in token there is but
one onely true Maiſter and Loꝛd in Heauen:
wħich

which only true Maister & Lord: God graunt
all other may followe bothe in life and name,
vntil they coe to perfect men in Iesus Christ.

Spud. The people beeing so set vpon coue∙
tousnes, as I gather by your speeches they be,
is it possible that they wil lend money with∙
out vsurie, or without some hostage, guage or
pawn ? for vsurie followeth couetousnes, as
the shadowe doth the bodie.

Great Vsurie

in Ailgna.

Philo.

I T is as impossible for any to borrowe
money there (for the most part) without
vsurie & loane, or with out some good hostage,
guage or pledge, as it is for a dead man to
speak with audible voice.

Spud.. I haue heard say, that the positiue,
and statute lawes there, doo permit them to
take vsurye, limitting them how much to
take for euery pound. **The positiue Lawes.**

Philo. Although the ciuile lawes (for the a∙
voiding of further inconueniences) doo permit
certain sommes of money, to be giuen ouer∙
plus beyond or aboue the principall, for the
loane of mony lent, yet are ỹ vsurers no more
						discharged

Vsury.

discharged from the gilt of vsurie before God
therby: then the adulterous Iewes were from
whordome, because Moyses gaue them a per-
missiue law for euery man to put away their
wiues, that would, for euery light trifle. And
yet the lawes there giue no libertie to commit vsurie, but seeing how much it rageth,
left it should exceed, rage further and, ouer
flowe the banks of all reason and godlynes.
As couetousnes is a raging sea and a botto-
lesse pit, and neuer satisfied nor cōtented, they
haue limitedthem within certain meeres, and
banks (to bridle the insatiable desires of couetous men) beyond the which, it is not law
ful for any to go:but this permissiō of y lawes
argueth not, that it is lawful to take vsury, no
more (I say) then y permission of Moyses ar-
gued that whordome & adulterie is lawfull &
good, because Moyses permitted them to put a
way their wiues, for y auoiding of greater e-
uil: for as christ said to y Iewes frō y begining
it was not so, so say I to these vsurers frō the
begining it was not so, nor yet ought so to be.

Spud. If no interest were permitted, then
no man would lend, & then how should y por
doe? wherfore the lawes y permit some small
ouer-plus therin do very wel.

Philo. Non faciendum est malum, vt inde ve
niat bonum, we must not do euil, that god
may come of it:yet the lawes in permitting
　　　　　　　　　　　　　　　　certain

The lawes of
Aligna per-
mit no vsurie.

certain reasonable gain to be receiued for the
loane of money lent, lest otherwise the poor
should quaile (for without some commoditie
the rich would not lend) haue not done much
amisse, but if they had quite cut it of, and not
yeelded at all to any such permission, they had
don better. But hærin the intent of the lawe
is to be perpended: which was to impale with
in the Forrest, or park of reasonable and con
scionable gain, men who cared not howmuch
they could extorte out of poore-mens hands,
for the loane of their money lent, and not to
authorise any man to comit vsurie, as though
it were lawful because it is permitted.

The lawes permit some ouerplus, but comaund it

Therfore, those that say that the lawes there
do allow of vsury, & licence men to commit it
fræly, do slaunder ye lawes, & are worthy of
reprehension: for though the lawes say, thou
shalt not take aboue ij.s. in ye pound, x. li. in
a hundred, and so so forth. Doth this proue
ye it is lawfulto take so much,or rather ye thou
shalt not take more then ye: if I say to a man,
thou shalt not giue him aboue one or two
blowes, doth this proue ye I licence him to
giue him one or two blowes,or rather that he
shal not giue him any at al,or if he do,he shal
not exceed or passe ye bãds of resonable mesure:
so this law doth but mitigate ye penalty s for
it saith ye the party ye taketh but x. li. for ye vse
of an C. li. loseth but ye x.li. not his principal.

Forbidding to outrage in mircheef, is not permissi on to comit mischeef.

                              Spud.

Spud. Then I perceiue, if Vsurie be not lawful by the lawes of the Realm, then is it not lawful by the lawes of God.

Philo. You may be sure of that. For our Sauiour Christe willeth vs to be so far from couetousnes and vsury, as he saith : giue to him that asketh thee, and from him that would borrow, turn not thy face away.

Again, Lend of thy goods to them who are not able to pay thee again, and thy reward shalbe great in heauen.   If wee must lend our goods then to them, who are not able to pay vs again, no not so much as the bare thing lent, where is the interest, the vsurie, the gaine and ouer-plus, which we fish for so much? Therfore our Sauiour Christe saith, beatius est dare, potius quam accipere. It is more blessed to giue, then to receiue. In y̅ 22. of Exodus, Deut. 24. 23. Leuit. 25. Nehe. 5. Eze. 22. 18. & many other places, we are forbidden to vse any kinde of vsury or interest, or to receiue again any ouer-plus, besides the principall, either in money, corne, wine, oyle beasts, cattel, meat, drink, cloth, or any thing els what soeuer. Dauid asketh a questi on of the Lord saying, Lord who shall dwell in thy Tabernacle, and who shall rest in thy holy hil? wherto he giueth the solution him self saying: euen he that leadeth an incorrupt life : & hath not giuen his mony vnto vsurie,

nor

Math. 5. 6.
Luc. 6.

The word of
God against
vsurie.

Exodus. 20.
Deut. 24. 23.
Leuit. 25.
Nehe. 5.
Ezech. 22. 18.

Psalm. 15.

nor taken reward againſt the innocent, who
ſo doth theſe things ſhall neuer fall. In the
15. of Deut. the Lord willeth vs not to craue
again the thing we haue lent to our neighbor,
for it is the Lords frée yéer. If it be not lawful
(then) to aſke again ỹ which is lent, (for it is
not the law of good conſcience for thée to exact
it, if thou be abler to beare it, then the other
to pay it) much leſſe is it lawful to demaund
any vſury or ouer-plus. And for this cauſe
the Lord ſaith, let there be no begger amõgſt
you, nor poore perſon amongſt the Tribes of
Iſrael. Thus you ſée the word of God abandõ-
neth vſurie euen to hel, and all writers bothe
diuine and prophane, yea the very heathen
people, moued onely by the inſtinct of nature
and rules of reaſon, haue alwaies abhord it.
Therfore Cato, béeing demaunded what vſurie was, aſked againe, what it was to kill a
man? making vſurie equiualent with murther: And good reaſon, for he that killeth a
a man, riddeth him out of his paines at once,
but he that taketh vſury is long in butchering
his pacient, ſuffering him by little e little to
languiſh, and ſucking out his hart blood; neuer leaueth him ſo long as he féeleth any vitall blood, (that is hure and gaine) comming
forth of him. The Vſurer killeth not one,
but many, bothe Huſband, Wife, Children,
ſeruants, famelis and all, not ſparing any,
And

When it is
not lawfull
to aſke again
our goods
lent.

Hethen men
againſt vſury
and intereſt.

vſury equall
with murther.

And if the poore man haue not wherewith to pay aswel the interest, as the principall, when soeuer this greedy cormorant doth demaund it; then sute shalbe commenced against him, out go butter-flies and writs, as thick as haile, so the poore man is apprehended, and brought coram nobis, and being once conuented, iudgement condemnatorie and diffinitiue sentence proceedeth against him, compelling him to pay, aswel the vsury and ý loane of the money, as the money lent. But if he haue not to satisfie aswel the one as th'other, then to Bocardo goeth he as round as a ball, where he shalbe sure to lye vntil he rotte one poote from an'other, without satisfaction bee made. Oh cursed Caitiue, no man but a deuil, no Christian but a cruel Tartarian, and mercilesse Turck: darest thou look vp toward heauen, or canst thou hope to be saued by the death of Christe, that sufferest thine owne flesh and blood, thine owne bretheren & sisters in the Law, and which is more, the flesh and blood of Christ Jesus, vessels of saluation, coheirs with him of his superiall kingdom, adoptiue sonnes of his grace, & finally, saints in heauen, to lye and rot in prison for want of payment of a little crosse, which at the day of doome, shall beare witnesse against thee, gnaw thy flesh like a canker, and condemn thee for euer? The very stones of the prison walles

Marginal notes:

Sute commenced against him that is not able to pay aswel the Vsury as the Principall.

To prison with him that cannot pay the vsury.

No mercy in imprisoning of poore men for vsury, &c.

M.2

walles shall rise vp against thée, and condemne thée for thy crueltie, Is this loue? Is this charitie? is this to doo to others as thou wouldest with others to doe to thée? or rather as thou wouldest with the Lord to doe vnto thée? Art thou a good member of the bodie, which not onely cuttest of thy selfe from the vine, as a rotten braunch and void lop, but also hewest off other members from the same true vine, Christe Iesus? No, no, thou art a member of the Deuil, a limme of Sathan, and a Childe of perdition.

No crueltie to be shewed, but mercy and compassion ought to be extended.

Wée ought not to handle our bretheren in such sorte, for any worldly matter whatsoeuer. Wée ought to shew mercie and not crueltie to our bretheren, to remit trespasses and offences, rather then to exact punishment, referring all reuenge to him, who saith: Mihi vindictam, et ego retribuam. Uengeance is mine, and I wil rewarde (saith the LORD.)

Beléeue mée, it gréeueth mée to heare (walking in the streats) the pitiful cryes, and miserable complaints of poore prisoners in durance for debt, and like so to continue all their life, destitute of libertie, meat, drink, (though of the meanest sorte) and clothing to their backs, lying in filthie strawe, and lothsome dong, wursse then anie Dogge, voide of all charitable consolation, and brotherly comfort

The pitiefull crying of Prisoners in prison for debt.

iij

in this World, wishing and thyrsting after death, to set them at libertie, and lose them from their shackles, giues and pron bands: Notwithstanding, some mercilesse tygers are

A tygerlicke tyrannicall saying.

growen to such barbarous crueltie, that they blush not to say, tush, he shall neuer pay me the whole, or els lye there till his heels rot fro his buttocks, and before I will release him, I woll make dice of his bones. But take heed thou Deuill (for I dare not call thee a Man) lest the Lord say to thee, as he said to that wicked Seruant (who hauing great sommes for-

Math. xviii.
Marc.xi.

giuen him, wold not forgiue his Brother his small debts, but catching him by the throte, said: pay that thou owest) bind him hands and feet, and cast him into vtter Darknes, where shalt be weeping, and gnashing of teeth.

An Vsurer worse than a Thief.

An Vsurer is worse thã a Thief, for the one stealeth, but for need, the other for couetous-nes and crueltie: the one stealeth, but in the night commonly, the other daylie and hourly, night and daye at all times indifferently.

An Vsurer worser than a Iew.

An Vsurer is worse than a Iew, for they to this daye, will not take anye vsurie of their Brethren, according to the lawe of G O D.

An Vsurer worser than Iudas.

They are worse than Iudas, for he betraied Christ, but once, made restitution, and repented for it (though his repentance sprang not of faith, but of despaire) but these Vsurers be-tray Christ in his members daylie and hourly without

without any remorſe oȝ reſtitution at all.
They are wurſſe then hel it ſelf, foȝ it puniſheth but only the wicked and repȝobate, but
the Vſurer maketh no difference of any, but
puniſheth all alike. They are crueller then
death, foȝ it deſtroyeth but the body, and goeth no further, but the vſurer deſtroyeth both
body and ſoule foȝ euer. And to be bȝæf, the
Vſurer is wurſſe then the Deuil himſelf, foȝ
the Deuill plagueth but onely thoſe that are
in his hands, oȝ els thoſe whome God per-
mitteth him, the Vſurer plagueth not onely
thoſe that are within his iuriſdiction alredy,
but euen all other without permiſſion of any.
Therfoȝe ſaith Ambroſe, if any man commit vſurie, it is extoȝtion, rauin & pillage,
and he ought to dye. Alphonſus called vſury
nothing els then a life of death. Lycurgus baniſhed all kind of vſury out of his lands. Cato
did the ſame. Ageſſilaus, Generall of the Lacedemonians, burned the Vſurers bokes in
the open market places.   Claudius Vaſpa-
tiannus, and after him Alexander Seuerus,
made ſharpe lawes againſt vſury, and vtterly extirped the ſame. Ariſtotle, Plato, Pythagoras, and generally, all wȝiters bothe holy and pȝophane, haue ſharply inueighed a-
gainſt this deuouring canker of vſury, & yet
cannot we, that fain would be called chȝiſti-
ans auoid it. And if it be true, that I heare

L.   ſay,

vſurers wurſſe then Hel.

An Vſurer wurſſe then Death.

An vſurer wurſe then the Deuil.

The ſayings of Godly Fa-thers and Writers a-gainſt vſury.

Vſurers puni-ſhed with ſun-dry tortures.

say, there be no men ſo great doers in this noble facultie and famous ſcience, as the Scriueners be: For it is ſayd (and I feare mee too true) that there are ſome, to whome is committed a hundzed oz two of poundes, of ſome moze, of ſome leſſe, they puttinge in good ſureties to the owners foz the repayment of the ſame againe, with certaine allowance foz the loane thereof, then come there pooze men to them, deſiring them to lende them ſuche a ſom of money, and they wil recompence them at their owne deſires, who making refuſall at the firſte, as though they had it not (to acuate the minds of the pooze petitioners withall) at laſt they lend them how much they deſire, receiuing of the pooze men what intereſt & aſſurãce they luſt themſelues, and binding them, their lands, Goodes, and all, with fozfaiture thereof, if they fayle of payment: where note by the way, the Scriuener is the Inſtrument wherby the Diuell wozketh the frame of this wicked woozke of Uſurie, hee beeing rewarded with a good fleece foz his labour: Foz, firſte

he hath a certaine allowance of the Archdiuel who owes the money, foz helping him to ſuch vent foz his coyne: Secondly, he hath a greate deale moze vſurie to himſelfe, of him who bozoweth the money, than he alloweth ẙ owner of the mony: And thirdly, he hath not the leaſt part foz making the wzitings betwene them,

And

And thus the poore man is ſo implicate and wrapped in on euerie ſide, as it is impoſſible for him euer to get out of the briers, without loſſe of all that euer hee hath to the very ſkin. Thus the riche are inriched, the poore beggered, and Chriſt Ieſus diſhonored euerie way, God be mercifull vnto vs.　　De his hactenus.

Spud. Hauing (by the grace of Chriſte) by therto ſpoken of ſundrie Abuſes of that countrie, let vs proceed a little further, howe do they ſanctiſie and keepe the Sabbaoth day? In godly Chriſtian exerciſes, or els in prophane paſtimes and pleaſures?

The Maner of ſan-

ctiſyng the Sabaoth in Ailgna.

Philo.

THE Sabaoth day, of ſome is well ſanctiſied, namely in hearing the Word of GOD read, preached and interpreted, in priuat and publique Prayers, in ſinging of Godly Pſalmes, in celebrating the ſacraments, & in collecting for the poore & indigent,

L.ij　　　　　　　　wh:ch

which are the true vses and ends wherto the
Sabaoth was ordained. But other some spend
the Sabaoth day (for the most part) in frequenting of baudie Stage-playes and enterludes,
in maintaining Lords of mis-rule (for so they
call a certaine kinde of play which they vse)
May-games, Church-ales, feasts and wakeesses: in pyping, dauncing, dicing, carding,
bowling, tennisse playing: in Beare-bayting, cock-fighting, hawking, hunting, and
such like. In kæping of Faires, and markets
on the sabaoth. In kæping Courts and Læts:
In fæt-ball playing, and such other deuilish
pastimes: reading of laciuious and wanton
bækes, and an infinit number of such like
practises and prophane exercises vsed vppon
that day, wherby the Lord God is dishonoured, his Sabaoth violated, his word neglected, his sacraments contemned and his People meruelously corrupted, and caryed away
from true vertue and godlynes.   Lord remooue these exercises from thy Sabaoth.

  Spud. You wil be dæmed tæ tæ Stoicall, if
you should restrain men from these exercises
vpon the Sabaoth, for they suppose, that, that
day was ordained and consecrate to that end
and purpose, only to vse what kinde of exerci
ses they think gæd thêselues, & was it not so?
Phi. After that the Lord our God had created
the world, and all things therin contained, in

(margin note) Prophane ex
ercises vpon
the Sabaoth
day.

                                                                    sir

ſir dayes, in the ſeuenth day he reſted from all his worꝛks, (that is from creating them, not from gouerning them) and therefoꝛe hée commaunded y̆ the ſeuenth day ſhould be kept holy in all ages to the end of the woꝛld: then after that in effect 2000. yéeres, he iterated this Commandement, when he gaue the law iu mount Horeb to Moyſes, & in him to all the Childꝛen of Iſrael, ſaying, remember (foꝛget it not) that thou kéep holy the ſeuenth day &c. If we muſt kéep it holy, then muſt we not ſpend it in ſuch bain exerciſes, as pleaſe our ſelues, but in ſuch godly exerciſes as he in his holy woꝛd hath commaunded. And (in my iudgement) the Loꝛd our God oꝛdained the ſeuenth day to be kept holy, foꝛ foure cauſes eſpecially.   Firſt to put vs in minde of his wunderful woꝛkmanſhip, & creation of the woꝛld and creatures beſides. Secondly, y̆ his woꝛd (the Church aſſēbling togither) might be pꝛeached, interpꝛeted & expounded, his ſacraments miniſtred ſincéerly accoꝛding to the pꝛeſcript of his woꝛd, & that ſuffrages & pꝛayers bothe pꝛiuat & publique might be offered to his excellent Maieſtie. Thirdly, foꝛ that euery chꝛiſtiã man might repoſe himſelf from coꝛpoꝛall labour, to the end they might y̆ better ſuſtain the trauailes of the wéek to enſue, and alſo to y̆ end, y̆ all beaſts & cattel, which the Loꝛd hath made foꝛ mans vſe, as helps &

When the Sabaoth was ordained.

Wherfore the Sabaoth was inſtituted.

L.3.   adiuments

adiuments vnto him in his daylie affaires &
businesse, might rest and refresh them selues,
the better to go thozow in their traueiles afterward. Foz, as the hethen Man knew very
wel, sine alterna requie,non est durabile quic-
quam. Without some rest oz repose, there is
not any thing durable, oz able to cōtinue lōg.
Fourthly,to th'end it might be a typical figure,oz signitoz to point (as it were) with the
finger, and to cypher foozth and shadowe vnto
vs that blessed rest & thzyse happie ioye which
the faithfull shall possesse after the day of iudgement in the kingdome of Heauen. Wherfoze,seeing the Sabaoth was instituted foz
these causes, it is manifest, that it was not
appointed foz the maintenance of wicked and
vngodly pastymes and vaine pleasures of the
flesh, which G O D abhozreth, and all good
men from their hartes do loth and detest.

Punishment foz violating the sabaoth.

The Man of whome we read in the law, foz
gathering of a few small sticks vpō the Sabaoth, was stoned to death, by the commaundement of God from the Theatoz of Heauen.

Violaters of the saboth.

Than if he were stoned foz gathering a few
sticks vppon the Sabaoth day, which in some
cases might be,foz necessities sake, and did it,
but once, what shall they be, who all the Sabaoth dayes of their lyfe giue them selues to
nothing els, but to wallow in all kind of wickednesse and sinne,to the great contempt both
of

of ȳ Lozd, and his Sabaoth? And though they haue played the lazic lurdens al the weke befoze, yet that day of ſet purpoſe, they wil toile and labour, in contempt of the Lozd and his Sabaoth. But let them be ſure, as he that gathered ſtickes vpon the Sabaoth, was ſtoned foz his contempt of the ſame, ſo ſhall they be ſtoned, yea grinded to pæces foz their contépt of the Lozd in his Sabaoth.

The Iewes, are verye ſtrict in kæping their Sabaoths, in ſo muche, as they will not dzeſſe ther meats and dzinks vppon the ſame day, but ſet it on the tables ȳ day befoz. They go not aboue ij. miles vpó ȳ ſabaoth day, they ſuffer not the body of any Malefactoz to hang vppon the gallowes vppon the Sabaoth day, with legions of ſuch like ſuperſticiós. Wherin, as I do acknowledge they are but too ſcrupelous, and ouerſhoot the marke, ſo we are therin plaine contempteous, and negligent, ſhooting ſhozt of the marke altogether. Yet I am not ſo ſtrait laced, that I would haue no kinde of wozke done vppon that daye, if pzeſent neceſſitie of the thing require it (foz Chziſte hath taught vs, the Sabaoth was made foz Man, not Man foz the Sabaoth) but not foz euery light trifle which may as well be done other dayes as vpon that day. And although ȳ day it ſelf in reſpect of ȳ very nature and oziginall therof be no better thā another

The Iewes very preciſe in keeping ſabaoth.

No work to be done vpon the ſabaoth, except neceſſite inforce it.

day

day, foʒ there is no difference of dayes except we become tempoʒizers, all bǽing alike gꝏd: yet becauſe the Loʒd our God hath commaun ded it to be ſanctified ⁊ kept holy to him ſelf, let vs (like obedient ⁊ obſequious Childʒen) ſubmit our ſelues to ſo louing a Father, foʒ els we ſpit againſt heauen, we ſtriue againſt the ſtream, and we contemn him in his oʒdi nances. But (perchance) you wil aſke me, whither the true vſe of the Sabaoth conſiſt in outward abſtaining from bodilye labour and trauaile? J anſwere no: the true vſe of the Sabaoth (foʒ Chʒiſtians are not bound onely to the Ceremonie of the day) conſiſteth as J haue ſaid, in hearing the woʒd of God truely pʒeached, therby to learn and to dꝏ his wil, in receiuing the ſacraments (as ſeales of his grace towards vs) rightly adminiſtred, in vſing publique and priuate prayer, in thankſgiuing to God foʒ all his benefits, in ſinging of gꝏdly Pſalmes and other ſpiritu all exerciſes and meditations, in collecting foʒ the pꝏʒe, in doing of gꝏd woʒkes: and bʒǽfly in the true obedience of the inward man. And yet notwithſtanding, wǽ muſt abſtain from the one, to attend vpon the other: that is, wǽ muſt refrain all bodily la bours, to the end that wǽ may the better bé reſtant at theſe ſpirituall exerciſes vppon the Sabaoth day.

Wherin the true vſe of the Sabaoth con- ſiſteth,

This

This is the true vse and end of the Lord his Saboth, who graūt that we may rest in him for euer.

Spud.   Hauing shewed the true vse of the Saboth, let vs go forward to speke of those Abuses particularlye, wherby the Saboth of the Lord is prophaned.   And first to begin with stage playes and enterluds : What is your opinion of them? Are they not good examples to youth to fray them from sinne?

Of Stage-playes and

Enterluds, with their wickednes.

Philo.

ALL Stage-playes, Enterluds and Commedies, are either of diuyne, or prophane matter: If they be of diuine matter, than are they most intollerable, or rather Sacrilegious, for that the blessed word of GOD, is to be handled, reuerently, grauely, and sagely, with veneration to the glorious Maiestie of God, which shineth therin, and not scoffingly, flowtingly, & iybingly, as it is vpon stages in Playes & Enterluds, without any reuerence, worship, or veneration to ý same: the word of our Saluation, the price of Christ his bloud, & the merits of his passion, were not giuen, to

L.b.   be

The deriding of the word of God in stage playes.

be derided, and iested at as they be in these filthie playes and enterluds on stages & scaffolds, or to be mixt and interlaced with bawdry, wanton shewes & vncomely gestures, as is vsed (euery Man knoweth) in these playes and enterludes. In the first of Ihon we are taught, that the word is GOD, and God is the word. Wherfore, who so euer abuseth this word of our God on stages in playes and enterluds, abuseth the Maiesty of GOD in the same, maketh a mocking stock of him, & purchaseth to himselfe, eternal damnation. And no marueil, for the sacred word of GOD, and

Reuerence to the maiestie of God due.

God himselfe, is neuer to be thought of, or once named, but with great feare, reuerence and obedience to the same. All the holy companie of Heauen, Angels, Archangels, Cherubins, Seraphins, and all other powers whatsoeuer, yea the Deuills themselues (as Iames saith) doo tremble & quake, at the naming of God, and at the presence of his wrath. and doo these Mockers and Flowters of his Maiesty, these dissembling Hipocrites, and flattering Gnatoes, think to escape vnpunished? beware therfore you masking Players, you painted

A warning to Players.

sepulchres, you doble dealing ambodexters, be warned betymes, and lik good computistes cast your accompts before what wil be the reward therof in the end, least God destroy you in his wrath: abuse God no more, corrupt his

people

people no longer with your dregges, and intermingle not his blessed word with such prophane vanities. For, at no hand, it is not lawfull, to mixt scurrilitie with diuinitie, nor diuinitie with scurrilitie.

Not lawfull to intermixt diuynitie, with scurrilitie

Theopompus, mingled Moyses law with his writinges, and therfore the LORD stroke him madd. Theodictes began the same practise, but the Lorde stroke him blind for it. With many others who attempting the like deuyses, were al ouerthrowne, and died miserably: besids, what is their iudgemét in the other World the Lord onely knoweth. Upon the other side, if their playes be of prophane matters, thã tend they to ý dishonor of God and norishing ofvice, both which are dãnable. So that whither they be the one or the other, they are quite contrarie to the Word of grace, and sucked out of the Deuills teates, to nourish vs in ydolatrie bethenrie, and sinne.

What if playes be of proophane matter.

And therfore, they cariyng the note, or brand of GOD his curse vppon their backs, which way soeuer they goe,. are to be hissed out of all Christian kingdomes, if they wil haue Christ to dwell amongst them.

Spud. Are you able to shewe, that euer any good Men from the beginning, haue resisted Playes and Enterluds.

Philo. Not onely the word of GOD doth ouerthrow thé, addiudging them, & the maintainers

tainers of them, to Hell, but also all holie coũ-
sels, and sinodes, both generall, nationall and
proũincia'l, togetyer, with all Wꝛiters both
diuyne and pꝛophane, euer since ẏ beginning
haue disalowed them, and wꝛit (almoſt) whole
volumes againſt them.

The word of God, al Wri-ters, counsels and Pathers haue writ a-gainſt playes, and enter-luds.

The learned Father Tertullian in his booke
de Speculo, saith, that playes, were consecrat
to that false ydoll Bacchus, foꝛ that he is said
to haue found out, and inuented ſtrõg dꝛinke.

Auguſtinus de ciuit. Dei, saith, that plaies
were oꝛdeined by the Deuill, and consecrat
to heathen Gods, to dꝛaw vs from Chꝛiſtia-
nitie to ydolatrie, and gentilisme. And in an
other place: Pecunias. Hiſtrionibus dare, vitium eſt innane, non virtus. To giue money
to Players, is a grǣuous sin.

Wherfore plaves were ordeined.

Chrisoſtome, calleth those playes, feſta
Sathani, feaſts of the Deuill. Lactantius, an
ancient learned Father, saith, Hiſtrionum
, impudiſſimi geſtus, nihil aliud nisi Libidi-
, nem mouent: The shameleſſe geſtures of
Plaiers, serue to nothing so much, as to moue
the fleſh to luſt, and vnclenneſſe. And
therfoꝛe, in the 30. Counsell of Carthage,
& Synode of Laodicea, it was decrǣd, that no
Chꝛiſten Man, oꝛ Woman, should resoꝛte to
plaves and enterludes, where is nothing but
blasphemie, scurrilitie and whoꝛdome maintained. Scioꝛo, ſeing the Romaines bente

Concilium.3. Cartha.Cap.11 Synode, Laodicea. Cap.54.

to

to erect Theaters, & places for plaies, dehorted them from it, with moſt prudent reaſons and forcible argumuents.   Valerius Maximus ſaith, playes were neuer brought vp, ſince regni rubore, without ſhame to the Cuntrey.

Ariſt. debarreth youth acceſſe to Playes & Enterluds, leaſt they ſæking to quench the thirſt of Venus, dœ quench it with a potle of fire.   Auguſtus, baniſhed Ouid, for making Bookes of loue, Enterluds and ſuch other amorous trumperie.

Conſtantius, ordeined that no Player ſhold be admitted to the table of the Lord. Than ſæing, that Playes were firſt inuented by the Deuil, practiſed by the heathen gentiles, and dedicat to their falſe ydols, Goddes and Goddeſſes: as the howſe, ſtage and apparell, to Venus: the muſicke, to Appollo: the penning, to Minerua, and the Muſes: the action and pronuntiation to Mercurie and ẙ reſt, it is more than manifeſt, that they are no fit exercyſes for a Chriſten Man to follow.   But if there were no euill in them, ſaue this, namely, that the arguments of tragedies, is anger, wrath, immunitie, crueltie, iniurie, inceſt, murther & ſuch like: the Perſons or Actors, are Goddes, Goddeſſes, Furies, Fyends, Hagges, Kings, Quænes, or Potentates. Of Commedies, the matter and ground is loue, bawdrie, coſenage, flattery, whordome, adulterie: the Perſons,

sons oʐ agẽts, whoʐes, queanes, bawdes, scullions, knaues, Curtezans, lecherous old men,
amoʐous yong men, with such like of infinit
varietie: If I say there were nothing els, but
this, it were sufficiẽt to withoʐaw a good chʐistian from the vsing of them. Foʐ so often, as
they goe to those howses where Players frequẽt, thei go to Venus pallace & sathãs synagogue to woʐship deuils, & betray Chʐist Iesus.

Theaters and
curtaines Venus pallaces.
Spud. But notwithstanding, I haue hard
some hold opinion that they be as good as sermons, and that many a good Example may be
learned out of them?

No playes coparable to the
word of God
Philo. Oh blasphemie intollerable: Are filthie playes & bawdy enterluds comparable to
the woʐd of God, ÿ foode of life, and life it selfe?
It is all one, as if they had said, bawdʐie, hethenrie, pagãrie, scurrilitie, and diuelrie it self,
is equall with the woʐd of God. Oʐ that the
Deuill, is equipolent with the Loʐd.

The Loʐd our God hath oʐdeined his blessed woʐd, and made it the oʐdenarie mean of
our Saluation, the Deuill hath inferred the
other, as, the oʐdenarie meane of our destruction, and will they yet compare the one with
He is cursed
that saith
playes and
enterluds are
comparable
to sermons.
ÿ other? If he be accursed, ÿ calleth light darkenes, & darknes light, truth, falsehod, & falshod
truth, swéet, sowʐe, and sowʐ sweete, than a
fortiori is he accur● d that saith that playes &
enterluds be equiualent with Sermons. Besides

ſtos this, there is no miſchief which theſe pla
es, maintain not. For, do they not noziſh ydle
nes? and otia dant vitia, ydlenes is the Mo
ther of vice. Do they not draw the people frō
hering the word of God, from godly Lectures,
and ſermons? for you ſhall haue them ſlocke
thither thick & threeſould, whē ẙ church of God
ſhalbe bare & emptie. And thoſe ẙ will neuer
come at ſermons wil ſlow thither apace. The
reaſon is, for that the nūber of Chriſt his elect
is but few, and the number of the reprobat is
many, the way ẙ leadeth to life is narow, and
few tread ẙ path, ẙ way that leadeth to death,
is brod, & many ſind it. This ſheweth, they are
not of God, who refuſe to here his word (for he
that is of God. hereth God his word ſaith our
Sauiour Chriſt) but of the deuill, whoſe exer
cyſes they go to viſite. Do they not maintaine
bawdrie, inſinuat folery, & renue ẙ remēbrance
of hethen ydolatrie? Do they not induce whor
dome & vnclennes? nay, are they not rather
plaine deuourers of maydenly virginitie and
chaſtitie? For proofe wherof, but marke the
ſlocking and rūning to Theaters & curtens,
daylie and hourely, night and daye, tyme and
tyde to ſee Playes and Enterludes, where
ſuch wanton geſtures, ſuch bawdie ſpeaches:
ſuch laughing and ſlæring: ſuch kiſſing and
buſſing: ſuch clipping and culling: Suche
winckinge and glancinge of wanton eyes,
　　　　　　　　　　　　　　and

Wherfore ſo many 'ſlock to ſee playes and enter-luds.

The fruite of theathers, & playes.

The Godly demeanoures vſed at playes and enterluds

and the like is vsed, as is wonderfull to behold. Than these goodly pageants being done,
euery mate sorts to his mate, euery one brin-
ges another homeward of their way verye
frendly, and in their secret conclaues (couert-
ly) they play þ Sodomits, or worse. And these
be the fruits of Playes and Enterluds, for
the most part.   And wheras, you say, there
are good Examples to be learned in them:

The goodly examples of Playes and Enterluds.

Trulie, so there are: if you will learne fal-
shood, if you will learn cosenage: if you will
learn to deceiue: if you will learn to play the
Hipocrit: to cogge, lye and falsifie: if you will
learn to iest, laugh and fleer, to grin, to nodd,
and mow: if you will learn to playe the vice,
to swear, teare, and blaspleme, both Heauen
and Earth : If you will learn to become a-
bawde, vncleane, and to deuerginat Mayds,
to deflour honest Wyues: if you will learne
to murther, slaie, kill, picke, steal, robbe and
roue: If you will learn to rebel against Prin-
ces, to commit treasons, to consume treasurs,
to practise ydlenes, to sing and talke of bawe-
dis loue and venery : if you will lerne to de-
ride, scoffe, mock & flowt, to flatter & smooth :
If you will learn to play the whore-maister,
the glutton, Drunkard, or incestuous person:
if you will learn to become proude, hawtie &
arrogant : and finally , if you will learne to
comtemne G O D and al his lawes, to care
neither

What things are to be ler-ned at playes.

neither foz heauen noz hel, and to commit al
kinde of ſinne and miſcheef you need to goe to
no other ſchole, foz all theſe good Cramples,
may you ſee painted befoze your eyes in enterludes and playes: wherfoze, that man who
giueth money foz the maintenance of them,
muſt needs incurre the damage of premunire,
that is, eternall damnation except they repet.
Foz the Apoſtle bidoeth vs beware, leaſt wee
communicat with other mens ſinnes, & this
their dooing, is not only to communicat with
other mens ſinnes, & maintain euil, to the di-
ſtruction of the ſelues & many others, but alſo
a maintaining of a great ſozte of idle lubbers
and buzzing dzonets to ſuck vp and deuoure
the good honie, wherupon the poz bees ſhould
liue.

Therfoze I beſeech all players & Founders of
plaies and enterludes, in the bowels of Jeſus
Chziſte, as they tender the ſaluation of their
ſoules, and others, to leaue of that curſed kind
of life, and giue them ſelues to ſuch honeſt er-
erciſes, and godly miſteries, as God hath cõ-
maunded them in his wozd to get their li-
uings wall : foz who wil call him a wiſeman
that plaieth the part of a foole and a vice: who
can call him a Chziſtian, who playeth y part
of a deuil, the ſwozne enemie of Chziſte: who
can call him a iuſt man, that playeth the part
of a diſſembling hipocrite ? And to be bzief,
　　　　　　P.　　　　　　who

Theaters
.ſcl.coleſo
Seminaries
of pſeudo
chriſtianit

A dyuine pre
munire.

What it is to
communicate
with other
mens ſinnes.

An Exhortati
on to plaiers.

The ignowy
due to Play-
ers.

who can call him a ſtraight deling man, who
playeth a Coſoners trick? And ſo of all ẙ reſt.
Away therfoꝛe with this ſo infamous an art,
Players liue vpon begging. foꝛ goe they neuer ſo bꝛaue, yet are they coũted and taken but foꝛ beggers. And is it not
true? liue they not vpon begging of euery one
that comes? Are they not taken by the lawes
of the Realm, foꝛ roagues and vacabounds? I
Players coun ted Rogues by the lawes of the Realm ſpeak of ſuch as trauaile the Cuntries, with
playes & enterludes, making an occupation
of it, and ought ſo to be puniſhed, if they had
their deſerts . But hoping that they will be
warned now at the laſt, I wil ſay no moꝛe of
them, beſæching them to conſider what a fearful thing it is to fall into the hands of God, &
to pꝛouoke his wꝛath and heauie diſpleaſure
againſt them ſelues and others , which the
Lord of his mercie turn from vs.

Spud. Of what ſoꝛte be the other kinde of
playes, which you call Loꝛds of Miſ-rule? foꝛ
mé thinke , the very name it ſelf caryeth a
taſte of ſome notoꝛious euil.

Lords of Miſ-rule
in Ailgna.
Philo.

Lords of Miſ-rule in Ailgna. THE name indæd is odious both to God
and good men, & ſuch as the very heathen
people would haue bluſhed at, once to
haue

haue named amongst them. And if the name
impozteth some euil, then what may ý thing
it self be, iudge you. But because you desire to
know the manner of them, I wil showe you
as I haue sæn them practised my self. First,
all the wilde-heds of the Parish, conuenting
togither, chuse them a Graund-Captain (of
all mischæfe) whome they innoble with the
title of my Lozd of Mis-rule, and him they
crowne with great solemnitie, and adopt foz
their king. This king anointed, chuseth fozth
twentie, fozitie, thræscoze oz a hundzed lustie
Guttes like to him self to waighte vppon his
lozdly Maiestie, and to guarde his noble per
son. Then euerie one of these his men, he in-
uesteth with his liueries, of græn, yellow oz
some other light wanton colour.   And as
though that were not (baudie) gaudie enough
I should say, they bedecke them selues with
scarfs, ribons ɇ laces hanged all ouer w̃ goldẽ
rings, przecious stones ɇ other iewels: this
dõn, they tye about either leg xx. oz xl. bels,
with rich handkercheifs in their hands, and
sometimes laid a crosse ouer their shoulders
ɇ necks, bozrowed foz the most parte of their
przetie Mopsies ɇ louing Besses, foz bussing
them in ý dark. Thus all things set in ozder,
then haue they their Hobby-hozses, dzagons
ɇ other Antiques, togither with their baudie
Pipers and thundering Dzummers to strike

The manner
how Lords of
Mis-rule are
vsed to be
played.

The monste-
rous a tyring
of my Lord
of Misrules
Men.

The rable-
ent of the
deuils guarde

vp the deuils daunce withall, then marche
these heathen company towarts the Church
and Church-yard, their pipers pipeing, their
d2ummers thund2ing, their stumps dauncing,

The beha-
uiour of the
Deuills band
in the temple
of God.

their bels iyngling, their handkercheiss swing
ing about their heds like madmen, their hob-
bie ho2ses and other monsters skirmishing a-
mongst the route: & in this so2te they go to the
Church (I say) & into the Church (though the
Minister be at p2aier o2 p2eaching) dancing &
swinging their hadkercheifs ouer their heds,
in the Church, like deuils incarnate w such a
confuse noise, y no man can hear his own voice.
Then the foolish people, they looke, they stare,
they laugh, they floer, & mount vpon sourmes
and pewes to see these goodly pageants solem-
3ed in this so2t. Then after this, about the

Receptacles.
in the Cemite
ries or church
yards for the
deuils agents

Church they goe againe and again. & so fo2th
into y church-yard, where they haue comonly
their Sõmer-haules, their bowrers, arbo2s, &
banqueting houses set vp, wherin they feast,
bãquet & daunce al that day, & (peraduenture)
all the night too. And thus these terrestriall
furies spend the Sabaoth day.

They haue also certain papers, wherin is
painted some babblerie o2 other, of Imagery

My Lord of
mis-rules cog
nizances.

wo2k, & these they call my Lo2d of mis-rules
badges, these they giue to euery one, that wil
giue money fo2 them, to maintaine them in
their hethenrie, diuelrie, who2dome, d2unken
nes,

nes, pride, and what not. And who will not
be burom to them, and giue them money for
theſe their deuilſh cognizances, they are mock
ed, ¢ flouted at, not a little. And ſo aſſoted are
ſome, that they not only giue them monie, to
maintain their abhomination withall, but alſo weare their badges ¢ cognizances in their
hats or caps openly. But let them take hœde,
for theſe are badges, ſcales, brands ¢ cognizances of the deuil, whereby he knoweth his
Seruants and Clyents, from the Childzen
of God. And ſo long as they weare them:

Sub vexillo diaboli militant contra Domi-
num et legem ſuam. They fight vnder ý báner
and ſtanderd of ý deuil againſt Chriſt Ieſus,
and all his lawes. Another ſorte of fantaſti-
call fœles bring to theſe hel-hounds (the Lord
of miſ-rule and his complices) ſome bread,
ſome gœd-ale, ſome new-chœſe, ſome olde,
ſome cuſtards ¢ fine cakes, ſome one thing,
ſome another: but if they knew that as often
as they bring any thing to the maintenance
of theſe execrable paſtimes, they offer ſacri-
fice to the deuil and ſathanas, they would re
pent and withdraw their hands, which God
graunt they may.

Spud. This is a horrible prophanation of
the ſabaoth (the Lord knoweth) ¢ more peſti-
lent then peſtilence it ſelf, but what? be there
any abuſes in their May-gāes like vnto theſe.

　　　　Philo

Philo. As many as in the other. The order of them is thus, Against May, Whitsonday or other time, all the yung men and maides, olde men and wiues run gadding ouer night to the woods, groues, hils & mountaines, where they spend all the night in plesant pastimes, & in the morning they return bringing with them birch & branches of trees, to deck their assemblies withall, and no meruaile, for there is a great Lord present amongst them, as superintendent and Lord ouer their pastimes and sportes, namely, Sathan prince of hel: But the cheifest iewel they bring from thence is their May-pole, which they bring home with great veneration, as thus. They haue twentie or fortie yoke of Oxen, euery Oxe hauing a swéet nose-gay of floures placed on the tip of his hornes, and these Oxen drawe home this May-pole (this stinking Ydol rather) which is couered all ouer with floures, and hearbs bound round about with strings from the top to the bottome, and sometime painted with variable colours, with two or thrée hundred men, women and children following it with great deuotion. And thus béing reared vp, with handkercheefs and flags houering on the top, they straw the grounde rounde about, binde gréen boughes about it, set vp sommer haules, bowers and arbors hard by it. And then fall they to raunce about it like as the heathen

Margin notes:

The order of their May-games.

A great Lord presét in May games, as superintenden therof.

The manner of bringing home their May-poles.

heathen people did at the dedication of the I-
dols, wherof this is a perfect pattern, oz ra-
ther the thing it self. I haue heard it credibly   May-poles a
repozted (and that, viua voce) by men of   pattern of the
great grauitie and reputation, that of foztie,   hethen Ydols
thzæscoze, oz a hundzed maides going to the
wood ouer night, there haue scarsly the third
part of them returned home againe vndefiled

These be the frutes which these cursed pa-
stimes bzing fozth.   Neither the Iewes, the   The frute of
Turckes, Sarasins, noz Pagans, noz any other   May-games.
natiõs how wicked, oz barbarous soeuer, haue
euer vsed such deuilish exercises as these, nay
they would haue bæn ashamed once to haue
named them, much lesse, haue vsed them. Yet
wæ that would be Chziftians, think them not
amisse. The Lord forgiue vs, and remooue
them from vs.

Spud, What is the manner of their church
ales, which you say they vse, foz they sæm vn
couth and straunge to mine eares?

The Manner of
Church-ales in Ailgna.

N. 4.   Philo.

Philoponus.

The manner
of Church-
ales in Ailg.

THE manner of them is thus, In certaine Townes where drunken Bachus
beares all the sway, against a Christmas, an Easter, Whitsonday, or some other
time, the Church-wardens (for so they call
them) of euery parish, with the consent of the
whole Parish, prouide half a score or twenty
quarters of mault, wherof some they buy of
the Church-stock, and some is giuen them of
the Parishioners them selues, euery one con-
ferring somewhat, according to his abilitie,
which mault bæing made into very strongale
or bære, it is set to sale, either in the Church
or some other place assigned to that purpose.

Then when the Nippitatum, this Huf-cap
(as they call it, and this nectar of lyfe, is set
abroche, wel is he that can get the soonest to
it, and spend the most at it, for he that sitteth
the closest to it, and spends the moste at it, he
The filthiest
beast, the god-
lyest man. is counted the godliest man of all the rest, but
who, either cannot for pinching pouertie, or
otherwise wil not stick to it, he is couted one
destitute bothe of vertue and godlynes. In so
much, as you shall haue many poormen make
hard shift for money to spend therat, for it, bæing put into this Corban, they are perswaded
it is meritorious & a good seruice to God. In
this kinde of practise, they cōtinue sir wéeks, a
quarter of a yéer, yea half a yéer togither, swilling

ling and gulling, night and day, till they be
as drunke as Apes, and as blockish as beasts.

Spud. Seeing they haue so good vtterance,
it should seeme they haue good gaines,. But I
pray you how doe they bestowe that money,
which is got therby?

Philo. Oh, well I warent you, if all be true
which they say: For they repaire their Churches and Chappels with it, they buy bookes
for seruice, cuppes for the celebration of the
Sacrament, surplesses for Sir Jhon, and such
other necessaries: And they maintaine other
extraordinarie charges in the parishes besydes. These be their exceptions, these be their
excuses, and these be their pretensed allega-
tions, wherby they blind the world, and con-
ueigh themselues away inuisibly in a clowd.
But if they daunce thus in a net, no doubt
they will be espied.

How the
monyy is spent
which is got
by Churcha-
les.

For if it wer so, y̆ they bestowed it as they
say, do they think that the Lord will haue his
howse build with drunkennesse, gluttony and
such like abhominatiō? Must we do euill, that
good may come of it? must we build this house
of lyme and stone, with the desolation, and vtter ouerthrow of his spirituall howse, clensed
and washed in the preciouse blood of our Sauiour Jesus Christ? But, who seeth not that
they bestow this money vpon nothing lesse,
than in building and repayring of Churches

Wil the Lord
haue his hou-
se build with
maintenance
of euill.

and

and Oratories? For, in most places, lye they not like swyn coates? their windowes rent, their dores broken, their walles fall downe, the roofe all bare, and what not, out of order? Who seeth not the booke of GOD, rent ragged and all betorn, couered in dust, so as this Epitaphe may be writ with ones finger vppon it, ecce nunc in puluere dormio: (Alas) behold I sleep in dust, and obliuion, not once scarse looked vppon, much lesse red vpon, and the least of all preached vppon. And on the other side, who seeth not, (for this I speak but in way of parenthesis) in ϕ meane tyme, their owne howses and mansion places, are curiously build, and sumpteously adorned: which plainly argueth, that they rather bestow this drunken got-money, vppon prophane vses and their own priuat affaires, than vpon the howse of prayer, or the temple of God: And yet this their doing is wel liked of and no mã may say, black is their eye. For why? Thei do all things well, and according to good order, as the say. And when time commeth, like good accountantes they make ther accountes, as please themselues.

The decay of Churches, which are lacerat, rent and torn.

Súpteousnes of their owne mansions.

Sp. Were it not better, & more consonant to ϕ truth, that euery one contributed somewhat according to his abilitie to ϕ maintenance of templaries & oratories, thã thus to maintaine thẽ, by drunkẽ churchales? as you say, thei do?

Philo.

Philo. It weare muche better: And ſo we read, the Fathers of the old Teſtament, euery one after his abilitie did impart ſome what, to the building and reſtauration of the Tabernacle, which Moyſes erected to the Lord. So, as in the end, there was ſuch aboundance of all things, as ÿ Artificers, conſulting with Moyſes were glad to requeſt the People, to ſtay their liberalitie, for they had more, than they knew what to do withall. Theſe People made no drunken Church-ales to build their edeſice withal: notwithſtanding, their importable charges and intollerable coſtes. But as their zæl was feruét, and very commendable in bringing to the Church, ſo our zeal is more than froſen & blame worthie in detracting frō the Church: and beſtowing it vpon whordom drunkenneſſe, gluttony, pride, and ſuch like abhominations: God amend it

Churges are to be maintained by mutuall contribution of euery one after his, power.

Spud. How do they ſolemniſe their feaſtes and wakeſſes there, and what order do they obſerue in them?

Our zeal waxen cold and froſen, in reſpect of the zeal of the former world

The maner of keep-
ing of Wakeſſes, and feaſts in Ailgna.

Philoponus.

This is their order therein: euery towne, pariſhe and Uillage, ſome at one tyme of the Yære, ſome at another (but
ſo

ſo that euery towne, pariſh & village kéep his
proper day aſſigned and appropriat to it ſelf,
(which they call their Wak day) bſe to make
great preparation, and ordenaunce for good
chéer. To the which all their Fræends and
kynſ-folks farre and néer are inuited, wher is
ſuch gluttony : ſuch drunkenneſſe : ſuch ſatu-
ritie and impletion bſed, as the like was neuer ſéen. In ſo muche, as the poore men that

Saturitie in
feaſts and
wakeſſes.

beare ȳ charges of theſe feaſts and wakeſſes,
are the poorer, and kéep the Worſer howſes
a long tyme after. And no marueil, for manie

The great
charges of
Wakeſſes.

ſpend more at one of theſe wakeſſes, than in
all the whole yéer beſides. This makes many
a one to thripple & pinch, to runne into debte
and daunger, and finallie, brings many a one
to btter ruine and decay.

Spud. Wold you not haue one fréend to bi-
ſite another at certen tymes of the yéer ?

Philo. I diſalowe it not, but much com-
méd it. But why at one determinat day, more

Againſt wa-
kes & feaſts.

than at another (except buſines brged it) why
ſhould one and ȳ ſame day continue for euer,
or be diſtinct from other dayes , by the name
of a wake day ? why ſhould there be more exceſſe of meats and drinks at that day, than at
another? why ſhould they abſtaine from bode-
ly labor. ij. or thrée dayes after, peraduenture,
the whole week, ſpending it in drunkenneſſe,
whordome, gluttony, and other filthie Sodo-
mi-

niticall exerexſes.

Spud. Sæing you allowe of one Frænd to
uiſite another, would you not haue thé to congratulat their comming with ſome good chéar?

Philo. Yes truely, but J allowe not of ſuch
excesſe of ryot & ſuperfluitie as is there vſed.
J thinke, it conuenient for one Frænd to viſite another (at ſometimes) as oportunitie &
occaſion ſhall offer it ſelfe, but wherfore ſhuld
the whole towne, pariſh, village and cuntrey,
kæpe one and the ſame day, and make ſuch
gluttonous ſeaſts as they doo? And therfore,
to conclude, they are to no end, except it be to
draw a great frequencie of whores, drabbes,
theiues and verlets together, to maintaine
whordome, bawdrie, gluttony, drunkennesſe,
thiefte, murther, ſwearing and all kind of miſchief and abhomination. For, theſe be the
ends wherto theſe feaſtes, and wakeſſes doo
tende.

Wherto wa-
keſſes and
feaſts do very
aptly tend.

Spud. From whence ſprang theſe feaſts and
wakeſſes firſt of all, can you tell?

Philo. J cannot tell, except from the Paganes and heathen People, who whan they
were aſſembled together, and had offred Sacrifices to their wodden Goddes and blockiſh
ydols, made feaſts and banquets together before them, in honour and reuerence of them,
ſo appointed the ſame yérly to be obſerued in
memoriall of the ſame, for euer: But whence
ſoeuer

From whence
theſe annuall
feaſts and ſta-
cionarie wa-
keſſes had
their be-
ginning.

soeuer they had their exordium,certē it is,the
druill was ẏ Father of them, to drown vs in
perdition and destruction of body and soule :
which G D D forefend.

Sp. As I remember,you spoke of dauncing
before,inferring ẏ the sabaoth is greatly prophaned therby: whereof I pray you shew mée
your iudgement.

The horrible Vice of

pestiferous dauncing, vsed in Ailgna.
Philoponus.

Dauncing,as it is vsed(or rather abused)
in these daies,is an introductiō to whordom,a preparatiue to wantonnes,a prouocatiue to vncleanes,& an introite to al kind
of lewdnes , rather than a pleasant exercyse
to ẏ mind,or a holsome practise for ẏ body:yet
notwithstanding,in Ailg. both men, wemen
& childrē,are so skilful in this laudable sciēce,
as they maye be thought nothing inferiour to
Cynœdus, ẏ prostitut ribauld, nor yet to Sar-
danapalus that effeminat tarlet.Yea thei are
not ashamed to erect scholes of dauncing,thin-
king it an ornament to their childrē, to be expert in this noble science of heathen diuelrie:
and yet this people glory of their christianitie
& integritie of life: Indead,verbo tenus Chri-
stiani boni vocitentur: But vita & moribus
Ethnicis,& paganis peiores reperiētur. Frō
the

Scholes of
dauncing
erected.

þ mouth outward, they may be said to be good
Christians, but in life & maners, farre woorser
than the heathen, or Paganes: Wherof, if they
repent not, & amend, it shalbe easier for that
Land of Sodoma and Gomorra at the day of
iudgement then for them.

Sp. I haue heard it said, þ dauncing is both
a recreation for the minde , & also an exercyse
for the body, very holsome, and not only that,
but also, a meane wherby loue is acquired.

Ph. I will not much denie, but being vsed
in a meane , in tyme and place conuenente,
it is a certē solace to the minds of such as take pleasure in such vanities, but it is no good
reason to say, some mē take pleasur in a thing
ergo, it is good, but the cōtrarie is true rather:
For this is (basis veritatis) a ground of truth,
þ whatsoeuer a carnall man with vncircum-
cised heart, either desireth, or taketh pleasure
in, is most abhominable & wicked before god:
As on the other side, what the spirituall man
regenerat, & borne anew in Christ, by the di-
rection of God his spirit desireth or taketh delight in , is good, and according to the will of
God. And seeing mās nature is too procliue of
it selfe to sinne, it hath no need of alluremēts
& allections to sin (as dauncing is) but rather
of restraints & inhibitiōs frō the same. which
are not there to be found. For what clipping,
what culling, what kissing and bussing, what

snou-

Dauncing a
pleasure to
them that de-
light in vani-
ties.

What allure-
ments to sin,
be in daun-
cing.

smouching & flabbering one of another, what filthie groping and vncleane handling is not practised euery wher in these dauncings? yea the very deed and action it selfe, which I will not name for offending chast eares, shall be purtrayed and shewed forth in their bawdye gestures of one to another. All which, whither they blow vp Venus cole, or not, who is so blind that seeth not? wherfore, let them not think that it is any recreation (which word is abusiuely vsed to expresse the ioyes, or delightes of the mind, which signifieth a making againe of that, which before was made) to the mind of a good Christian, but rather a corrosiue most sharp and nipping. For seing that it is euill in it self, it is not a thing wherin a Christia Mans heart may take any comfort.

Dauncing no recreation, but a corrosiue to a good Christian.

The onely, summum bonum, wherin a true Christians heart is recreated and comforted, is the meditatio of the passion of Iesus Christ, the effusion of his blood, the remission of sins, and the contemplation of the ineffable ioyes and beatituds after this life, prepared for the faithfull, in the blood of Iesus Christ. This is the only thing, wherin a Christian ma ought to reioyse, and take delight in, all other pleasures & delights of this lyfe set a parte, as a marulent and bitter, bringing forth fruit to eternall destruction. but the other, to eternall lyfe: And wheras they conclude, it is a holesome

The onely thing, wherin a good christian doth delight.

ſome exerciſe for the bodie, the contrary is
moſte true, for I haue knowen diuers by the
immoderate vſe therof, haue in ſhort time become decrepit and lame, ſo remaining to their
dying day. Some haue broke their legs with
ſkipping, leaping, turning and vawting, and
ſome haue come by one hurt, ſome by another
but neuer any came from thence without ſome
parte of his minde broken and lame, ſuch a
wholſome exerciſe it is. But ſay they it induceth loue, ſo I ſay alſo, but what loue?
Truely a luſtful loue, a venereous loue, a con-
cupiſcencious, baudie & beaſtiall loue, ſuch as
proceedeth from the ſtinking pump and loth-
ſome ſink of carnall affection, and fleſhly ap-
petite, and not ſuch as diſtilleth from the bowels of the hart ingenerat by the ſpirit of God.

Wherfore, I exhort them in the bowels of
Jeſus Chriſt to eſchue not only from euil, but
alſo from all apperance of euil, as the Apoſtle
willeth them, procæding from one vertue to
another, vntil they growe to perfect men in
Chriſte Jeſus, knowing that we muſt giue
accoũts at þ day of iudgment of euery minut
and iote of time, from the day of our birth to
the time of our death: for there is nothing
more precious, then time, which is giuen
vs to glorifie God in good-workes, and not to
ſpend in luxurious exerciſes after our owne
fantaſies and delights.

Dancing no
holſom exer-
ciſe for the
Bodie.

What loue
dancing pro-
cureth.

We muſt ren-
der accounts
for time heer
lent vs.

N   Spud.

Spud. But I haue heard then: affirme that dauncing is prouable by the word of God: for (say they) did not the women come foorth of all the Cities of Israel to meet king Saule?and Dauid returning from the slaughter of Goliath,with psalteries, flutes,tabrets,Cymbals and other musicall Instruments, dauncing & leaping before them? Did not the Israelites hauing passed ouer the red sea bring foorth their Instruments and danced for ioy of their deliuerance?

1 Sa. 18.

Exo. 15.

Exo. 32.

Againe, did they not daunce before the golden Calf,which they had made, in Horeb or Sinai?   Did not king Dauid daunce before the Ark of the Lord? Did not the Daughter of Iephtah daunce with tabret and harp at the return of her Father from the field? Did not the women of the Israelits dance comming to visit good Iudith? Did not the Damsel daunce before King Herod? Did not Christ blame ye people for their not dancing,when he said, wee haue pyped vnto you, but you haue not daunced?

2. Sa. 6.

Iudic, 11.
Iudic. 15,

Mat. 14,

Luc. 7.

Eccle. 3.

Saith not Salomon, there is a time to weep 'and a time to laughe, a time to mourne 'and a time to daunce?

And doth not the Prophet Dauid in many places of his Psalmes commend and commaund dauncing and playing vpon Instruments of Musick.

Wherfore

Wherfore(for thus they conclude)seeing these
holy Fathers (wherof some were guided by
the instinction of God his Spirit) haue not
only taught it in doctrine,but also expressed it
by their Examples of life, who may open his
mouth once to speake against it.

No man with
out errors
both in lyfe
and doctrin

    Philo.   The Fathers as they were men
had their errors and erred as men, for Hominis est errare, decipi et labi: it is naturall
for man to erre, to be deceiued & to slide from
the trueth. Therfore the Apostle saith:follow
mée in all things as I follow Christ: but to ÿ
intent that they who perpend the Examples
of the Fathers,and Scripture falsly wrested,
to maintaine their deuilish dauncings withall,may sée their owne impietie & grosse igno-
rance discouered,I wil compendiously set down
the true sence and meaning of euery place, as
they haue cyted them perticulerly. For the
first:wheras they say that the Women came
foorth in daunces with timbrels and Instruments of Ioy to méet Dauid and Saule , I
aske them for what cause they did so ?

1.Sa. 18.
The first pil
lare of daun
cing ouer-
throwen.

    Was it for wantonnes or for very ioye of
hart, for their Victorie gotten ouer the Phili-
stines their sworne Enemies ?   Was it
in prayse of G O D:or to stirre vp filthie lust
in them selues, or for nicenes onely , as our
daunces bée ?

               N. 2.   Did

Did men and women daunce togither, as is
now vsed to be don: or rather was it not don
amongst women only? for so saith the text,
the women came forth &c.   But admit it
were neither so, nor so, wil they conclude a
generall rule, of a particuler example? it is
no good reason to say such and such did so, ther
fore it is good, or we may do so, but all things
are to be poysed in ý balance of holy scripture
and therby to be allowed or disalowed, according to the meaning of the holy Ghost, who is
only to be heard and obeyed in his word.

*good cō-
ment to say
ers did so,
o it is
od, or wee
y doo the
c.*

The Israelitish women hearing of the fame
of Dauid, and how he had killed their deadly
enemie Goliath, came forth to meet him play
ing vpon instrumēts, dancing & singing songs
of ioye and thanks-giuing to the Lord who
had giuen them victorie and deliuered them,
from the deadly hostilitie of him, who sought
their distruction euery way. Now what maketh this, for our lewd, wanton, nice and vbi-
quitarie dauncings, for so, I may call them
because they be vsed euery where, let the god
ly iudge: who seeth not rather ý this example,
(let Cerberus the dog of hel alatrate what he
list to the cōtrary) clean ouerthroweth them.

*he differēce
tween the
nnces of our
orefathers,
nd ours.*

Theirs was a godly kind of dācing in praise
of God: ours a lustful, bawdie kinde of dea-
menour, in praise of our selues: theirs to shew
their inward ioy of minde for the blessings of
God.

God bestowed vpon them, ours to show our actiuitie, agilitie and curious nicitie and to procure lustful loue and such like wickednes infinit: But to their second allegation: ŷ Children (say they) of Israel danced being deliuered out of the seruitude of Pharo and hauing passed ouer the red sea: I graunt they did so, and good cause they had so to do: For were they not emancipate and set free from three great calamities and extreame miseries? First frō the seruile bondage of Egipt, from the sword of Pharo, who pursued the rereward of their hoste, and from the danger of the red sea, their enemies being ouerwhelmed in the same.

For these great and inestimable benefits and blessings receiued at the hands of God, they played vpon Instruments of musick, leaped, daunced, and sung godly songs vnto ŷ Lord, shewing by these outward gestures ŷ inward ioy of their harts and mindes.   Now what conduceth this, for the allowance of our luxurious dauncings? Is it not directly against them? They danced for ioy in thanks to god, wee for vaingloriei: they for loue to God, wee for loue of our selues: they to shew the interior ioy of the minde for God his blessing, heaped vpon them: we to shew our concinitie, dexteritie, and vain curiositie in the same: they to stir vp and to make them selues the apter to praise God, we to stir vp carnall appetites

Their sece
Pillar shal

How the Is
elits danced

and fleshlie motions : they to shewe their humilitie before God, and we to shew our pride both before God and ye world. But how so euer it be, sure I am, their dauncing was not like ours, consisting in measures, capers, quauers, & I cannot tel what, for thei had no such leasure in Egist to learne such vaine curiositie in that lust full bawdie schoole, for making of brick and tyles. And notwithstanding, it is

The dauncing of our Forfathers mai not be called a dancing, but rather a Godly triûphing, & reioycing of heart for ioy.

ambiguous whether this may be called a dauncing or not, at lest not like ours, but rather a certê kind of modest leaping, skipping, or moving of the body to expresse the ioye of ye mind in prayse of God, as the Man did, who being healed by the power of our Sauiour Christe, walked in the Temple, leapping, skipping, & praising God.

We neuer read, that they euer daunced, but at some wonderfull portent, or straunge iudgment of God, and therfore, made not a common practise of it, or a daylie occupation as it were, much lesse set vp schools of it, and frequenting nothing els night and day, Sabaoth day, and other, as we do.

Their.3. Reason. examined.

But to their third Reason : The Israelits daûced before the Calf in Horeb. And what than ? They made a Golden Calf, and adored it, maye we therfore do the like ? They committed ydolatrie there , therfore is ydolatrie good, because they committed it ?

Adam

Adam, diſobyed G☉D, and obeyed the
ƌeuil: is obedience therfore to the deuil good,
becauſe hæ did ſo?

Therfore wæ muſt not take hǽde what
man hath don hǽretofore, but what God hath
commaunded in his word to be don, and that
followe, euen to the death. But to be ſhort,
as it is a friuilous thing to ſay, becauſe they
committed Jdolatrie, therfore may wæ do
the like, ſo it is no leſſe ridiculous, to ſay, becauſe they daunced, therfore wæ may do the
ſame: for as it is not lawful to commit Jdolatrie, becauſe they did ſo, ſo is it not lawfull
to daunce, becauſe they daunced.

So that if this place inferre any thing for
dauncing, it inferreth that wæ muſt neuer
daunce but before a golden Calf, as they did:
but J think by this time, they are aſhamed of
their dances: therfore, of this place J nǽd to
ſayno more, giuing thē to note, that this their
dauncing in reſpect of the end therof, was
farre diſſonant from ours: for they daunced
in honour of their Jdol, wæ clean contrary
though neither the one nor the other be at a-
ny hand tollerable.

Their fourth reaſon, Did not Dauid   Their.4.
daunce before the Ark, ſay they? very true: Reaſon.
and this place (as the reſt before) reſelleth
their cuſtomarie dauncings of men and women togither moſte excellentlie.   For
                                      Dauid

Dauid danced him selfe alone, without either woman, or musicall Instrument to effeminate the minde. And this dauncing of Dauid was no vsuall thing, nor frequented euery day but that one time, and that in prayse of God, for the deliuerie of the Ark of God his testament out of the hands of the Infidels and heathen people: the ioy of this holy Prophet was so vehement, for this great blessing of GOD (such a feruent zeale he bore to the trueth) that it burst forth into exterior action, y more to induce others to prayse God also. Would God we would dance as Dauid daunced heer, for the deliuerie of his assaining word out of the hands of that Italian Philistin & archenemy of all trueth, the Pope of Roome, for in this respect I would make one to daunce, to leap, to skip, to triumph, and reioyce as Dauid did before the Ark. By this I trust any indifferent man seeth, that by this place, they gain as much for the maintenance of their leude dancings, and baudie chorusses, as they did by citing the former places, that is iust nothing at all, which they may put in their eies and see neuer the wursse?

Their fift reason. Did not Ieptath his daughter meet her Father when he came from war dancing before him, and playing vppon Instruments of Ioy.   Ieptath going forth to warre against the Amonites promised the

Lord

Lord (making a rashe vowe) that if it would
pleafe his Maieftie to giue him victorie ouer
his Ennemies, he wold facrifice the firſt lyuing thing that fhuld meet him frō his houſe:
It pleaſed G D D that his ſole daughter and
heire hearing of her Fathers profperous re-
turn(as the maner of the Cuntrey was) ran
forth to meete her Father, playing vppon inſtruments, in praiſe of GDD, and dauncing
before him for ioye. Now what proueth this
for their daunces? Truely, it ouerthroweth
them if it be well confidered: for firſt, we read
that fhe did this but once, we daylie : She in
prayſe of God, we in prayſes of our ſelues:
fhe for ioy of her Fathers good fucceſſe, we to
ftere vp filthie and vncleane motions:　She
with a virginall grauitie, we with a babifh
leuitie:fhe in comly maner, we in bawdie ge-
ſture. And moreouer, this fheweth, that women are to daunce by themſelues(if they wil
needs daunce·) and men by themſelues, for ſo
importeth the Text, making no mention of
any other her collegues, or Companions dancing with her.

Wherfore &] how the Daughters of Iepthath, dau ced.

Their.vi.Reaſon: Did not ẙ Iſraelitifh wemen daunce before Iudith, comming to viſit
her? I graunt they did ſo: the ſtorie is thus.

Ther. 6, reaſon. Iudith. Ca. ij.

Holofernes, oppoſing himſelfe, againſt the
Iſraelits, the choſen people of G D D, and in-
tending to ouerthrowe them, and to blot out.
　　　　　　N.b.　　　　　their

their remembrance for euer from vnder heauen, assembled a huge power, and besieged
them on euery side.

    The Israelits, seeing themselues circum-
valled and in great daunger on eachside, su-
borned good Iudith, a vertous Godlye Woman (for without some stratagem, or pol-
licie wrought, it was vnpossible for them in
the eyes of ẙ world, to haue escaped) to repaire to Holofernes, & by some meanes or other
to work his destruction : who guided by the
hand of God, attempted the thing & brought
it happely to passe.   For she cut of his head
with his owne fauchine, wrapping his body
in the canopie, wherin he lay sleepingly possest
as he was with ẙ spirit of drunkennesse: this
done, the Women of Israell came together,
and went to visit this worthie Woman, and
to congratulat her prosperous successe, with instruments of musick, singing of Godly songs,
and dauncing for ioye, in honor and prayse to
God, for this great victorie obtained.   Now
who seeth not, that these women sang, dauced,
and played vppon instrumentes in prayse of
God, & not for any other lewdnes, or wantonnes, as comonly the world doth now adaies?
This also ouerthroweth the dauncinges of
Men and Women together in one companie:
for though there was an infinite number of
People by, yet the Text saith, there daunced
none

Iudith cut-
teth of the
head of holo-
fernes.

The vnlaw-
fullnes of
dauncing of
men and wo-
men together

ne, but onely Women, which plainly ar-
ieth the vnlawfulneſſe of it in reſpecte of
Man.   And this being but a particular fact
i a ſort of impꝛudent Women, ſhall we
:aw it into example of lyfe, and thinke it
ilwfull, oꝛ good, becauſe they did pꝛactiſe it ?
It was a cuſtome in thoſe dayes, when God
ad powꝛed foꝛth any notable bleſſing vpon
is People from his Heauenly Pallace, thē
People in honour, pꝛaiſe and thankeſgiuing
o God foꝛ them. would, play vppon their in-
truments, ſing Godly Songs, daunce, leape,
ſkip and triumphe, ſhewing foꝛth the ioye of
heir mindes, with their thankefulneſſe to
GOD, by all exteriour geſtures, that they
:ould deuyſe.   Which kinde of thankefull
daunting, oꝛ ſpirituall reioycing, wold God,
we did follow, leauing all other wanton daū-
:ing to their Father the Deuill.

A cuſtome tẏ
daunce in
prayſe of
God.

    Their. vj. Reaſon : Did not (quothe
they) the Damoſell daunce befoꝛe kinge
Herode, when the head of Iohn Baptiſt was
cut of ?   She daunced indeed : And herein
they maye ſee the fruite of daunting, what
goodneſſe it bꝛingeth :   Foꝛ, was not this
the cauſe of the beheading of Iohn the Baptiſt ? Se whether daunting, ſtyꝛeth not vp
luſt and inflameth the mind.

Ther. 7.
reaſon.

Dauncing
ſtyꝛreth
luſt.

    Foꝛ, if Herode with ſeeing her daunce, was
ſo inflamed in her loue, and rauiſhed in her
                                  beha-

behauiour, that he promised her, to giue h
whatsoeuer she wold desire, though it wer
half of his Emperie,oz kingdome:what wol
he haue béene, if he had daunced with her
and what are those that daunce with them
hand in hand, chéek by chéek, with busin
and kissing, slabbering and smearing, mo
beastly to behold? in so much,as I haue hear
many impudently say, that they haue chose
their Wyues,and wyues their Husbands b
daucing: Which plainely proueth the wic
kednesse of it. Their. viij. reason: Did no
Christ rebuke the People, foz not daucing
saying:we haue pyped vnto you,but you hau
not daunced.   They may as well conclud
that Christ in this place, was a Pyper, oz
Minstrell, as that he alowed of daucing, o
reprooued them,foz not excercysing the same.

Their.8.
Reason.
Luc. 7.

This is a Metaphozicall, oz Allegozicall
kinde of speach, wherin our Sauiour Christ,
goeth about to reprooue and checke the styf
neckednes,the rebellion and pertinacious có
tumacy of ẙ Scribes and Phariseis, who were
neither mooued to receiue the glad tydings
of the Gospell by the austeritie of Iohn the
Baptiste, who came preaching vnto them the
doctrine of repentaunce, in mourning sozt:nei
ther yet at the preaching of our Sauiour him
selfe,breaking vnto them the pure Ambrosia,
the Cœlestial Manna,the woz of life in ioy-
full

The more
than obdurat
hardnes of
the Iewes.

all, and gladsome maner.

Ihon the Baptist he piped vnto them, that
, he preached vnto them, austeritie of life, to
mourn for their sinnes, to repent, to fast, pray
and such like. Our Sauiour Christ he py-
ed (that is) preached vnto them, the glad &
comfortable tidyngs of ye Gospell, yet at neither of these kinde of concions, they were any
whit moued, either to imbrace Christ, or his
Gospell: Wherfore he, sharply rebuketh them,
by a similitude of foolishe Children sitting in
the market place, and piping vnto them that
would not daunce. This is the true vndoubted
sence of this place, which, whether it ouerthrow not all kinde of lewd dauncing (at lest
maketh nothing for them) allowing a certen
kind of spirituall dauncing, and reioysing of
the heart vnto God (that I may suspend my
owne iudgement) let wyse men determine.
Their. ix. Reason: Saith not Salomon, there
is a time to weep, & a time to laugh, a time to
mourn, and a time to daunce? This place is
directly against their vsuall kinde of dauncing. For, saith not the Text, there is a time,
meaning, somtime, now and than, as the Israelites did in prayse to GOD, when anie
notable thing happened vnto them, and not
euery daye and howre as we do, making an
occupatiō of it, neuer leauing it, vntil it leaue
vs. But what, and if Salomon speaketh here

Eccle. 3.
Their. 9.
Reason.

Salomō mea-
neth a certen
kind of a spi-
tuall daūcing
or reioying
of the heart.

of

of a certen kind of spiritual dauncing, and re
ioysing of ẙ heart in praise to G D D ? Thi
is easily gathered by the circumstances of th
place, but specially by the sentence preceden
(vz. there is a time to mourn, & a time to da
ce &c.) that is, a time to mourn for our sinnes
& a tyme to dauce or reioyse, for the vnspeak
able treasures purchased vnto vs by ẙ death
& passion of Jesus christ. How much this pla
re maketh for defence of their nocturnall, diu
turnall, wanten, lewde and lascibious daun
rings (if it be censured in the imparciall bal
lance of true iudgement) all ẙ world may se
and iudge. And now to draw to an end, J wil

Their vltimũ   come vnto their vltimum refugium. That is
refugium.   Doth not Dauid both commend, and also cõ
maunde dauncing and playing vpon instru
ments in diuerse of his Psal. Jn all those pla
ces, ẙ Prophet speaketh of a certẽ kind of spi
rituall dauncing and reioysing of the heart to
ẙ Lord for his graces & benefits in mercie be
stowed vpon vs.   This is the true kinde of
dauncing, which the word of God doth allow
of in any place, and not that we should trippe
like rammes, skip like goats, & leap like mad

Why our feet   men. For, to ẙ end our feet were not giuẽ vs
were giuẽ vs.   but rather to represent ẙimage of God in vs
to keep Companie with the Angels, & to glo
rifie our heuenly Father thorow good workes

Spud. Do you condemne al kinde of daun
                                    cing

ring, as wicked and prophane?

Ph. All lewde, wanton, & lasciuious dauncing in publique assemblies & conuenticles,
without respect either of sex, kind, time, place,
Person, or any thing els, I by the warrant of
the word of God, do vtterly condemne: But
that kind of dauncing which is vsed to praise
and laud the name of God withall (as weare
the dauces of the people of the former world)
either priuatly or publiquely is at no hand to
be dysallowed, but rather to be greatly commended. Or if it be vsed for mans comfort,
recreation, and Godly pleasure: priuatly (euery sex distincted by themselues) whether with
musick, or otherwyse, it cannot be but a very
tollerable exercise, being vsed moderatly, and
in y feare of God. And thus, though, I condé-
ne all filthie, luxurious and vncleane dauncing, yet I condemne not al kind of dauncing
generally. For certen it is, the exercyse it self,
in it own nature, qualitie & proprietie, though
to some it is lawfull, to othersome vnlawfull
in dyuerse respects, is both ancient & general,
hauing been vsed euer in all ages, as wel of y
Godly, as of y wicked, almost from the beginning. Wherfore, when I códemne the same
in some, my meaning is, in respecte of the
manifold abuses therof.   And in my iudgement as it is vsed now a dayes, an occupatió
being made of it, and a continuall exercyse,
                                        without

What daun-
cing is con-
demned by
the word of
God.

without any difference oʒ reſpect had either to
time, Perſon, ſex oʒ place in publique aſſemblies and frequencies of People . with ſuche
beaſtlie ſlabberings , buſſings & ſmouchings
and other filthie geſtures & miſdeameanoʒs
therein accuſtomed , it is as vnpoſſible to be
vſed without doing of infinit hurt, as it is foʒ
a naked Man to lye in the middeſt of a hote
burning fire, and not to conſume. But theſe
abuſes with other ẙ like (as there be legions
moe in it) being cut of from the exerciſe it
ſelfe, the thing remayneth very commendable
in ſome reſpectes. Oʒ els , if our daunces
tended, as I haue ſaid , to the ſetting foʒth of
GOD his gloʒie (as the daunces vſed in pʒe-
ter time did) to dʒaw others to pietie and ſan-
citie of life, and to pʒaiſe and reioyce in God,
to recreat ẙ minde oppʒeſſed with ſome great
toyle; oʒ laboʒ taken in true virtue and godlynes, I would not (being don in the feare of
GOD, men by them ſelues, and Wemen by
thē ſelues, foʒ els it is not poſſible to be without ſinne) much gainſtand it. But I ſee the
contrarie is euery where vſed to ẙ great diſ-

**Why men
ſhould daunce
by themſelfes
and women
by themſelus.** honoʒ of God, and coʒruption of good maners,
which God amend.

Spud. And wherfoʒe, would you haue Men
to daunce by them ſelues , and Women by
them ſelus?

Philo. Becauſe it is without all doubte, a
pʒo-

prouocation to luſt and venery, and the fire
of luſt once conceiued, (by ſome irruption
oʒ other) burſteth foʒthe into open action
of whoʒedome and foʒnication. And therfoʒe
a certain godly Father ſaidwel, Omnis ſaltus in chorea, eſt ſaltus in profundum inferni,
Euery leap oʒ ſkip in dance, is a leap toward
hel. Yet notwithſtanding in Ailgna it is coū
ted & vertue, and an oʒnament to a man, yea,
and the onely way to attaine to pʒomotion &
aduancement, as experience teacheth.

Why men
ſhould dance
by the ſelues
and Women
by the ſelues,

Spud, Notwithſtanding, foʒ my further in-
ſtruction, I pʒay you ſhowe mē what Fathers and Councels haue iudged of it, and
what they haue wʒit and decrēd againſt it.

Philo. If I ſhould goe foʒth to ſhew all the
inuectiues of Fathers, all the decrēs of councels, and all the places of holy Scripture a-
gainſt the ſame, I ſhould neuer make an end:
wherfoʒe, of many I wil ſelect a few, hoping
that they wil ſuffice any reaſonable man.

Teſtimonies
of Fathers
councels, and
Writers a-
gainſt daun-
cing.

Syrach ſaith, frequent not the company of a
woman, that is a ſinger oʒ a dauncer, neither
heare her, leaſt thou be intrapped in her craf-
tines. Chriſoſtome, dylating vpon Mathew
ſaith: In euery dance, the deuil daunceth by,
foʒ companie, though not viſible to ỹ eye, yet
palpable to ỹ minde. Theophilus, wʒiting v-
pon Mark ỹ firſt Chapter ſaith, Mira coļluſio
ſaltat per puellam Diabolus This is a wun-

Eccle. 131

Mat.

D.　　　　　　　　　　　　derfull

derful deceit, for the deuil danceth amongst the
for company. Augustine writing vpon the
32. Psalme, saith, it is better to digge all the
Sabaoth day, then to dance. Erasmus, in his
Booke, de contemptu Mundi, saith, Whose
minde is so well disposed, so stable, or
wel setled, which these wanton dances, with
swinging of armes, kicking of legs, playing
vpon instruments, and such like would not o
uercome and corrupt: Wherfore saith hee, as
thou desirest thine owne credit, and welfare,
eschew these scabbed and scuruy companie of
daunders.

Ludouicus Viues saith, amongst all pleasures, dauncing and voluptuousnes is the
kingdome of Venus, and the empire of Cu-
pid: wherfore, saith hee, it were better for thee
to stay at home, and to break either a leg, or
an arme of thy body, then to break the legges
and armes of thy minde & soule, as thou dost
in filthie scuruy dauncings.   And as in all
Feasts and pastimes, dauncing is the last, so
it is the extream of all other vice: And again,
there were (saith he) from far cuntries, certain men brought into our parts of ye world,
who when they saw men daunce, ran away,
meruelously affraid: crying out and thinking
the to haue bin mad. And no meruaile, for
who seing them leap, skip & trip like Goates &
and hindes, if hee neuer saw the before, would
not

Augustine.

Erasmus,

Lodouicus
viues.

Daunders
thought to be
mad-men.

not think them either mad, or els possest with
some furie? Bullinger, paraphrasting vpō Mathew, 14. saith ,   After feasting swilling and
gulling commeth dancing, the root of all filthy-
nes and vncleannes.   Bullinger.

Maister Caluin, writing vpon Iob , Ser. 8.   Caluin.
Cap. 12. calleth dauncing the cheefe mischeef
of all mischeefs , saying there be such vnchast
gestures in it , as are nothing els, but incite-
ments to whordome.

Marlorate, vpon Mathew saith , whosoeuer
hath any care either of honestie , sobrietie or
grauitie , haue long since bad adieu to all filthie dauncing .

No man (saith a certaine heathen Writer)
if hée be sober daunceth, except hée be mad.

Salustius, commending Sempronia that
renowmed whore, for many goodly gifts, con   Salust-
demneth her for her ouer great skil in dauncing : concluding, that dauncing is the Instrument of lecherie.

Cicero, saith, a good man would not dance
in open assembles , though hée might by it   Cicero.
get infinite treasure.

The Council of Laodecea decréd that it
should not be lawful for any Christiā to dance
at mariages or at any sollemne feast.

In an other Councel it was enacted , that
no man should daunce at any marriage, nor
yet at any other time.

                    D. 2.   The

The Emperour Iustinian decreed, that for no respect in feasts or assemblies, there should be any dauncing, for feare of corrupting the Beholders, and inticing men to sinne.

All Writers bothe holy and prophane against daun cing.

Thus you may see, bothe Scripture, councels and Fathers, holy and prophane, heathen and other, euen all ingenerall, haue detested and abhorred this filthie dauncing, as the quauemire or plash of all abhomination: and therfore, it is no exercise for any Christians to followe: for it stirreth vp the motions of ý flesh, it induceth lust, it inferreth baudrie, afforceth ribaldrie, maintaineth wantonnes, & ministreth oile to ý stinking lamp of deceitful pride: and in summa', nourisheth a world of wickednes and sinne.

Dauncing a World of sin

Spud Now that the wickednes of it, is so manifestly shewed, that no man can denie it, I pray you who inuented this noble science, or from whence sprang it?

Who inuented dauncing and from whome it sprang,

Philo. Haereof, there be sundry and diuers opinions: for some holde an opinion (and very likely) that it sprang from the heathen idolatrous Pagans and Infidels, who hauing offred vp their sacrifices victimats and holocaustes to their false Gods, in reuerence of them, and for ioy of their so doing, vsed to daunce, leape, and skip before them.

And this may be proued by the Israelits themselues, who hauing seen and learned the same

practise

practiſe in Egipt, feared not to imitate the like in the wildernes of Horeb: ſome again, ſuppoſe that Pyrrhus one of Sibils Preiſts deviſed it in Creet. Others holde that the Prieſts of Mars, who in Roome were had in great eſtimation for their derteritie in dauncing, innented it: Others think ẏ one Hiero a truculent and bloody Tirant in Sicilia, who to ſet vp his tyrannie the more, inhibited the people to ſpeake one to an other, for feare of inſurrections and commotions in his kingdome was the occaſiõ of ẏ inuenting therof: for whẽ the Sicilians, ſawe that they might not vnder pain of death one ſpeak to another, they inueted dauncing to expreſſe the inward meaning and intentiõs of the minde by outward leeks and exteriour geſtures of the body, which vſe afterward grew into cuſtome, and now into nature.   But what ſoeuer men ſay of it, or from whence ſoeuer it ſprang, S. Chriſoſtom ſaith plainly (to whom J willingly ſubſcribe) that it ſprang from the teates of the Deuils breſt, from whence all miſchæfels doth flow: Therfore to conclude, if of the egges of a Cokatrice, may be made good meat for man to eat, and if of the web of a ſpider, can be made good cloth for mans body, then may it be proued that dancing is good and an exerciſe fitte for a chriſtian man to followe, but not before:

Wherfore God of his mercy take it away

D. 3.   from

from vs.

Spud, What say you of Musick, is it not a laudable science?

Of Musick in

Ailgna, and how it allu-
reth to vanitie.

Philo.

I Say of Musick, as Plato , Aristotle, Ga-
len and many others haue said of it , that
it is very il for yung heds, for a certaine
kinde of nice, sinowthe sweetnes in alluring
the auditorie to nicenes, effeminacie, pusil-
lanimitie, & lothsomnes of life, so as it may not
improperly be compared to a swæt electuarie
of honie, or rather to honie it self, for as honie and such like swæt things recciued into ye
stomack, dœth delight at the first, but afterward they make the stomack so quasie , nice
and weake, that it is not able to admit meat
of hard digesture .   So swæt Musick, at the
first delighteth the eares, but afterward corrupteth and depraueth the minde , making it
weake, and quasie , and inclined to all licen-
tiousnes of lyfe whatsoeuer.

And right as good edges are not sharpned,
but

A comparison betwixt hony and dancing.

Wits dulled by Musick.

(but obtufed) by bæing whetted vpon fofte ſtones , ſo gꝏd wits by hearing of ſoft muſick are rather dulled then ſharpned, and made apt to all wantonnes and ſinne. And therfore Writers affirme Sappho to haue bæn expert in muſick, and therfore whoriſh.

Authors of the bringing in of muſick.

Tyrus Maximius ſaith , the bringing in of muſick, was a cup of poyſon to all the world.

Clytomachus , if hæ euer heard any talking of loue, or playing vpon muſicall Inſtruments, would run his way and bidde them farwel.

Plutarchus , complaineth of Muſick , and ſaith, that it dꝏth rather femenine the minde as pricks vnto vice, then conduce to godlines as ſpurres vnto Uertue.

Pythagoras, condemnes them for fꝏles , and bequeathes them a cloſe-bag, that meaſure Muſick by ſound and eare . Thus you heare the iudgement of the wiſe, concerning Muſick , now iudge therof as you liſt your ſelf.

Spud. I haue heard it ſaid,(and I thought it very true) that Muſick dꝏth delight bothe man and beaſt, reuiueth the ſpirits, comforteth the hart , and maketh it apter to the ſeruice of GOD.

Philo. I graunt Muſick is a gꝏd gift of GOD, and that it delighteth bothe man and

Muſick the gꝏd gift of God.

and beaſt, reuiueth the ſpirits, comforteth þ hart, and maketh it redyer to ſerue GOD, and therfore did Dauid bothe vſe muſick him ſelf, & alſo commend the vſe of it to his poſteritie (and bæing vſed to that end, for mans priuat recreation muſick is very laudable.)

Of muſick in publique aſſemblies, and conuenticles.

But bæing vſed in publique aſſemblies and priuate conuenticles as directories to filthie dauncing, thorow the ſwæt harmonie & ſmoothe melodie therof, it eſtraungeth þ mind ſtireth vp filthie luſt, womanniſheth þ minds rauiſheth the hart, enflameth concupiſence, and bringeth in vncleannes. But if muſick openly were vſed (as I haue ſaid) to þ praſis and glory of God as our Fathers vſed it, and

How muſicke were tollerable & good.

as was intended by it at the firſt, or priuatly in a mans ſecret Chamber or houſe for his owne ſolace or comfort to driue away the fantaſies of idle thoughts, ſolicitude, care, ſorrowe and ſuch other perturbations and moleſtations of the minde, the only ends wherto true Muſick tends, it were very commendable and tollerable. If Muſick were thus vſed it would comfort man wunderfully, and moue his hart to ſerue God the better, but bæing vſed as it is, it corrupteth good minds, maketh them womanniſh and inclined to all kinde of whordome and miſchæf.

Spud, What ſay you then of Muſitions, & Minſtrels who liue only vpon the ſame art?

Philo.

Philo. I thinke that all good minſtrelles, ſober and chaſt muſitions (ſpeking of ſuche drunken ſockets, and bawdye paraſits as raͤge the Cuntreyes, ryming and ſinging of vncleane, corrupt, and filthie ſongs in Tauernes, Ale-houſes, Innes, and other publique aſſemblies) may daͤuce þ wild Moris thorow a naͤdles eye. For how ſhould thei bere chaſte minds, ſaͤing that their crercyſe is the pathway to all vncleanes. Their is no ſhip, ſo balanced with maſſie matter, as their heads ure fraught with all kind of bawdic ſongs, filthie ballads, and ſcuruie rymes, ſeruing for euery purpoſe, and for euery Cumpanie.

Who be more bawdie than they? who vncleaner than they, who more licentious, and looſe minded? who more incontinent thã they? and brieſely, who more inclyned to all kind of inſolencie and lewdnes than they? wherfore, if you wold haue your ſonne, ſofte, womanniſh, vncleane, ſmoth mouthed, affected to bawdrie, ſcurrilitie, filthie rimes, and vnſeemely talking: briſly, if you wold haue him, as it weare tranſnatured into a womã, or worſe, and inclyned to all kind of whordome and abhomination, ſet him to dauncing ſchool, and to learn muſicke, and than ſhall you not faile of your purpoſe. And if you would haue your daughter whooriſh, bawdie, and vncleane, and a filthie ſpeaker, and ſuch like, bring her vp in muſick

The ſcarſity of good muſitions and minſtrelles.

The marchãdiſe of minſtrelles, and muſitions.

The wickednes of muſitions and minſtrels.

How to haue Children leaned in all wickednes.

musick and dauncing, and my life for youres, you haue wun the goale.

And yet notwithstanding it weare better (in respecte of acceptation) to be a Pyper, or bawdye minstrell , than a deuyne , for the one is loued for his ribauldrie , the other hated for his grauitie , wisdome , and sobrietie.

The scarcytie of dyuines.

Euery towne , Citie and Countrey is full of these minstrelles to pype vp a dance to the Deuill , but of dyuines , so few there be as they maye hardly be seene.

But some of them will reply and say, what Sir ? we haue lycenses from iustices of peace to pype, & vse our minstralsie to our best commoditie ? Cursed be those licences, which lycense any man to get his lyuing, with the destruction of many thousands.

But haue you a lycence from the Arch-iustice of peace Christe Jesus ? If you haue so, you may be glad, if you haue not (for the Worde of GOD is against your vngodly exercyses , and condemneth them to Hell) than may you as rogues, extrauagantes, and straglers from the Heauenlye Country be arrested of the high iustice of peace Christ Jesus, and be punished with eternall death, notwithstanding your presented licēces of earthly men. Who shall stand betwixt you , and the Iustice of GOD at the daye of Iudgement ?   Who shall excuse you , for drawing

Licences graunted to musitions & minstrels to exercyse their mistery or facultie of mischief.

ing

ing so manye thousandes to Hell? shall the
Iustices of peace? shall their licenses? Oh no:
For neither ought they to graunt anye licen-
cens to anie to doo hurt withall, neither (if
they would)ought any to take them.

No lycences to do hurte withall are to be graun-ted.

Giue ouer therfore your Occupations, you
Pypers, you Fidlers, you minstrelles, and
you musitions, you Drummers, you Tabret-
ters, you Fluters, and all other of that wicked broode, for the bloud of all those, whome
you drawe to destruction thorow your prouo-
cations, and intysing allurementes shalbe
powred vppon your heads, at the day of Iudgement, but hereof enough, and perchaunce
more than will like their humour.

A Cauet to musitions, minstrelles & all others of twat stampe.

Spud. Is it not lawfull vppon the Sabaoth daye to playe at Dice, Cardes, Tables,
Bowles, Tennisse, and suche other plea-
saunt exercyses, wherein Man taketh pleasure and delight?

Cards, Dice, Tables,
Tennisse, Bowles, and other ex-
ercyses, vsed vnlawfully
in Ailgna.
(*⁎*)

Philo.

Philoponus.

THese be no Sabaothlike exercyses for
any Christian man to follow any day at
all, much lesse vppon the Sabaoth daye,
which the Lord wold haue to be consecrat to
himselfe, and to be spent in holy and Godly
exercyses according to his will. As for cards,
dice, tables, bowls, tennisse, and such like, thei
are furta officiosa, a certê kind of smoth deceiptfull, and sleightie theste, wherby many a
one is spoiled of all that euer he hath, sometimes of his life withall, yea of body and soul
for euer : And yet (more is the pitie) these be ŷ
onely exercyses vsed in euery mans howse, al
the yær thorow. But specially in Christmas
tyme there is nothing els vsed but cards, dice
tables, masking, mumming, bowling, ŷ such
like foeleries: And the reason is, they think
they haue a commission and prerogatiue that
time, to do what they lust, and to folow what
vanitie they will. But (alas) do they thinke
that they are priuiledged at that tyme, to doo
euill? the holier the time is (if one time were
holier than another, as it is not) the holier
ought their workes to be. Can anie time di-
spense with them or giue them libertie to sin.
No, no : the soule which sinneth shall dye, at
what time so euer it offêdeth. But what will
thei say? Is it not Christmas? must we not be
mery ŷ truly it is: we ought both than, and at
all

(Marginal notes, left column:)

Exercises vn-
lawfull vpon
the Sabaoth
day.

Furta offi-
ciosa.

All wicked
games vsed
in Christmas
syme.

No tyme pri-
uiledged a
man to sinne.

all tymes besides to be merie in the Lord, but not otherwyse, not to swil and gull more that time thã at any other time, not to lauish foorth more at that time, than at another times.

But the true celebratiõ of the Feast of Christmas is, to meditat (and as it were to ruminat) vppon the incarnation and byrthe of Jesus Christ, not onely that time, but all the tymes and daies of our life, and to shewe our selues thankeful to his Maiestie for the same: Notwithstanding, who is ignorant, that more mischiefe is that time committed than in all the yeere besides? what masking and mumming, wherby robberie, whoredome, murther, and what no, tis committed: what dicing & carding, what eating and drinking, what bãqueting and feasting is than vsed more than in all the yeere besydes? to the great dishonor of GOD, and impouerishing of the realme.

The true keeping of Christmas.

Wickednes in Christmas.

Spud. Is it not lawfull for one Christian to play with another at anye kinde of game, or to winne his monie, if he can?

Philo. To play at tables, cards, dice, bowls or the liks (though a good Christian man will not so ydely, and vainely spend his golden dayes) one Christian with another, for their priuat recreations, after some oppression of studie, to driue awaye fantasies, and suche like, I doubt not, but they may, vsing it moderatly, with intermission, and in the feare of

Vnlawful for one Christian to play with another to win his money.

God

GOD? But to play for lucre of gaine, and for desire onely of his Brothers substaunce (rather than for any other cause) it is at no hand lawfull, or to be suffered.

For as it is not lawful to robbe, steale and purloine by deceit, or slaight, so is it not lawfull to get thy Brothers goods from him, by carding, dicing, tabling, bowling, or any other kynd of thefte, for these playes are no better, nay worser than open theft, for open theft euery Man can be ware of, but this being a craftie pollitick theft, and comonly don vnder pretence of Frændship, few, or none at all can beware of it. The commaundement saith, thou shalt not couet, nor desire any thing that belongeth to thy Neighbour. Now, it is manifest, that those that playe for monie, not onelye couet their Brothers monie, but also vse craft falshod and deceit to wyne the same.

The Apostle, forbiddeth vs to vse deceipt in bargaining, in buying, or selling, much lesse than ought we to vse deceipt in gaming.

Our Sauiour Christ biddeth euery man, do to an other, as he would another shonld do vnto him.   Which rule if it weare dulie obserued, weare sufficient to withdraw men both from all kynd of gameing, and also from all kynd of indyrect, and vniust dealing.

A rule to restraine vnlawfull gamening.

For as thou woldest not that another man should winne thy money, so thou oughtest not

to

to desire the winning of his, for thou must do
as thou wouldest be done by.

Spud. If gameing for money be so vnlawfull, wherfore are there howses, and places appointed for maintenance of the same?

Philo. That excuseth not the fault, but ag-
grauateth it rather.　　　And truely great pitie
it is, that these brothel howres (for so I call all
gaming howses) are suffred as they be.

For, are they not the very seminaries, and
nurseries of all kynd of abhomination, whatsoeuer heart can thinke, or tongue exprelse.

And therfore I maruecile y those who keep
and maintaine these gaming howses, can euer
haue light hearts, or once to loke vp towards
Heauen, y not onely suffer this manifest theft
in their howses (for gaming is no better) but
also maintaine and nourish the same.

The Apostle saith, not onely they that do
euill, digni sunt morte, are worthie of death,
but also, qui consentiunt facientibus, those
who consent to them that do it.

Call to mind, than what euills come of this
wicked exercyse I beseeche you.

For doth not swearing, tearing, and blas-
pheminge of the Name of ☉☉☉, doth
not stinkinge Whordome, Thefte, Robberie, Deceipt, Fraude, Cosenage, fighting Quareling, and sometymes Murder,
doth

doth not pride, rapine, drunkns, beggerye, and
in fine, a shamefull end followe it, as the shadowe doth follow the body? wherfore I will
not doubte to call these gaming howses, the
slaughter howses the shambles or blockhow-
ses of the Deuill, wherin he buchereth Christen mēs soules infinit waies, God knoweth,
the Lord suppresse them.

Spud. Weare there euer anie lawes made
against the inordinat abuse hereof, or haue
the Godly in any age misliked it?

Philo. In all ages and times, both the godly sober Christians haue detested it, and holsome lawes haue ben promulgat against it.

Octauius Augustus, was greatly reproched
of the Writers of his time, for his great delight in gaming, notwithstanding, his manifold vertues besides.

Cicero, obiected to Marcus Antonius, his
often gaming, as a note of infamie vnto him.

The noble Lacedemonians sent their Am-
bassadours to Corinth, to conclud a peace, who
coming thither, and finding the People playing at dice, and cards, and vnthriftie games,
returned back again (infecta pace) their peace vnconcluded, saying, it should neuer be re-
ported, that they wold ioyne in league with
Dice-players and gamesters.

The same Lacedemonians, sent to Deme-
trius in derision of his diceplaying, a paire o f
dice

Lawes and
sanctions di-
uulgat a-
gainst ga-
ming.

The Infamy
purchased by
gaming.

dice of gold. Sir, Thomas Eliot (that worthie knight) in his Book of gonernance, aſketh, who will not think him a light man of ſmall credit, diſſolut, remiſe and vaine, that is a Dici-player, or gameſter.

Publius ſaith. Quantò peritior eſt aleator in ſua arte, tanto nequior eſt, & vita & moribus. How much cõninger a mã is in gaming and diceplaying, ſo much corrupter he is both in life and maners. Iuſtinian made a lawe, that none ſhould play at dice, nor cards for no cauſe, neither priuately, nor openly.

Laws againſt gaming.

Alexander Seuerus, baniſhed all gameſters out of his dominions. And if anie were found playing, their goods were confiſcat and they counted as mad men euer after, neuer truſted, nor eſtæmed of anie.

Ludouicus, ordeined ý al gameſters ſhold depart his lãd, for feare of corrupting of others.

K. Richard the ſecond, forbad all kynd of gaming, and namely dice-playing.

K. Henrie the fourth, ordeined ý euery Dice-player ſhould be impriſoned ſix daies for euery ſeuerall time he offended in gaming.

Puniſhment for gaming.

K. Edward the fourth, ordeined who ſo kept gaming howſes, ſhould ſuffer impriſonment three yeeres, and forfait. xx.li. & the Players to be impriſoned. two yeers, & forfait x.pound.

K. Henri the ſeuenth, ordeined ý euery Dice-player ſhould be impriſoned all a day, and the

The penalty for thoſe that keep gaming howſes.

P.   the

Kéeper of the dicing house to forfeit for euery
offence vi.ſhil. viij.d. and to be bou̅d by recog-
nizance to good behauiour.

K. Henrie the eight, ordeined that euery
one that kept dicing houſes, ſhould forfait.xl.
ſhil. and the Players to forfait vi. ſhil. viij.d.
with many good lawes and ſanctio̅s ſet forth
againſt this raging Abuſe of gaming, which
to auoid tediouſnes I omit, beſeeching y̅ Lord
to root vp, and ſupplant theſe, and all other
ſtumbling blocks in his church what ſo euer.

Sp. As I reme̅ber in the Catalogue of abuſes before, you ſaid, y̅ ſabaoth day was prophaned, by bearbaiting, cockfighting, hauking,
hunting, kéeping of faires, courts, & markets
vpõ y̅ ſaid day. Is it not lawful thõ to follow
theſe exerciſes vpon the ſabaoth day, neither?

Beare baiting and o-

ther exercyſes, vſed vnlawfully in AILGNA.

Philoponus.

Theſe Hethnicall exercyſes vpon the Sabaoth day, which y̅ Lord hath co̅ſecrat to
holy vſes, for the glory of his Name, and our
ſpirituall comfort, are not in any reſpect tollerable, n̅ to be ſuffered. For, is not the baiting
of a Bear, beſides that it is a filthie, ſtinking

         and

and lothsome game, a daungerous, & perilous
exercyse: wherein a man is in daunger of his
life euery minut of an houre: which thing
though it weare not so, yet what exercyse is
this meet for any Christiã: what christē heart
cã take pleasure to sée one poore beast to rent,
teare, and kill another, and all for his foolish
pleasure? And although they be bloody beasts
to mankind, & séeke his destructiõ, yet we are
not to abuse them, for his sake who made thē,
& whose creatures they are. For notwithstanding that they be euill to vs, & thirst after our
blood, yet are thei good creatures in their own
nature & kind, & made to set foorth the glorie &
magnificence of the great God, & for our vse, &
therfore for his sake not to be abused. It is a
mon saying amongst all men, borowed frõ ȳ
frēch: Qui aime Iean, aime son chiē, loue me,
loue my dog, so loue God, loue his creatures.

No Creature
to be abused.

If any should abuse, but the dog of another
mans, wold not he who oweth the dog, think
ȳ the abuse therof resulteth to himselfe? And
shall we abuse ȳ creatures of God, yea take
pleasure in abusing thē, & yet think ȳ the contumely don to thē, redoūdeth not to him who
made them? but admit it weare graūted that
it weare lawfull to abuse the good Creatures
of God, yet is it not lawfull for vs to spend
our golden yéers in such ydle and vaine exercyses dayhe and hourelie, as we do.

God is abused
when his
Creatures are
misused.

P.ij.   And

Keeping of
maſtyues &
bandogs.

And ſome who take themſelues for no ſmall
fooles are ſo farre aſſotted , that they will not
ſtick to keep a doſen, or a ſcore of great maſti-
ues and bādogs, to their no ſmall charges, for
the maintenance of this goodly game (for-
ſooth)and will not make anie bones of. xx. xl.
C. pound. at once to hazard at a bait : with
ſeight dog , ſeight beare (ſay they) the deuill part all.   And to be plaine, I thinke the
Deuill is the Maiſter of the game, bearewarde
and all.   A goodly paſtyme, forſoth, worthie
of commendation, and wel ſitting theſe Gentlemen of ſuch reputation. But how muche
the Lord is offended for the prophanation of
his Sabaoth by ſuch vnſauorie exercyſes, his
Heauenly Maieſtie of late hath reueiled, pou-
ring forth his heauie wrath, his fearfull iudgements, and dreadfull vengeance vppon the
Beholders of theſe vanities.

A Fearfull Example

of G O D his Iudgement vpon the
prophaners of his
Sabaoth.

VPon the. 13. day of Ianuarie laſt, being
the Sabaoth day. Anno. 1 5 8 3. the People, Men , Wemen and Children , both
yonge and old, an infinit number, ſlocking to
theſe

thoſe infamous places, where theſe wicked
exercyſes are vſuallie practiſed (for they haue
their courts, gardens & yards for ẏ ſame purpoſe:) when they were all come together, and
mounted aloft vpon their ſcaffolds, and galle-
ries, and in middeſt of al their iolytie & paſtime, all the whole building (not one ſtick ſtan-
ding) fell down with a moſt wonderfull and
fearefull confuſiõ. So, that either two or thrẽ
hundred, men, wemẽ and childre̅ (by eſtima-
tiõ) wherof ſeuẽ were killed dead, ſome were
wounded, ſome lamed, and otherſome bru-
ſed and cruſhed, almoſt to the death.   Some
had their braines daſht out, ſome their heads
all to ſquaſht, ſome their legges broken, ſome
their arms, ſome their backs, ſome their ſhoul
ders, ſome one hurt, ſome another.   So, that
you ſhould haue hard a woful crie, euen pear-
cing the ſkyes, parents bewayling their children, Children their louing Parents: wyues
their Huſbands, and Huſbands their wyues,
marueilous to behould. This wofull ſpectacle
and heauie iudgement, pitifull to heare of, but
moſt ruefull to behold, did ẏ Lord ſend down
from Heauen to ſhew vnto the whole World
how grẽuouſly he is offended with thoſe that
ſpend his Sabaoth in ſuch wicked exerciſes:
In ẏ meane tyme leauing his temple deſolat
and emptie.   God graunt all men, may take
warning hereby to ſhun the ſame, for feare of

A wofull
crie.

P.iy.   like

like oz wozſer Judgement, to come.

A fearfull Iudgement

of GOD, ſhewed at the Theaters.

THY like Judgement (almoſt) did the
Lozd ſhew vnto them a litle befoz, being
aſſembled at their Theaters, to ſée their
bawdie enterluds, and other trumperies pza-
ctiſed. Foz, he cauſed ý earth mightely to ſhak
and quauer, as though all would haue fallen
down, wherat the People ſoze amazed, ſome
A woſull ſpe- leapt down (frō the top of ý turrets, pinacles,
ctacle.   and towzes, wher they ſtood) to the ground,
Wherof ſome had their legs bzoke, ſome their
arms, ſome their backs, ſome hurt one where,
ſome another, ∉ many ſoze cruſht and bzuſed:
but not any, but they wēt away ſtoze affraid,
∉ wourded in cōſcience. And yet cā neither ý
one, noz ý other, fray them frō theſe diueliſh
exercyſes, vntill the Lozde conſume them all
in his wzath: which God forbid. The Lozd
of his mercie, opē the eyes of the maieſtrats,
to pluck down theſe places of abuſe, that god
may be honozed, and their conſciēces diſbur-
Cockſeigh- thened.
ting vpon the   Beſids theſe exerciſes, thei flock thick ∉ thzée
Sabaoth.   fold to ý cockſeights an exercyſe nothing inferiour to ý reſt, wher nothing is vſed, but ſwe-
rīg, fozſwering, deceit fraude, colluſion, coſe-
                            nage,

nage, ſcoulding, railing, conuitious talking, feighting, b:awling, quarreling, d:inking, who:ing, ₡ which is wo:ſt of all, robbing of one an other of their gœds , ₡ ÿ not by direct, but indirect means ₡ attēpts : ₡ yet to blaūch ₡ ſet out theſ miſchiefs with all (as though they were vertues)thei haue their appointed daies ₡ ſet how:s, when theſe d:uelries muſt be exerciſed. They haue houſes erected to ÿ purpoſe, flags ₡ enſignes hanged out. to giue notice of it to others , and p:oclamation goes out to p:oclaim ÿ ſame, to th'end ÿ many may come to the dedication of this ſolemne feaſt of miſchief: the Lo:d ſupplant them. And as fo: hawking ₡ hunting vpō the ſabaoth day, it is an exerciſe vpon ÿ day, no leſſe vnlawful thā the other. Fo:, no mā ought to ſpend any day of his life, much leſſe euery day in his life, as many do, in ſuch vaine ₡ ydle paſtimes: wher fo:e, let Gentlemen take heed, fo: be ſure accoūts muſt be giuen at the day of iudgemēt fo: euery minut of time , both how they haue ſpent it ₡ in what exerciſes. And let them be ſure no mo:e libertie is giuen thē, to miſpend an how:e ,o: one iote of the Lo:d his gœds , than is giuen to the poo:eſt, and meaneſt perſon ÿ liueth vpō the face of the earth. J neuer read of any in ÿ volume of ÿ ſacred ſcripture that was a gœd man, and a Hunter.

Eſau, was a great hunter, but a rep:obat: Iſ-
P.iiij.   maell,

Appointed times for exerciſe of dyuelries.

Hawking & hunting vppō the ſabaoth.

No more libertie giuen to one than another for miſpēding of their goods.

maell a great hunter,but a miscreant: Nemrode a great hunter,but yet a reprobat, and a vessell of wrath. Thus I speake not to condemne hawking and hunting altogether, being vsed for recreation, now and than, but against the continuall vse therof daylie, hourly, wéekly, yéerly, yea all the time of their life, without intermissio. And such a felicitie haue some in it, as they make it all their ioye, bestowing more vpõ hawkes and hounds , and a sort of idle lubbers to followe them in one yéer,than they will impart to the poore members of Christ Iesus in vij.yéers,peraduenture in all the dayes of their life.So long as mã in Paradice persisted in innocency,all beasts what so euer,weare obedist to him,and came and prostrated themselues before him. But euer since his fall,they haue fled from him, & disobeyd him,because of his sin: that séeing he disobeyed the Lord,they again disobeied him. For,so long as man obeied God, so long they obeied him:but so soone as mã disobeyed God, they disobeyed him,& becam enemies to him, as it were séeking to reuége y iniurie which mã had don vnto G O D, in disobeying his lawes. Wherfore,the cause why all beasts do fly from vs , and are become Enemies to vs, is our disobedience to the L O R D, which we are rather to sorow for,than to hunt after their deaths by the sheading of their blud.

If

No good hunters, scripture.

Cost bestowed in hauks and dogges.

When all beasts weare obedient to man & wherfore they rebell.

n If necessitie or want of other meats infor-
ceth vs to seek after their liues, it is lawfull
to vse them in the feare of God, w thanks to
his name: but for our pastimes and vain
pleasures sake, wæ are not in any wise to
spoyle or hurt them. Is he a christian man
or rather a pseudo-christian, that delighteth
in blood? Is he a Christian that spendeth all
his life in wanton pleasures and plesaunt delights? Is hæ a Christian that buieth vp the
corne of ý poor, turning it into bread (as many
do) to fæd dogs for his pleasure? Is hæ a christian that liueth to the hurt of his Neighbour
in treading and breaking down his hedges,
in casting open his gates in trampling of his
corne & otherwise, in preiudicing him as hunters do? wherfore God giue them grace to sæ
to it, and to mend it betimes ere it be to late,
for they know mora trahit periculum, delay
bringeth danger. Let vs not deferre to leaue
the euil and to do good, least the wrath of the
Lord be kindled against vs, and consume vs
from of the vpper face of the Earth?

Spud, What say you to kæping of Markets, of Fayres, Courtes and Lætes vpon ý
Sabaoth day? Think you it is not lawful to
vse the same vpon any day?

Philo. No truely, for can you serue God &
the deuil togither, can wæ carrie to God and
serrie to the deuil, can we serue two Maisters
and

For pleasure sake only no man ought to abuse any of the cretures of God.

Hurt by hunting to poore Men.

Not lawfull to keep courtes, Leets Markets and Fayres vppon the Sabaoth day,

and neither offend the one nor the other? can we serue God and Mammon? can we please God and the world bothe at one time? The Lord wil not be serued by peecemeale, for either he wil haue the wholeman, or els none. For saith he, Thou shalt looue the Lord thy God with all thy soule, withall thy minde, withail thy power, withall thy strength, and so forth, or els with none at all. Then seeing that we are to giue ouer our selues so wholely and totally to the seruice of God, al ý daies of our life, but especially vppon the Sabaoth day, being consecrate to that end, we may not intermedle with these prophane exercises vpon that day. For it is more then manifest ý these faires, markets, courtes and leetes vpon the Sabaoth day, are not only a hinderãce vnto vs in the true seruice of God, and an abuse of ý Sabaoth, but also lead vs the path way to hel. For what cosonage is not there practised? what falshod, deceit & fraude is not there exercised? what dissimulation in bargaining? what setting forth of fucate & deceiuable wares, is not there frequented? what lying swering, forswering, drunkennes, whordom, theft, & sometimes murther, either there or by ý way thither, is not euery where vsed?   In courtes & leets what enuie malice & hatred is norished? what expostulation, railing, scoulding, periuring & reperiuring is maintained?
what

Abuse of the Sabaoth by Fayres, markets.

The euil in Fayres and Markets.

The euils in Courtes and Leets practised.

what opꝛeſſion of ẙ pooꝛe, what fauouring the rich, what iniuſtice ⁊ indirect dealing? what bꝛibing, deceiuing, what poling ⁊ pilling is there pꝛactiſed? it would make a chꝛiſtiã hart to blæd in beholding it. And yet notwithſtanding we muſt haue theſe gœdly pageãts played vpon ẙ ſabaoth day (in a wanion) becauſe there are no mo daies in ẙ wæk. And hærby ẙ ſabaoth is cõtaminat. Gods woꝛd contemned, his cõmandemẽts diſanulled, his ſacramẽts cõculcate, his oꝛdinãces neglected, ⁊ in ſuma, his blœd trod vnder fæt and all miſchæf maintained. The Lord cut of theſe with all other ſin, both from their ſoules and thy Sabaoth, that thy name may be gloriſied, & thy Church truely ediſied.

Spud. Is ẙ playing at fœtball, reding of mery bœkes ⁊ ſuch like delectations, a violation oꝛ pꝛophanation of the Sabaoth day?

Ph. Any exerciſe which wiðꝛaweth vs from godlines, either vpon ẙ ſabaoth, oꝛ any other day els, is wicked ⁊ to be foꝛbiden. Now who is ſo groſly blinde, ẙ ſæth not, ẙ theſe afoꝛeſaid exerciſes not only wiðꝛaw vs froꝛ godlines ⁊ vertue, but alſo baile ⁊ allure vs to wickednes and ſin: foꝛ as cõcerning fœtball playing: I pꝛoteſt vnto you, it may rather be called a frændly kinde of fight, then a play oꝛ recreation. A blœdy and murthering pꝛactiſe, then a felowly ſpoꝛte oꝛ paſtime.

Playing at Foot-ball.

Foot-ball a freendly kind of fight.

Foꝛ

For: doth not euery one lye in waight for his Aduersarie, seeking to ouerthrowe him & to picke him on his nose, though it be vppon hard stones, in ditch or dale, in valley or hil, or what place soeuer it be, hée careth not so he haue him down. And he that can serue the most of this fashion, he is counted the only felow, and who but he? so that by this meanes, somtimes their necks are broken, sometimes their backs, sometime their legs, sometime their armes, sometime one part thrust out of ioynt, sometime an other, sometime the noses gush out with blood, sometime their eyes start out: and sometimes hurt in one place, sometimes in another. But whosoeuer scapeth away the best goeth not scotfrée, but is either sore woũded, craised and brused, so as he dyeth of it, or els scapeth very hardly: and no meruails, for they haue the sleights to méet one betwixt two, to dashe him against the hart with their elbowes, to hit him vnder the short ribbes with their griped fists, and with their knées to catch him vpon the hip, and to pick him on his neck, with a hundred such murdering deuices: and hereof, groweth enuie, malice, rãcour, choler, hatred, displeasure, enmitie and what not els? and sometimes fighting, brawling, contention, quarrel picking, murther, homicide and great effusion of blood, as experience dayly teacheth.

Hurt by foot ball playing.

Foot-Ball playing a murthering Play.

30

Is this murthering play now an exercise for the Sabaoth day? is this a christian dealing for one brother to mayme and hurt another, and that vpon prepensed malice, or set purpose: is this to do to another, as we would wish another to do to vs, God make vs more careful ouer the bodyes of our Bretheren.

And as for the reading of wicked Bookes, they are vtterly vnlawfull, not onely to bee read, but once to be named, & that not (onely) vpon the Sabaoth day, but also vppon any other day: as which tende to the dishonour of God, depravation of good manners and corruption of christian soules.   For as corrupt meates do annoy the stomack, and infect the body, so the reading of wicked and vngodly Bookes (which are to the minde, as meat is to the body) infect the soule, & corrupt y minde, hailing it to distruction: if the great mercy of God be not present.

And yet notwithstanding, whosoeuer wil set pen to paper now a dayes, how vnhonest soeuer, or vnseemly of christian eares his argument be, is permitted to goe forward, and his work plausibly admitted and freendly licensed, and gladly imprinted without any prohibition or contradiction at all : wherby it is growen to this issue, that bookes & pamphlets of scurrilitie and baudrie, are better esteemed and more vendible then the godlyest and sagest

Reading of wicked bookes

The euil comming by reading euil Bookes,

gest bookes that be : for if it be a godly trea-
tise , reproouing vice , and teaching vertue, a-
way with it, for no man(almost)though they
make a flourish of vertue, and godlynes, will
buy it , nor (which is lesse) so much as once
touch it . This maketh the Bible , the blessed
Book of God, to be so little estéamed.   That
woorthie Booke of Martyrs made by that famous Father & excellent Instrument in God
his Church, Maister Iohn Fox, so little to be
accepted and all other good books little or nothing to be reuerenced : whilst other toyes ,
fantasies and bableries wherof the world is
ful, are suffered to be printed. These prophäe
schedules, sacraligious libels, and hethnical
pamphlets of toyes & bableries (the Authors
wherof may vendicate to them selues no smal
commendations, at the hands of the deuil for
inuenting the same) corrupt mens mindes ,
peruert good wits., allure to baudrie , induce
to whordome , suppresse vertue & erect vice :
which thing how should it be otherwise? for
are they not innéted & excogitat by Belzebub
writté by Lucifer,licésed by Pluto,printed by
Cerberus & set a broche to sale by the infernal
furies themselues to ẙ poysning of the whole
world : But let the Inuétors,the licésors,the
printers & the sellers of these vaine toyes. and
more then Hethnicall impieties take héed for
the blood of all those which perish or take hurt
thorow

ſhozow theſe wicked bꝏkes,ſhalbe powꝛed v-
pon their heads at the day of iudgement, and
be required at their hands.

Spud. I pꝛay you how might al theſe inoꝛ-
mities, and Abuſes be refoꝛmed? Foꝛ, it is
to ſmall purpoſe to ſhew ꝑ abuſes,ercept you
ſhewe withall how they might be refoꝛmed.

Philo. By putting in pꝛactiſe and executing
thoſe gꝏd lawes, wholſome ſanctions, and
Goldy ſtatutes, which haue bæne heretofoꝛe,
and daily are ſet foꝛth and eſtabliſhed, as
GOD be thanked, they are manie.

The want of the due execution wherof, is
ꝑ cauſe of all theſe miſchiefs,which both rage
and raigne amongſt vs.

Spud. What is the cauſe why theſe lawes
are not executed,as they ought to be?

Philo. Truely I cannot tell, erccpte it be
ſhoꝛow the nigligence, and contempt of the
inferiour Magiſtrates.   Oꝛ els, perhaps
(which thing happeneth now and than) foꝛ
money they are bought out, diſfranchiſed and
diſpenſed withall,foꝛ as the ſaying is, quid
non pecunia poteſt? what is it, but money
will bꝛing to paſſe? And yet notwithſtanding ſhall it be don inuiſibly in a clowde (vnder benedicite I ſpeake it) the Pꝛince being
boꝛne in hand, that the ſame are dalie erecuted. This fault is the coꝛruption of thoſe that
are put in truſt to ſæ thē erecuted, as I haue
          M.   tculd

toulo you, and (notwithstanding) do not.

Spud. This is a great corruption & Abuse, doubtles, and woorthie of great punishment.

Ph. It is so truely, for if they be good lawes tending to the glorie of GOD, the publique weale of the Cuntrey, and correctiō of vices, it is great pytie that money should buy them out. For what is that els, but to sell vertue, for lucre: Godlynes, for drosse, yea mens seuls for corruptible money? Therfore those that sell them, are not onely Traitors to GOD, to their Prince and Countrey: but are also the Deuils Marchants, and ferrie the bodies, and soules of Christians, as it were in Charons boate to the Stigian flood of Hell, burning with fire and brimstone for euer.

And those that buy them are Traitors to GOD, their Prince and Countrey also.

For if the lawes were at the firk good (as GOD be praised al the lawes in Ailgna be) why should they be suppressed for money, and if they were euill, why were they diuulged, but had rather bæne buried in the wombe of their Mother before thy had euer sæne ŷ light.

And why were lawes instituted, but to be executed? Els it were as good to haue no lawes at all (the People lyuing orderly) as to haue good lawes, and thē not executed.

The Prince ordeining a law, may lawfully repeale & adnull the same againe, vpō speciall

causes

cauſes & conſiderations, but no inferiour ma=
ieſtrat or ſubiecte what ſo euer, may ſtop the
courſe of any lawe made by the Prince with
out daunger of damnation to his owne ſoule,
as the Word of G D D beareth witneſſe.

And therfore, wo be to thoſe men, that will
not execut the ſentence of the lawe (being ſo
Godly, and ſo Chriſtian as thei be in Ailgna)
vppon Malefactors and Offenders.

Uerely they are as guiltie of their blood be=
fore G D D, as euer was Iudas of the death
of Chriſte Ieſus.

Spud. Seing it is ſo, that al fleſh hath cor=
rupted his way before the face of God, and
that there is ſuch abhomination amongeſt
them, I am perſwaded the daye of Iudgement is not farre of. For when iniquity ſhall
haue filled vp his meaſure, than ſhall the end
of all appeare, as Chriſt witneſſeth in his
Euangelic.

Philo. The day of the Lord cannot be farre
of, that is moſt certen: For what wonderfull
portents, ſtrang miracles, fearful ſignes, and
dreadfull Iudgements hath he ſente of late
daies, as Preachers & fortellers of his wrath
due vnto vs, for our impenitēce & wickedneſ
of life. Hath he not cauſed the earth to tréble
and quake? the ſaine Earth to remoue from
place to place? the ſeas and waters to roare,
ſwell & bruſt out, and euerflow their bankes

to the destruction of many thousands? hath he not caused the Elements and Skyes, to send foorth flashing fire? to raine downe wheat, a wonderfull thing as euer was heard, and the like? hath he not caused wonderfull Eclypses in the Sunne and Moon, with most dreadfull coniunctions of Starres and Planets, as the like this thousand yeeres, haue not been heard of? haue not the clowdes distilled downe a-boundance of rayne and showres, with all kinde of vnseasonable wether, to the destroy-ing (almost) of al thinges vppon the Earth? haue we not seene Commets, blasing starres, firie Drakes, men, feighting in the ayre, most fearfully to behold? Hath not dame Nature her selfe denied vnto vs her operation, in sen-ding foorth abortiues, vntimely births, vggle-some monsters and fearfull mishapen Crea-tures both in man & beast. So, that it seemeth all the Creatures of God are angrie with vs and threaten vs with destruction, and yet we are nothing at all amended (alas) that shal be-come of vs? Remember we not there is a God that shal iudge vs righteously? that there is a Deuill, who shall torment vs after this lyfe vnspeakably, if we repent not? At that day, the wicked shall find that there is a Material Hell, a place of all kinds of tortures, wherein they shal be punished in fire and brimstone a-mongest the terrible Company of vgglesome

Deuills

Deuils world without end, how light ſo euer they make account of it in this World.

For ſome ſuch there be, that when thei heare mention of Hell, or of the paines therof in the other World, they make a mocke at it, thinking they be but metaphoricall ſpeaches, onely ſpoke to terrifie vs withall, not otherwyſe. But certen it is, as there is a God, that will reward his Children, ſo there is a Deuill that will remunerat his Seruaunts: And as there is a Heauen, a Materiall place of perfect ioye prepared for the Godly, ſo there is a Hell, a Materiall place of puniſhmēt for thē wicked and reprobat, prepared for the Deuil & his Angels, or els the word of God is in no wyſe to be credited, which blaſphemie, once to think, God kæp all his Children from.

Spud. But they will eaſily auoid this, for they ſay, it is writ, at what time ſo euer a ſinner doth repent him of his ſinne, J wil put all his ſin out of my remembrance ſaith ÿ Lord.

So that, if they maye haue thræ words at the laſt, they will wiſh no more. What think you of theſe felowes?

Philo. J think them no men, but Deuills, no Chriſtians, but worſe thā Tartarians, and more to be auoided than ÿ poiſon of a ſerpent: for the one ſlayeth but the body, but the other, both body & ſoul for euer. Wherfore, let euery god Chriſten Man take heed of them, and
　　　　　D.iij.　　　　　auoid

auoid them.　For, it is truely said, cum bonis bonus eris, & cum peruersis, peruerseris: with the good, thou shall learne good, but with the wicked, thou shall be peruerted.

Spud. Do you think than, that that cannot be a true repentance, which is deferred to the last gaspe.

Ph. No truely: For true repentance must spring out of a liuelie faith, with an inward lothing, hating and detesting of sinne. But this deferred repentance springeth not of faith, but rather of the feare of death which he seeth imminent before his eyes, of the grief and tediousnes of paine, of the Horror of Hell, and feare of God his ineuitable iudgement, which he knoweth now he must néeds abyde: And therfore, this can be no true repentance. For there is two maner of repentances, ye one a true repentance to life, the other a false repentance to death: As we maye sée by Iudas, who is said, to haue repented, and which is more, to haue confessed his faulte, and which is most of all, to haue made restitution, and yet was it a false repentance. And why? because it sprang not out of true faith, but as before.

Peter repented, and wept bitterly, and was saued therby, though he neither made confession, nor satisfaction: and why? Because it sprang of a true and liuely faith. So these felowes may say they repent, but except it be a
true

true repentance springing of faith, it can serue thē no moze to life than the pretensed repentance of Iudas did serue him to saluation. Let them beware, foz Cain repented, yet is he condemned.

Esau, did repent, yet is he condemned.

Antiochus, did repent, yet is he condemned : Iudas did repent, yet is he condemned, with infinite moe : And why so? Because their prolonged repentaunce spzange not of faith, &c.

Thus they may sée, that euerye light affection, is no true repentance: And that it is not ynough to say at the last, I repent, I repent. Foz, vnles it be a true repentāce indeed, it is wozth nothing. But indeed, if it weare so, that man had, liberū arbitrium, frée wil of himself, to repent truely when he wold, and that God pzomised in his wozd to accept of that repentance, it weare another matter. But repentance is, donum Dei, the gifte of God, de sursum veniens à patre luminum, comming from aboue frō the Father of light, & therfoze it is not in our powers to repent when we will. It is the Lozd ẏ giueth the gift, when, where & to whom it pleaseth him: & of him are we to craue it incessantly by faithfull pzayer, & not otherwise to pzesume of our owne repentāce, when indeed we haue nothing lesse, than a true repentance.

Spud.

Spud. Than thus much I gather by your words, that as true repentance (which is a certen inward grief, and sorrow of the heart, côceiued for our sinnes, with a hatred and loathing of thesame) erueth to saluation thorow the mercie of GOD in Christ, so fained repentance saueth not from perdition.

And therfore, we must repent dayly and howrely , and not to deferre our repentaunce to the last gaspe as many do, than which, nothing is more perilous.

Philo. True it is , for maye not he be called a great Foole , that by deferring and prolonging of repentance to the last cast (as they say) will hazard his body and soule to eternall damnation for euer ? Wheras by daily repentaunce he maye assure him selfe both of the fauour of GOD , and of life euerlasting (by faith) in the mercy of GOD, thorow the most precious blood of his deare Sonne, Iesus Christ, our alone Sauiour and Redemer, to whome be praise for euer.

Spud. Now must I needs say as the Wyse King Salomon said, all things are vaine and transitorie, and nothing is permanent vnder the Sonne, the workes of men are vnperfect and lead to destruction , their exercyses are vaine, and wicked altogether.

Wherfore , I setting apart all the vanities of this lyfe, will from benceforth consecrate

All things are vaine and vanitie it selfe.

ꝫ

of Abuses.   A Chriſtian proteſtation.

my ſelfe to the ſeruice of my God, and to
follow him in his Word, which onely is permanent and leadeth vnto life.

And I moſt hartelie thanke the Lord God
for your good Company this day, and for your
graue inſtructions, promiſing by the aſſiſtance of God his grace, to followe and obey them
to my poſſible power all the daies of my life.

Philo. God giue you grace ſo to do, and euery Chriſten man els, and to auoid all the vanities, and deceiuable pleaſures of this life: for
certenly they tread the path to eternal deſtruction, both of body and ſoule for euer, to as
many as obey them.

For, it is vnpoſſible to wallowe in the
delights and pleaſures of this World, and to
lyue in ioy for euer in ÿ Kingdom of Heauen.
And thus we hauing ſpent the daye, and alſo
cõſummate our iorney, we muſt now depart,
beſeaching God that we may both meete
againe in the kingdome of Heauen, there to
ralgne and lyue with him for euer, through

Ieſus Chriſte our Lorde, to whome with
the Father, and the holy Spirit be
all honour & glorie for
euer more
Amen.

FINIS.

R.i.   ¶Faults

The ioyes of this life tread the path to death.

¶ Faults escaped in printing.

Letter.	Page.	Line	Fault.	Correction.
In B,	vij.	6	the in Lord	in the Lord.
In B,	xi.	5	what is ther,	what thing is there
In D,	xi.	3	initimur	nitimur.
In D	xiiij.	9	tátæ meriades	tátæque meryades
In D,	xv.	16	supplyed	applyed.
In F,	i.	19		Read thus.

} Spud. I pray you shew me the opinions of the Fathers, concerning this coloring of faces.

In F,	ix.	3	Antiquities	Antiques.
In F,	xvi.	5	pesteruing	pestering.
In L	iij.	26	refug meat	refuse meate.
In I,	iij.	27	patrings	parings.
In I,	viij.	16	appetitum	appetitui.

Perufed, authorifed, &
allowed, according to the order
appoincted in the Queenes
Maiefties Iniun-
ctions.

At London

Printed by Richarde

Iones : dwellinge at the Signe of the
Rofe and the Crowne, neare vnto
Holborne Bridge.
1 5 8 3.